# PULPIT, MOSQUE AND NATION

# PULPIT, MOSQUE AND NATION

*Turkish Friday Sermons as Text and Ritual*

**Elisabeth Özdalga**

EDINBURGH
University Press

Edinburgh University Press is one of the leading university presses in the UK. We publish academic books and journals in our selected subject areas across the humanities and social sciences, combining cutting-edge scholarship with high editorial and production values to produce academic works of lasting importance. For more information visit our website: edinburghuniversitypress.com

Edinburgh University Press Ltd
The Tun – Holyrood Road
12 (2f) Jackson's Entry
Edinburgh EH8 8PJ

First published in hardback by Edinburgh University Press 2022

Typeset in 11/15 Adobe Garamond by
IDSUK (DataConnection) Ltd, and
printed and bound by CPI Group (UK) Ltd, Croydon, CR0 4YY

A CIP record for this book is available from the British Library

ISBN 978 1 4744 8820 4 (hardback)
ISBN 978 1 4744 8821 1 (paperback)
ISBN 978 1 4744 8823 5 (webready PDF)
ISBN 978 1 4744 8822 8 (epub)

# CONTENTS

# ACKNOWLEDGEMENTS

The research analysed in this volume touches upon a variety of fields within the humanities and social sciences. The interdisciplinary character of the study has therefore involved contacts with scholars and individuals from a wide range of institutions. To start with, I gratefully want to mention faculty and staff at the Near Eastern Studies Department at Princeton University, where I stayed as visiting fellow during the spring of 2015, and the university's renowned Firestone Library, which not only provides abundant collections but also accommodating lending services. I also want to extend my thanks to the Islamic Research Centre (İslam Araştırmaları Merkezi, İSAM) in Istanbul, which arranged for access to *Diyanet Gazetesi* and other publications of central importance to the research. Likewise, as acting Chair of the Department of Political Science at Bilkent University (2011–13), I took advantage of this institution's well-endowed library facilities. Special thanks must go to the Department of Sociology and Work Science at Gothenburg University, and particularly to the then Head of Department, Associate Professor Jan Carle, for kindly providing office space and other facilities during a period when it was difficult to sustain research in Turkey. Apart from that, the University Library in Gothenburg has continued to be a reliable source of support, for which I am always grateful.

What has laid the groundwork for this study in the first place, however, is the generous funding afforded by Riksbankens Jubileumsfond (The Central

Bank Foundation for the Advancement of the Humanities and Social Sciences) in Stockholm. I therefore owe this institution and the managing organisation, the Swedish Research Institute in Istanbul, heartfelt thanks. I especially want to express my appreciation to the Chairman of the Board of Trustees, Professor Daniel Tarschys, Ambassador Kjell Anneling (treasurer), Research Officer Helin Topal (Istanbul office) and Controller Lena Andersson (Stockholm office), all four from the Swedish Research Institute in Istanbul, for their – in their different ways – assistance and encouragement.

Throughout the project, I have been offered opportunities to participate in seminars and workshops organised by the Department of Cross-Cultural and Regional Studies (Section for the History of Religions), University of Copenhagen. I am particularly grateful to Professor Catharina Raudvere, Associate Professor Simon Stjernholm and Professor Jakob Skovgaard Petersen for their interest and constructive feedback.

My appreciation also goes to Professor of Theology Mehmet Aydın, who, for several years, has kindly responded to my questions relating to Muslim and Turkish homiletics, and who also read parts of the manuscript of this book. Heartfelt thanks are also directed to those students and other audiences who willingly took part in the interviews I conducted during the summer of 2014. My gratitude is especially directed to Professor Bünyamin Erul of the Faculty of Theology at Ankara University, who generously shared his views on what Friday preaching is like in Turkey today. In addition, Professor Erul kindly completed references missing in official Friday sermon texts. I also want to thank Professor Mehmet Sait Özervarlı, Department of Humanities and Social Sciences, Yıldız Technical University, Istanbul, who, on various occasions generously extended a hand of support, and Professor Necdet Subaşı for providing valuable source material during various stages of the research.

Scholars who, at different times, have helpfully commented on my work are: Professor Göran Larsson and Researcher Claes Grinell at the Department of Literature, History of Ideas, and Religion at the University of Gothenburg; Ingvild Flaskerud, Senior Lecturer at the Faculty of Theology, University of Oslo, who hosted me for a whole day in the Norwegian capital and generously shared her views on early drafts of the manuscript; my friend and colleague of many years at the Department of Sociology, University of Gothenburg, Rolf Törnqvist, who contributed straightforward and useful comments; and Senior Lecturer Ann-Kristin Jonasson from the Department of Political Science of the same university, also a board member of the Swedish Research Institute in Istanbul, who read and commented on the final draft, for which I am especially grateful.

Last, but not least, I want to express my appreciation to Allison Kanner-Botan, PhD candidate in the Divinity School and the Department of Near Eastern Languages and Civilizations, University of Chicago, for her conscientious translations from Turkish into English of the sermonising texts quoted throughout the book. Many thanks also to Zehra Aydın, who carefully transcribed the recorded interviews.

*Elisabeth Özdalga*
*Gothenburg, April 2021*

# NOTE ON TRANSLITERATION, PRONUNCIATION AND TRANSLATIONS

**Transliteration**

In this book transliteration of Turkish and Arabic words has been somewhat eclectic. The rule has been to remain as close as possible to modern Turkish orthography, while at the same time refrain from transliterating terms that are commonly used in English such as the Koran, Muhammad, sharia, Sunna, mufti and jihad. Apart from such Anglified terms, modern Turkish orthography has been used both for words of Turkish origin and Arabic words that are used in Turkish contexts, for example *hutbe, hatip, hadis, ezan, minber, medrese* and *müderris*.

In citations of works in Turkish or Ottoman Turkish that do not follow the orthography of modern Turkish, original transliterations have been followed as closely as possible. This is especially the case for references given by the authors of the quoted sermons, where styles of transliteration vary extensively, and for references to the Turkish *İslam Ansiklopedisi*. The same principle has been followed in citations of names from Brill's *Encyclopaedia of Islam*.

Concerning the extracts of sermons and sermon topics in the original Turkish (Appendices I, II and III), spelling, especially in relation to diacritics, has been left unedited, that is, the texts have been preserved in their original form.

**Pronunciation of Modern Turkish Letters**

Ç/ç      <u>ch</u>, as in *child*

Ş/ş      <u>sh</u>, as in *short*

I/ı      <u>io</u>, as in *portion*

Ö/ö      German <u>ö</u>, as in *König*

Ü/ü      German <u>ü</u>, as in *über*

Ğ/ğ      inaudible, prolongs the preceding vowel

**Translations**

All translations from Turkish to English of Friday sermons (*hutbe*s), Chapter 2 and Chapter 4, have been made by Allison Kanner-Botan, PhD candidate in the Divinity School and the Department of Near Eastern Languages and Civilizations, University of Chicago. All other translations, including interviews in Chapter 6, are made by the author.

'These things he said in words. But much in his heart remained unsaid.'

Kahlil Gibran: *The Prophet* (1926)

'The service had begun, he looked down at the people. Cruel torments seized him then. He wanted to speak to them, console them in their poverty and hopelessness.'

Selma Lagerlöf: *The Saga of Gösta Berling* (1891)

'The nation-state is more deeply fastened to the inner life of people than was the multiethnic empire of the past or today's common markets. By associating the nation and the state, nationalism has integrated the emotional life of people with political life.'

Gregory Jusdanis: *The Necessary Nation* (2001)

# INTRODUCTION:
## PULPIT UNDER RED BANNER

Alongside the spread of Islamic radicalism, Muslim Friday sermons have caught the attention of growing audiences. Because these weekly gatherings are suitable platforms for political agitation and propaganda-making, they have also become the scenes of mass demonstrations and sensational suicide bombings. Since the end of the 1970s, the most dramatic headlines have been drawn from Friday sermons in Egypt, Iran, Iraq, Afghanistan and Pakistan. In Turkey, however, which is the focus of this book, the situation has been different. Not in the sense that this Muslim majority country situated on the border between Europe and the Middle East has been spared political conflict and social unrest, but in the sense that mosques to a great extent have been kept outside of such political turbulence. This, undoubtedly, is related to the overbearing character of the Turkish state, both in its lengthy role as guardian of a secular order and, more recently, as a protagonist of an authoritarian Islamist regime.

For almost a century, state hegemony was expressed in the form of a secularist doctrine. A decade into the twenty-first century, however, the state was transformed into an instrument for Islamist agendas in the hands of the Justice and Development Party (Adalet ve Kalkınma Partisi, AKP). A dismantling of democracy took place, which goes back to the vicious suppression of the Gezi protests in May–June 2013 followed by the covering up of serious corruption allegations directed at the AKP leadership in December of the same year, and culminating in the sequel to the failed coup attempt in July 2016, which occasioned the AKP leadership to take measures leading to a serious undermining of the rule of law (martial law and ruling by decree). These agonising events marked a watershed in Turkey's modern political history. The consequences of this breach of democracy will be dealt with in the last chapter of this book. The main concern, however, is not with the AKP, but with an almost century-long period of state–religion relationships, and within that framework the practice of Friday preaching. As much as authoritarian AKPism is a new development with still unknown consequences for Turkey's eighty-five million citizens, this book calls attention to more longstanding aspects of its nation-building process. In that perspective, secularism stands out as the most distinguishing characteristic of Turkey's modern history, a doctrine that was launched by the founders of the Republic in 1923 and added as an immutable principle to the constitution in 1937. After the end of the Second World War, when Turkey turned more clearly towards the West, multi-party democracy was added to this order as a fundamental regime aim.

Secularism in the Turkish context has not built so much on a separation between state and religion as on state control over religion, an order safeguarded by Diyanet İşleri Başkanlığı (the Directorate of Religious Affairs). The fact that a state especially committed to secularism for such a long time has held the upper hand in the organisation of religion may seem paradoxical. However, what the Turkish case shows is that a secularist agenda may not render the penetration of religious influences, here studied in the form of weekly oratory, less pervasive. Looking back over the decades, the officially overseen homilies in Turkey are admittedly not as colourful and imaginative as those practised in less secularised Egypt (Gaffney 1994), or more 'civil Islam'-oriented Indonesia (Hefner 2000), but they are not less significant in the formation of religious and social identities. The question, however, is how? This constitutes the fundamental issue of this book, which studies the formation of citizenship and national identities in modern Turkey by focusing on the Friday sermons (Turkish: *hutbe*), which the Republic, in spite of its secularism, has viewed as an avenue for reaching out to the common people. Modern collective identities are complex, expressed in and through cultural fields such as historical writing, religion, fiction, film, theatre and the media. With this study, a hitherto mainly overlooked field of research, that of Friday sermons, is added to the study of national (political and cultural) identities.

## The *Hutbe*

Before commenting on the empirical and analytical aspects of this book, the core concept requires clarification. The *hutbe* is the sermonising part of a longer ritual, the Friday noon service, also known as *cuma*, the name for Friday in the Turkish language. Friday is the day of the week's most important prayer, but it is historically not regarded as the day of rest like the Jewish Sabbath or the Christian Sunday. That Friday, in terms of work and business, is not differentiated from other weekdays is especially striking in modern Turkey, where Sunday is the official holiday, an effect of its Western-oriented secularism. People therefore generally join the prayer right from the street, or in the middle of work, something which also gives special meaning to an old piece of advice to preachers to keep their *hutbe*s short. The service should not detain people from their daily dealings.

The obligatory (*farz*) character of the Friday sermon is laid down in the canonical law, sharia. Major elements of the liturgy are also based on or prescribed by Islamic law. This issue is discussed further in the following chapters, but it is important to emphasise from the very beginning the intimate connection between the liturgical and the juridical, specifically the binding role of canonical law on *hutbe* ritual practices. Another distinguishing feature of the Friday noon prayer is that participation is evaluated as a collective effort, preferably involving a large number of worshippers. Indeed, a service does not count as a valid act of worship if the number of participants is too small. On the other hand, when performed in accordance with canonical rules, the act of worship is valid for all members of the community. The Friday sermon is therefore a shared or communal ritual in a double sense: it is valueless or futile when delivered in solitude (for example, at home or at work), but once performed collectively, its blessing befalls the whole community. The various Islamic *mezheps*[1] differ as to the number of believers demanded for a service to be valid: the Shafii and Hanbali schools require forty, but the Hanefi (the majority of Turkish Muslims belong to this school) three and the Maliki twelve.[2] Irrespective of minimum numbers, it is desirable to deliver the Friday sermon to a large congregation, that is, in a large mosque. Certain greater mosques are thus preferred as ceremonial Friday mosques, a preference that also confers on them superior status. People therefore often travel from villages to nearby towns or cities, where larger mosques are situated, in order to attend the Friday sermon.

The Friday sermon is a ceremony only for men. As a rule, women are not forbidden from participating in the Friday noon prayer, and most mosques have a detached space where women can conduct their prayer (*namaz*), but the participation of women in the ritual is not essential to its canonical validity. The *hutbe* is a ceremony carried out by free, adult Muslim men for the good of the whole community, including women. Women, by contrast, are denied the opportunity to play an active role in this essential ritual (Jones 2006: 33).[3]

The political character of the Friday sermons must also be mentioned. Throughout history, rulers and governors have mounted the pulpit in order to declare their own hegemony over conquered areas, or to exhort people to holy war (jihad). In addition, *hutbe*s have traditionally included intercessions for rulers. However, over and above such common expressions of loyalty to the existing political authority, the *hutbe* has also been used as a platform in the struggle between contesting groups, for example between the religiously learned ulema and other elite groups, various Sufi circles and radical ideologues or firebrands.[4] The Friday prayer is an essential part of the politically oriented public sphere.

The *hutbe* represents a ritualised form of preaching, therefore the term 'liturgical preaching' (Jones 2012: 9) is used to separate the *hutbe* from other forms of Islamic homiletics. A freer, and more common form of oratory speech is *vaaz*: freer in terms of length; topic chosen; preacher initiative, including consent to speak extemporaneously; and time and place of delivery. The fact that in contemporary Turkey women with a religious education are allowed to engage in *vaaz*, but not in *hutbe*, also bears witness to the greater freedom allowed to the former kind of preaching.

### *Hutbe*s as Officially Authorised Texts

Who is responsible for the Friday sermons and how are they prepared? Mostly, when looking around the Muslim world, the chief imam or worship leader of any particular mosque is responsible for the weekly service, meaning that he would have to see to it that a preacher (Turkish: *hatip*), a cleric particularly skilled in or appointed for preaching, is engaged for this task. This may be a permanently employed preacher or someone enrolled from outside. If a professional preacher is not present, often the case for small mosques and congregations, the imam will conduct the *hutbe*. Whoever is appointed to lead the week's Friday *hutbe* would then prepare the sermon. This could be as a written text to be read out to the congregation, or as a speech delivered straight from the heart, extemporaneously.

Turkey, however, differs from this pattern – a situation that constitutes a leading theme in this book. Turkish practices differ because preachers generally do not prepare their own sermons. Instead, ever since the early years of the Republic, it has been an ambition of the official authorities to offer ready-made texts. While the technical means to do so were limited during the mid-war period, they have advanced significantly over the post-war decades. Technical means allude not only to printing, but also distribution facilities. In the mid-war period, the government had to suffice with producing authorised collections of *hutbe*s to be distributed to clerics around the country. Imams and *hatip*s were then enjoined to use these texts for their Friday services. Immediately after the Second World War, steps were taken to reach out to the local congregations with a regularly appearing periodical containing sermons in tune with the times. However, it was not until the end of the 1960s that Diyanet was able to get such a project going.

When the Internet made it possible for the central office in Ankara to instantly reach out to local congregations with the same sermon, this brought new opportunities, but, in the end, also problems. A common understanding in governmental and religious circles was that conveying the same message to the whole nation would have calming and unifying effects. Eventually, however, groups within and around Diyanet realised that too much standardisation might be dysfunctional – the simple reason being the social, economic and cultural heterogeneity. Problems encountered by people living in one part of the country could be very different from those of another part, be it eastern or western, urban or rural areas, rendering the texts irrelevant for large sections of the audiences. Around 2006 each one of the eighty-one administrative provinces was therefore enjoined to take responsibility for its own sermons, and sermon committees were set up in each provincial capital, however with little success.

## *Hutbe* Practices under a Secularist Regime

The secularist course, which the political elite around Mustafa Kemal Atatürk embarked upon after the establishment of the Republic in 1923, meant a hard blow to religious institutions and networks. The traditional religious scholars, the ulema, were more or less eliminated; religious education almost came to an end; Sufism (Islamic mysticism) was banned; and Islamic law, sharia, was shelved. Among the few religious practices allowed to continue were the daily prayers, *namaz*, including the Friday *hutbe*. That the restrictions were not pushed even further was probably out of respect for religion as a time-honoured institution, in combination with a recognition of the potential inherent in Friday preaching. Here was a medium that could be harnessed by the government in its consolidation of Turkey as a modern nation state. A frequently cited anecdote recalls how the national leader Atatürk, only a few months after the War of Independence (1919–22), expounded on this issue in an address to the congregation gathered in the Zağnos Paşa mosque in Balıkesir, western Turkey. There he enunciated a kind of '*hutbe* manifesto', in which he advocated including topics vital to the 'nation' in Friday sermons. Mosques were not built only for religious worship, he claimed, but were also meant to be places where citizens discussed and exchanged ideas on matters important to their social, economic and political life. To carve out the aims of the nation was a duty to be shouldered by all members of society, not just a narrow elite. The Prophet, Atatürk lectured, had conducted his deeds from two houses: his own house and Allah's house (mosque). It was from Allah's house that he managed things relating to the nation.[5]

Atatürk's aim to use Friday sermons for education, enlightenment (with only 13 per cent literacy in 1927) and rallying purposes was not new. As a matter of fact, it was part of the intellectual and political heritage of the Young Turk period. Especially after the 1908 Revolution, which marked the advent of the Second Constitutional Period and the coming to power of the Committee of Union and Progress, a wide range of intellectuals (pan-Islamist, nationalist and liberal) appealed to the ulema to include pressing social and political topics in their *hutbe*s (Doğan 1998; Yazıcı 1996). This idea was carried over to the leaders of the secular Republic.

Through the *hutbe*s, Turkish authorities have sought to engage with people on various topics: religious and ethical issues; matters related to family, women, health; dress codes; education; business, industry, agriculture; and the environment. Even if politics, in the name of secularism, was banned from mosques and sermons, questions of how to be a good citizen and to merge into, honour and support the nation have been of utmost importance. It is especially the last-mentioned topics – citizenship and nationhood – that stand at the centre of attention in this study.

## Nation and Nationalism: Analytical Perspectives

'Nationalism is primarily a political principle, which holds that the political and the national unit should be congruent' (Gellner 1983: 1). Nationalism, defined as a doctrine, movement and an essential feature of the state-formation process, is part of modernity: it emerges when pre-modern divisions of labour based on family, village, tribe and feudal estates break down, leaving individuals to form new alignments with state and society (Smith 1971; Kedourie 1993; Hobsbawm 1990; Breuilly 1993). Applied to modern Turkey, it can be said that the 1923 proclaimed Republic inherited from the Ottoman Empire a relatively strong, partly modernised state apparatus. Thus, the state was there from the start. The nation, however, still had to be created. Numerous literary narratives speak of the absence of a sense of common nationhood among Anatolian peasants during the early republican decades (Karaosmanoğlu 2008; Makal 1954). The prospects of a Gellnerian 'happy marriage' between state and nation were uncertain, representing a major challenge for republican leaders.

The above-mentioned theories represent long-term perspectives in historical sociology and anthropology, with important bearings on theories of nationalism also focusing on contemporary contexts. Therefore, a common distinction in current political science is that between the nation as a political and as a cultural community (Heywood 2007: 109ff.). The first concerns the relationship of individuals to the state and deals with mutual rights and obligations. In this perspective, the nation is a group of people bound together as citizens, irrespective of their cultural, ethnic and other loyalties. The nation as cultural community, by contrast, relates to a sense of shared belonging, mostly through linguistic, ethnic and/or religious identities.

## The Nation as a Political Community

The vision of the future Turkish society adumbrated in Atatürk's Balıkesir sermon built on the notion of the modern individual as detached from traditional sociopolitical institutions. Every individual was to be regarded as autonomous, standing in an equal relationship to the state. The republican leaders were not unfamiliar with Enlightenment philosophy. Many had spent time abroad (some in exile) and had established contacts with various intellectual circles. Since the early Tanzimat reform period (initiated in 1839), Paris had been a favourite destination for the Turkish intelligentsia. The 1908 Revolution strongly echoed the French Revolution's mottoes of liberty, equality, fraternity, to which was added justice (Zürcher 2019: 484). The theory of the social contract, strongly identified with Enlightenment thinking, was part of the reformers' intellectual baggage. Rousseau's philosophy had an important impact on their worldview.

The Kemalist leaders of the early 1920s were thus bearers of the idea that henceforth politics must be 'in a new style',[6] and be carried out in the name of the people or nation. The system they were entitled to rule over represented a 'moral order' different from the partly constitutional,[7] but largely despotic Ottoman regime they had actively struggled to overthrow. The question was how these insights could be conveyed to the larger public.

Even if Kemalists supported republican and progressive values, in their political practice they were no democrats. The reform programme promoting secularism and modernisation was implemented with a rod of iron. Under such conditions, the good citizen was the obedient and passive citizen, themes that well suited the patronising character of traditional homiletic admonitions. However, with the transition to a multi-party system in 1946 (first free election, 1950), the people became a political factor to count upon, but the question is how citizen-friendly the official outlook in fact became. Marshall (1950: 8–9) provides a useful approach in his classic theory of citizenship rights that distinguishes between three sets of rights: civil rights (freedom of speech, assembly, movement, conscience, equality before the law and right to own property); political rights (to participate in political life, to vote, to stand for election, to hold public office); and social rights (those state undertakings necessary to guarantee individuals a minimum of social status as a basis for exercising civil and political rights). These categories are useful tools in the analysis of how the balance was struck between rights and duties, freedom and obedience in the Turkish context and, as a manifestation of that, how such citizenship-related issues touched or penetrated the *hutbe* sermons.

## The Nation as a Cultural Community

The key parameters of the nation as cultural community are language, ethnicity and religion, that is, Turkish and Muslim identities. The War of Independence (1919–22) was carried out in defence of the motherland (*vatan*), a notion that appealed to an intricate intertwining of Turkish and Islamic values. However, after the war this double identity was challenged by the Kemalists. When Turkey's territorial borders were internationally recognised (Lausanne Treaty, 1923) and the leaders were firmly in the saddle, they launched a programme for the cultural unification of the people, which emphasised the ethnic dimension of nationhood (language and pre-Ottoman Turkic history). In the period following the 1908 Revolution, three conceptions of nationalism had competed: Ottomanism, pan-Islamism and Turkishness. Out of the turmoil caused by the Balkan Wars, the First World War and the War of Independence, the last version triumphed (Karpat 2001: 353ff.).

Consequently, in schools and other official contexts (military and civil commemorations and other ceremonials), secular and ethnic Turkish attributes were celebrated. This was done against the backdrop of an officially sanctioned amnesia, relating to the recently (1915) carried out atrocities against Armenian and other Christian minorities, and, more generally the dynastic and Islamic character of the Ottoman Empire. The emphasis on language and ethnicity in combination with forced oblivion came to occupy the 'downstage' of Turkish nationalism. Religious sentiments, however, were largely contained within the mosques, which were reduced to an 'upstage' or even 'backstage' phenomenon. Religion was not totally suppressed, as in the neighbouring Soviet Union, but neither was it allowed much visibility in official contexts. After the transition to multi-party democracy at the end of the Second World War, however, this order could hardly persist. Bit by bit, religion reclaimed a place at the front of the stage of Turkish nationhood. This struggle over which cultural values should determine Turkish national identity ran through much of post-war ideological controversy and politics. The focus of the following chapters is therefore especially on the balances struck between Turkish and Islamic identities, but also on how exclusionary they were defined in relation to other ethnic and religious groups, such as the Kurdish, Arab, Alid-oriented Alevi, Shafii[8] and Christian (Greek Orthodox, Armenian) minorities.

The national poet Mehmet Akif Ersoy (1873–1936), author of the national anthem, appealed to both Islamic and Turkish sentiments. When Kemalist leaders opted for a secularist order, he went into exile in Cairo. However, 'Mehmet Akif' is still the favourite poet quoted in Friday sermons. The close affiliation between Islamic and Turkish values has always been at the foundation of Turkish national consciousness. The *hutbe*s offer important insights into how religious and ethnic sentiments have interacted and affected each other.

### Discourse, Ritual and Officialdom in Historical Perspective

The overall concern of this book is with official *hutbe* oratory and how the study of this rhetorical genre contributes to the understanding of religious, ethnic and national identities. The problems are approached from four different perspectives. The first is the verbal message conveyed through the sermon, that is the discursive content of the *hutbe*. The second, which constitutes the vessel for the homiletic message, is the liturgical ritual with roots in early Islam. The third is Diyanet, the governmental agency through which the state reaches out to audiences or congregations. The fourth concerns the historical dimension. Neither the sermonising texts and the rituals, nor the official institution Diyanet, can meaningfully be understood outside of their historical contexts.

In the analysis of the first aspect, the discursive messages of the *hutbe*s, questions are related to images of the ideal believer, and how that is related to notions of the ideal citizen. What kind of social orientation and belonging is encouraged? Is the focus on the local, small-scale society, or are individuals encouraged to engage themselves in developments taking part on the macro, national level? How is the ideal nation imagined? What about ethnic, religious and social differences? Are they ignored, denied even, or are they tolerated, and in that case, to what degree? In other words, how inclusive, or exclusive is the image of the Turkish nation as communicated by the official *hutbe* texts? Which images are conveyed of modern Turkey's ancestor, the Ottoman Empire? Which are the visions for the future? Is the stress on democracy and an open society, or on order and hierarchies? One of the most prevailing themes in the corpus of official sermons is 'unity and togetherness'. How much is this unity and togetherness imagined as a consensus? What do the threats to the unity of the nation look like? How should the nation's enemies – external as well as internal – be fought? How much conflict or antagonism is regarded as endurable? Answers to these questions offer clues to the amalgamation of ethnic and religious components of the imagined nation; to the mixture of local, urban and metropolitan orientations and loyalties; and to the commitments to liberal versus authoritarian values.

The second dimension is related to the relationship between sermon and ritual in the Friday noon prayer. The liturgy, including praise of God, intercession for the Prophet, prayers for the believers and citations from the Koran, renders authoritative and emotive power to delivered messages. How do these rituals, with roots in early Islam, interplay with the sermon itself, that is the exhortation to piety? What are the effects of these ceremonies on the collective consciousness, religious and national? What about the power generated by the act of praying itself, which brings the believers together in disciplined and compact rows? In other words, how do the prayer rituals contribute to the experience of being part of a close-knit community of believers? By addressing these questions, the role of religious rituals in the formation of national identities are elucidated. It also helps to illuminate how the experience of being part of a religious community at the level of the local mosque is connected to a sense of solidarity with the community of believers on the national level.

The third dimension is related to Diyanet, the institution situated lower down in the official bureaucracy, hegemonised by the presidency, the military and the government. In its dealings with this agency, 'the state' appears with many faces and the questions addressed in relation to this topic are which state officials especially bring pressure to bear on Diyanet. Is there a difference between bureaucrats operating from the central and the local administrations? How about managers within the public media and representatives for the military, the government and the presidency? What kinds of demands are especially called for? Requests for appointments to ranks (positions) within

Diyanet are common, but what else? Has the content of the sermons been under particular pressure, and in that case how and in what direction? Diyanet has always been subject to governmental control, which its leaders as well as rank and file have either willingly or reluctantly accepted or tried to ward off more or less successfully. How much resistance has Diyanet been able to rally against such pressures? Another question addressed is which shifts, if any, there have been between Diyanet and other official institutions in terms of heavy-handedness and more reciprocal cooperation based on mutual understanding. State and religion have remained intertwined with each other, but the relative strength of each side has shifted. Even if the state weighs heavily, especially the military in its capacity as the special guardian of the secular state, the question is how and on what terms Diyanet has been able to resist some of these external demands and pressures.

The fourth and more comprehensive dimension is related to the historical context. None of the above-mentioned aspects of preaching can be meaningfully elaborated upon without taking history into account. Thanks to certain outstanding events, Turkey's modern history lends itself relatively easily to a well-arranged periodisation. The mid-war period was dominated by a one-party regime under the Republican People's Party (Cumhuriyet Halk Partisi, CHP) and its Kemalist leadership, the cadre that laid the foundation to the modern, secular Republic. The post-war period was dominated by closer relations to the West, including becoming a member of the Council of Europe (1949), signing the European Convention of Human Rights (1953), joining the European Court of Human Rights (1959), becoming a member of NATO (1952), and introducing multi-party parliamentarianism with free elections (1950). Due to the fact that it has been lined with hitches, the democratic process has been interrupted by military interventions almost with a kind of uniformity (1960, 1971, 1980 and 1997), clearly separating the subsequent decades with their special actors and agendas from each other. The *hutbe*s have been written and audited under the impact of these changing social and political circumstances. However, exactly how context sensitive the *hutbe*s are, when it comes to the political and societal environment, constitutes one of the basic problems addressed in this book. How much has specific social and political events and public issues been reflected in the sermons? By contrast, what stands out as chiefly recurrent, standard themes, more or less untouched by the times? Answers to these questions offer clues to the general efficacy or sensitivity of the *hutbe*s as a medium for conveying official nationhood-related messages.

## Presentation of Chapters

The book starts with a longer discussion of what distinguishes the *hutbe* from other forms of Muslim preaching, such as *vaaz* and homiletic storytelling (*kasas*). Research on *hutbe* oratory is generally under-represented in the academic literature. There are, as a matter of fact, but a handful of scholarly works on this issue. However, within the existing limits, Chapter 1 offers a broader account of the variety of social and political contexts in which the Friday *hutbe* has stood out as a celebrated religious – and political – manifestation. The chapter has two principal aims: first, to convey a sense of what constitutes the core of the Friday sermon, and to do so by emphasising the great variations of geographical and historical contexts; and second, to emphasise its long-standing roots in the Islamic tradition.

The second chapter deals with authorised *hutbe*s from the early years of modern Turkey and concentrates on two renowned and widely spread authorised *hutbe* collections dating from the early republican period. Since these sermons were written by one of the most respected religious personalities of the period, Ahmet Hamdi Akseki (1887–1951), head of Diyanet from 1947 until his death, they have also served as models or paragons of *hutbe*s produced after that. In other words, Akseki's *hutbe* collections set the tone for Turkish official homiletics for a long time. For that reason, the second chapter goes into some detail in the description and analysis of themes and rhetoric dominating these texts. Emphasis has been laid on providing an assessment of the sermonising discourse, which is as comprehensive and inclusive as possible, without losing sight of the core question of citizenship and social and national identities. The analysis is carried out against the backdrop of significant political events and developments of the first years of the Republic, including a discussion of the changes taking place in the structure of legitimate authority between the pre-republican – imperial – and the republican period.

At the centre of attention of the third chapter is the popular resistance waged against some of the secularising reforms, especially those directed against the Turkification of liturgical or ritual language. The linguistic reform that caused most unease and discontent was the vernacularisation of the call to prayer (*ezan*), that is the ban, issued in 1932, against having this first, invitatory part of the ritual prayer (*namaz*) in general and the Friday *hutbe* in particular, in the Arabic original. When people opposed the Turkification of the *ezan*, it was not supposedly anti-nationalist or anti-secular sentiments that were at stake, but rather the preservation of long-standing ceremonies with links to the Koran. The way in which this conflict was played out, as described in some detail in the chapter, lends support to the idea that deep emotional values were attached to the liturgical ritual, while the sermonising part was met with less fervour. Concerning the ritual and its language, common people insisted on preserving the original Arabic because of the solemnity it rendered to the sermon as a whole, including a sense of eminence to the community of believers themselves. The question elaborated upon is therefore whether the 'voice' implicit in the ritual was more penetrating than that of the message delivered through the sermon.

In Chapter 4, attention is especially paid to *hutbe*s of the 1970s, an unusually turbulent and violent decade in Turkish modern history. This period coincides with important changes in the organisation and institutionalisation of Diyanet. A firmer organisation was introduced in 1965, a couple of years later followed by the regular publication of *Diyanet Gazetesi*. With this publication, it became possible, for the first time, to read *hutbe*s in the light of important social and political developments on a week-by-week or month-by-month basis. In this chapter, the *hutbe*s are 'read' as a current exhortative commentary to certain outstanding citizenship- and nationhood-related events of the period.

Chapter 5 deals with Diyanet. The two turbulent decades following the radicalisation of the student movements in 1968 and the ensuing political, sectarian and ethnic polarisations, are particularly interesting to follow from the point of view of how Diyanet tried to balance the demands of the secular state and its authoritarian leadership, on the one hand, and the pressures coming from below, especially the agitated cadres of the 1972 formed pro-Islamic National Salvation Party (Milli Selamet Partisi, MSP), on the other. The military coup of 1980 turned into a kind of testing ground concerning Diyanet's ability to navigate the unruly waters of these showdowns. The *hutbe*s must be approached with these power struggles in mind, even though such contests never really reached the lines of the official *hutbe* texts.

Up to now, the chapters have dealt with Friday sermons as texts and rituals, analysed in the light of social, political and historical contexts. In the sixth chapter, the focus is changed to individuals partaking in the *hutbe* ceremonies. What are, in the eyes of imams, sermon writers and audiences, the merits and shortcomings of the *hutbe*s delivered by Diyanet? Based on a smaller survey carried out in the summer of 2014 the chapter aims at shedding some light on how engaged believers understand and evaluate these performances. Six interviews have been reproduced in detail and commented upon: one with an experienced religious scholar and sermon writer, one with a middle-class professional and four with university students. The interviewees share the opinion that the topics of the sermons more often than not are irrelevant both to their own personal lives and to issues occupying the nation at large. The chapter opens with an overview of the highly eventful and staggering political developments of the last two decades of the twentieth and the first decade of the twenty-first century. Such a backdrop has been inserted in order to better illustrate the distance between the discourses of the official *hutbe*s and the social and political realities of the country's citizens.

Chapter 7 focuses on the Justice and Development Party (AKP), through which political Islam, for the first time, assumed power in Turkey. The AKP formed its first government in 2002 based on an overwhelming majority in parliament, and received positive salutes at home and abroad for its wary, but still liberal and democratic, profile. However, it did not take too long before the party's Islamist agenda stood out more sharply – a change closely connected with a shift to a more authoritarian stance. Diyanet was especially targeted in this process and came every so often to serve as an agent in the government's propaganda campaigns, especially evident in its flashy and populistic use of mass media. Diyanet not only grew in terms of expenditure and personnel, it was also drawn into areas of police and intelligence services, not least in and around Turkey's foreign missions, whereby it lost its earlier acquired autonomy. As a matter of fact, this utilisation of Diyanet was part of a larger process, through which official institutions were systematically subordinated to the particular interests of the governing political party with negative effects on the rule of law and the future integrity of the nation. Finally, the main contentions are reviewed in a concluding chapter.

## Notes

1. There are four recognised law schools (*mezhep*, Arabic: *madhhab*) in Sunni Islam: the Hanbali, Hanefi, Maliki and Shafii. The majority of Turkish Muslims belong to the Hanefi *mezhep*.
2. *İslam Ansiklopedisi*: Vol. 18, pp. 425–8.
3. In recent years liberal-minded or feminist Muslim women have started to question this order of things because of its gender discrimination. In Denmark, for example, women have founded their own mosques, where they conduct their prayers, including the Friday *hutbe*.
4. *İslam Ansiklopedisi*: Vol. 18, pp. 425–8; Zilfi 1988: 129ff.
5. 'Atatürk'ün Balıkesir Hutbesi', *Diyanet Aylık Dergi*, Şubat [February] 2003, pp. 40–1.
6. For this phrase, see Kedourie (1993: 1).
7. Sharia had ensured a kind of rule of law (Gerber 2002: 66–75).
8. The Shafii *mezhep*, common among some Kurdish groups in the south-east.

# 1

## THE *HUTBE* IN HISTORICAL PERSPECTIVE

The aim of this chapter is to give an idea about what a *hutbe* amounts to in a broader perspective, and also outside the context of modern Turkey. This will be done by providing some glimpses into its long history. The chapter therefore starts with a description of the special ritual and canonical character of the *hutbe*, with references to the early period of Islam, and continues by touching briefly on medieval history, after which it reaches the Ottoman Empire, including Egypt, and finally modern Turkey. The objective is twofold: to bring to mind the wider traditions and contexts into which *hutbe* preaching in modern Turkey is embedded; and, when doing so, outline the scholarly coordinates on which this book is based.[1]

As already mentioned, the Friday sermon – *hutbe* – is a special form of preaching. It is delivered from the pulpit (*minber*), is embedded in a well-defined liturgy, and represents an officially authorised kind of speech.[2] *Vaaz*, on the other hand, represents a less regulated form of address, which is not tied to a special time in the weekly or yearly liturgical schedule and is not necessarily performed in a mosque, even if that is the most common practice. Homiletic storytelling (*kasas*) is a third, even freer form of speech, which can be performed in a variety of ways and settings, such as someone's home, a tea-house, an outdoor square or other public space. This kind of oratory does not require the storyteller to have special competence in religious learning.

The *hutbe* belongs to the Friday noon service. However, *hutbe*s are also held on other occasions, for example, at weddings or at the morning services of the two great festivals, the *Ramazan Bayramı* at the end of the fasting month, and the *Kurban Bayramı*, the feast of sacrifice.[3] In the Friday service, the *hutbe* precedes the ritual *namaz* prayer (Arabic: *ṣalāt*), but on all other occasions it is performed after the prayer (Wensinck 1986: 74–5). The following is a short summary of the ritual steps in a Friday noon service.[4]

## Liturgical Preaching

All daily prayers, including the Friday noon prayer, start with the call to prayer (*ezan*). The *ezan* consists of several praises to Allah and the Prophet, testimonies of faith, and calls to prayer according to the following scheme:

1. Allah is most great (four times)
2. I testify that there is no god besides Allah (twice)
3. I testify that Muhammad is the apostle of Allah (twice)
4. Come to prayer (twice)
5. Come to salvation (twice)
6. Allah is most great (twice)
7. There is no god besides Allah (once) (Juynboll 1986)

Differing from the other five daily prayers, the Friday noon prayer starts with an additional call, a *sala*, a special liturgical phrase expressing praise to the Prophet. This is not an *ezan* in the proper sense of the word. It is recited from the minaret about an hour or an hour-and-a-half before the regular Friday noon *ezan* and is meant as a reminder, allowing people ample time to prepare for participation. An extra reminder has already been recited on Thursday nights before the evening prayer.

When the noon *ezan* is called out from the minaret most people are already gathered, ready to participate in the prayer. The *ezan* is then followed by four prostrations (*rekat*).[5] These are performed collectively, but by each individual at his/her[6] own pace, and are only supererogatory (*sünnet*), not obligatory (*farz*).[7] After that, the imam slowly mounts the pulpit and sits. In the meantime, a special *hutbe ezanı* preceding the sermon is recited by the muezzin from within the mosque (from the *mahfil* – special elevated place – if there is one).

This is followed by the *hutbe* itself, which is divided into two parts. It is obligatory (*farz*) for both parts to include thanksgiving to God (*elhamdülillah*), intercession and blessings for the Prophet (*selat-ü selam, salavat*), and admonitions to piety on the part of the worshippers. The preaching or sermon proper is usually performed in the first part of the *hutbe* and contains admonitions on religious, ethical, social and political issues. The first part should also include prayers (*dua*) for the faithful, including the sovereign or the rulers,[8] and recitations from the Koran. Further, it is commendable (*sünnet*) for the imam to stand up while speaking, greet the audience from the pulpit, support himself with a sword or a spire,[9] position himself facing the congregation, pray on behalf of all Muslims and keep his *hutbe* short. An oft-repeated saying by the Prophet is: 'Make your prayer long and your sermon short.' In addition, for the ritual to be canonically valid, the imam/*hatip* must be in a state of ritual purity; must dress according to given prescriptions; and must perform the two *hutbes* standing, while sitting down during the intermission (Wensinck 1986).

Having finished the *hutbe*, the imam descends from the pulpit and leads the congregation in the obligatory (*farz*) Friday ritual prayer, which is performed in unison and involves two prostrations. However, this prayer is preceded by *kamet*, an *ezan*-like call recited by the muezzin within the mosque, expressing willingness and intention of the congregation to perform the obligatory prayer.[10] Thereafter follows another four supererogatory *rekats*. The only obligatory *namaz* during the Friday service is performed by all directly after the *hutbe*. All other prostrations are supererogatory.

The rituals also require certain preparations, both mental and physical. For the worship to be valid, ritual cleaning is mandatory. Timeliness is also important. According to one *hadis* (Arabic: *hadith*) narrated by Abu Hurayra (d. 678), companion of Muhammad and prolific narrator of traditions about the Prophet:[11]

Allah's Apostle (p.b.u.h.) said: 'Any person who takes a bath on Friday like the bath of Janaba[12] and then goes for the prayer (in the first hour, that is, early), it is as if he had sacrificed a camel (in Allah's cause); and whoever goes in the second hour, it is as if he had sacrificed a cow; and whoever goes in the third hour, then it is as if he had sacrificed a horned ram; and if one goes in the fourth hour, then it is as if he had sacrificed a hen; and whoever goes in the fifth hour, then it is as if he had offered an egg. When the Imam comes out, the angels present themselves to listen to the Khutba.' (al-Bukhari 1979: Vol. XIII, p. 8)

Except for cleanliness, promptness and considerateness about where to kneel in an already crowded mosque (it is not acceptable to squeeze in between praying individuals), the congregation is also expected to maintain silence during the sermon – even to the point of refraining from interfering with someone disturbing the ceremony – as reported in the following exhortation, again narrated by Abu Hurayra: 'Allah's Apostle (p.b.u.h.) said: "When the Imam is delivering the Khutba and you ask your companion to keep quiet and listen, then no doubt you have done an evil act"' (al-Bukhari 1979: Vol. XIII, p. 56).

### Historical Origins of the *Hutbe*

According to the Islamic tradition, all liturgical elements can be traced back to the time of Muhammad and his close followers. However, according to historians the ritual organisation of the Friday sermon as it has been transmitted through the centuries was not fully elaborated during Muhammad's lifetime (Wensinck 1986; Becker 2006).

> The more thoroughly we study the beginnings of Islam the more clearly we see how unfinished Muhammad's work was at the time of his death and how mistaken Islamic tradition is whenever it tries to trace back present-day ideas and practices as far as possible to the Prophet himself. This is particularly true in the field of public religious services, where so far only little research has been done. Everything appears so simple and clear that we could be tempted to believe that we are dealing with one instance of a tradition that really does date back to Muhammad himself. (Becker 2006: 49)

The Friday *hutbe* is not mentioned in the Koran. The Friday service, however, is mentioned once in Sura 62: 9 (Retsö 2020: 20). Wensinck argued that the absence of the Friday *hutbe* did not indicate the lack of a sermon as part of worship in Muhammad's time, but rather that the different elements of worship had not yet been set in a fixed order. Most probably, this did not occur until the Umayyad period (661–750). A *hadis* from *Sahih Muslim*, cited by Wensinck, describes the Friday service of the time of the Prophet as a simple ceremony; a form that he assumes lasted until Marwan's time (r. 684–95), when a highly official style was introduced (Wensinck 1986).[13]

The renowned Orientalist Carl Becker (1876–1933) based his theory on a comparison of the rituals of Friday sermons, on one hand, and of the two holy feasts on the other. Common to the Friday celebration and the two feasts is the delivery of a sermon in two parts, with an obligatory ritual prayer. The differences, however, are summarised as follows:

1. On Fridays the *khuṭba* is linked to the midday prayer, on the feasts with the morning prayer.
2. On Fridays the *khuṭba* takes place before the *ṣalāt* [Turkish: *namaz*], on the feasts after the *ṣalāt*.
3. On Fridays *adhān* [Turkish: *ezan*] and *iqāma* [Turkish: *kamet*] are linked to the service, whereas this is not so on the feasts, when there is a shortened *adhān*.
4. The Friday service is held in the mosque, the service on the feasts – originally at least – outside on the *muṣallā* [courtyard]. All the implements of worship, such as the minbar, from which the Friday *khuṭba* is delivered, are missing on the *muṣallā*. (Becker 2006: 50)

Becker argued that there are strong reasons to believe that the feast celebrations were simpler, and more authentic than the Friday services, which seem to have been more consciously arranged.

> [The] ritual of the Friday celebration is no primitive creation in any of its aspects. On the contrary, it betrays a tendency towards organised worship, which takes into account not only the needs of town-dwellers but also their experience in the field of worship. Going out onto the *muṣallā* is a primitive action that does not really fit with city conditions. (Becker 2006: 50)

After giving the Friday sermon more elaborate form, the Umayyad rulers and scholars strove to do much the same for the feast celebrations,[14] but without much success. 'There must have been an established and old tradition against which even the all-mighty caliphate was powerless' (Becker 2006: 51). In this historical context, the Friday sermon was a 'newcomer', partly invented and partly inspired by practices of other religious communities. A major objective of Becker's article was to call attention to external Jewish and Christian influences, but implicit in his discussion was also the observation that Muslims allegedly strove to form new communal ties across tribal boundaries. Thus, one may conclude that the rituals surrounding the Friday sermon resulted from conscious efforts initiated by the Prophet himself and continued by early and later followers to modify older traditions for the purpose of strengthening the new Muslim community.

That ritual practices were shaped in an effort to create a new, trans-tribal religious community distinct from the Jewish and Christian is illustrated by the way the call for prayer was devised. Arriving in Medina in 622, the Prophet is said to have deliberated with his companions about how to summon Muslims to prayer in a distinctive way. Blowing a horn, lighting a fire or clapping long pieces of wood were already practised by others. In a dream, one of the companions saw someone mounting the roof of the mosque and using his own voice to summon the believers to prayer. Bilal famously became the first muezzin. This practice has remained a distinctive and enduring feature of Islam until our own day (Juynboll 1986).

### Canonical Foundations of the *Hutbe*

Conclusions drawn by historians on the canonical foundations of the *hutbe* do not necessarily correspond to the beliefs of practitioners of Islam. What lends authority to the whole universe of correct behaviour is that it is anchored in the Koran and Sunna. In Ibn Ishaq's (d. 768) Muhammad biography (*sira*, pl. *siyer*), the *hutbe* delivered by the Prophet after his arrival in Medina in 622 is narrated as follows:

> [The Apostle] praised and glorified God as was His due and then said:[15] O men, send forward (good works) for yourselves. You know, by God, that one of you may be smitten and will leave his flock without a shepherd. Then his Lord will say to him – there will be no interpreter or chamberlain to veil him from Him – Did not My apostle come to you with a message, and did not I give you wealth and show you favour? What have you sent forward for yourself? Then will he look to the right and left and see nothing; he will look in front of him and see nothing but hell. He who can shield his face from the fire even with a little piece of date let him do so; and he who cannot find that then with a good word; for the good deed will be rewarded tenfold yea to twice seven hundred fold. Peace be upon you and God's mercy and blessing. (Ibn Hisham [after Ibn Ishaq] 1955: 231)

In a lengthy *hadis* from Imam Muslim's (d. 875) collection *Sahih Muslim*, the Prophet's allegedly last sermon has been reported as part of the narrative about his pilgrimage to Mecca shortly before his death:

> Verily your blood, your property are as sacred and inviolable as the sacredness of this day of yours, in this month of yours, in this town of yours. Behold! Everything pertaining to the Days of Ignorance is under my feet completely abolished. Abolished are also the blood-revenges of the Days of Ignorance. The first claim of ours on blood-revenge which I abolish is that of the son of Rabi'a b. al-Harith,[16] who was nursed among the tribe of Sa'd and was killed by Hudhail. And the usury of the pre-Islamic period is abolished, and the first of our usury I abolish is that of 'Abbas b. 'Abd al-Muttalib,[17] for it is all abolished. Fear Allah concerning women! Verily you have taken them on the security of Allah, and intercourse with them has been made lawful unto you by words of Allah. You too have right over them, and that they should not allow anyone to sit on your bed whom you do not like. But if they do that, you can chastise them but not severely. Their rights upon you are that you should provide them with food and clothing in a fitting manner. I have left among you the Book of Allah, and if you hold fast to it, you would never go astray. And you would be asked about me (on the Day of Resurrection), (now tell me) what would you say? They (the audience) said: 'We will bear witness that you have conveyed (the message), discharged (the ministry of Prophethood) and given wise (sincere) counsel.' He (the narrator) said: 'He (the Holy Prophet) then raised his forefinger towards the sky and pointing it at the people (said): "O Allah, be witness. O Allah, be witness," saying it thrice.' (Bilal then) pronounced Adhan and later on Iqama and he (the Holy Prophet) led the noon prayer. He (Bilal) then uttered Iqama and he (the Holy Prophet) led the afternoon prayer and he observed no other prayer in between the two. (Muslim 1971–5: Vol. II, p. 616)

These examples illustrate how liturgical practices were founded in *siyer* and *hadis* collections, sources that together with the Koran constitute the foundations of Islamic jurisprudence (*fıkıh*, Arabic: *fiqh*).[18] In other words, the Friday sermon has been – and still is – strongly entrenched in sharia, the canonical law.[19]

### Preachers' Qualifications – Medieval Perspectives

Sharia was interpreted and implemented by the ulema, but it was protected and guarded by the sovereigns of those caliphates, sultanates and emirates that emerged as Islam spread to Egypt, North Africa (Maghreb), Spain, Iraq and Persia. The Friday sermon was the symbolic expression of this particular order based on a politically and militarily guarded religion. To lead a Friday sermon therefore required extra qualifications and responsibility and was based on appointment, most often by the supreme leader.[20]

The Islamic tradition has not called for an appointed imam to lead the *namaz*. In the absence of an imam, any congregational member could fulfil that duty. To qualify as a liturgical preacher, however, a person had to have in-depth knowledge of Islam's original texts, not only as proof of his scholarly erudition, but to enable him to prepare high quality sermons. He also had to have a strong voice, suitable for chanting the holy texts (*kıraat, tilavet*) to large audiences, and was expected to master the seven recitation styles of the Koran. Command of non-canonical styles added even more prestige (Jones 2012: 196–201).

In the early and medieval periods learning was mostly transmitted through personal relationships. Young men intent on a religious career would call upon renowned sheikhs and other professionals for guidance; but recognised teachers could also invite promising young men to study with them. One consequence of this system was that the novice had to travel, sometimes to faraway places. As a matter of fact, after acquiring profound knowledge of the Koran and the Sunna, students were encouraged to travel in order to study with a wide range of learned experts. Such scholarly experience and familiarity with the ways of the world served as social and symbolic capital, and played an important role in appointments (Jones 2012: 197–201). For aspiring liturgical preachers learning could also be achieved through apprenticeship, listening to or studying an elder *hatip*'s written sources. Some clerics had their sermons written down, for example, with the help of students. This suggests that *hutbe* collections – an issue to be dealt with in Chapter 2 – date back to the relatively early centuries of Islam (Jones 2012: 205–7).

### Institutionalisation of Religious Learning under Ottoman Rule

With the emergence of the Ottoman Empire, a new page in the history of Islam was opened. The Ottoman polity had its roots in medieval Central Asian and Persian state traditions, but its expansion during the fifteenth and sixteenth centuries coincided with the development of early modernity.

A more bureaucratic polity took form, which especially left strong imprints on the organisation of the army. Ottoman state building also had effects on the organisation of religion (Inalcık 1973; Hodgson 1974).[21]

Under Ottoman rule, the ulema developed from a loose network of scholars into a more integrated class. In the late-medieval Muslim world, the religiously educated had been thrown upon their own resources, both during training and in their professional lives. However, by the time the Ottoman Empire was firmly established, and after it had conquered Mecca and Medina and taken on the responsibility of the caliphate (1517),[22] religion was given a firmer institutional framework. What distinguished the Ottomans from other Islamic states was that they set out to organise the ulema into an elite hierarchical institution, the *ilmiye*. This was coupled with the organisation of *medrese*s into a more formal and hierarchical educational institution. To be recognised as a member of the religious elite – the ulema – a person required a diploma from one of the state-authorised higher schools of learning.

The *ilmiye* was headed by the sheikh ül-Islam, the grand mufti, and just below him the two chief justices of the army (*kadıasker*), one for Rumelia (the Balkans and beyond) and one for Anatolia and other eastern parts of the empire. Next in the hierarchy were the judges (*kadı*) of imperial cities such as Istanbul, Mecca, Cairo and Damascus, and below them the scholars (*müderris*) of the most prestigious *medrese*s, most of them in Istanbul. The number of ulema in the upper echelons was limited and concentrated in the main imperial centres. At the provincial level, however, there were numerous cadres of judges, juris consults and teachers who, since they generally lacked a full *medrese* education, were not permitted to use the title ulema. To this subcategory also belonged people attached to the innumerable foundations (*vakıf*) and the mosque preachers,[23] who conceptually must be kept apart from the officially appointed liturgical preacher, *hatip*. As deliverer of the Friday sermon, the *hatip* ritually represented the authority of the Prophet. He was also an expression of the subjects' allegiance to the ruler. By virtue of his official position and symbolic power, a liturgical preacher could gain both visibility and influence. In the Ottoman Empire an exceptional and prestigious position was held by those liturgical preachers enjoined to address the Friday congregations of the imperial mosques in Istanbul, such as the Aya Sofya, Sultan Ahmed ('Blue Mosque'), Beyazid, Fatih, Selim I, Valide and Şehzade mosques (Inalcık 1973: 168–72; Zilfi 1988: 24–5). Under Ottoman rule the ulema enjoyed more respect, honour and veneration among the rulers than had been the case in other Sunni states (Zilfi 1988: 24). However, these developments also paved the way for nepotism and other abuses of power.

### Potential Divisions among Ottoman Ulema

The ulema were, as indicated, active in legal and educational institutions. By holding the religious heritage in trust through educational institutions and sharia courts, the ulema contributed to the lawful or 'constitutional' character of the Ottoman state. The sultan was dependent on the law for his power; but the ulema were dependent on the maintenance of the imperial order. A balance was struck between *din-ü-devlet*, religion and state. Within the cabinet (*divan*), the sheikh ül-Islam was equal in power to the grand vizier, but his function was that of juris consult, not judge. However, to reach this elevated position, he had to serve in various positions in the *ilmiye* hierarchy, including as supreme justice of the military. As grand mufti, the highest interpreter of sharia, he even had the authority to declare the sultan unworthy of office, although he did not have the means to depose him (Zilfi 1988: 27).

As an embodiment of the community of believers, the ulema represented the people, but as appointees of the state they were part of the ruling elite (Zilfi 1988: 31). The nearer they drew to the state, the greater the risk that they became corrupted (Zilfi 1988: 28). Judges were especially exposed. Abuse did not pass unnoticed and led to discontent and division within religious cadres and the emergence of sometimes influential opposition movements. Common people were not unaffected by such developments, since the disputes could overflow into the mosques, where preachers with various leanings operated.

These observations show that the ulema and other clerics did not form a united stratum. On the contrary, several dividing lines cut through their ranks: First, there was competition within the ulema, especially between the senior judges and scholars (higher ulema) and those who had not attained such lofty offices (lower ulema), but, on the other hand, they maintained closer contact with their congregations. This was also reflected in the separation between a 'Friday mosque' or *cami* – a word alluding to *cuma* (Friday) as well as *cemaat* (congregation) – and smaller and less distinguished abodes, *mescit*s,[24] which often lacked a pulpit and therefore the entitlement to perform the Friday *hutbe*.[25] Second, there were tensions between the 'high (official) religion' of the *medrese*-educated ulema and 'folk religion' represented by Sufism. Third, frictions also befell the Sufi brotherhoods (*tarikat*s) themselves, between those with a more formal education and those lacking such credentials, including members of innumerable dervish lodges, noted for their emotional fervour (Zilfi 1988: 13–14).

To be sure, the mentioned divides did not reflect a rigorous, hierarchical order. As a matter of fact, there was ample space for social mobility in Ottoman society as shown in Zilfi's study of the seventeenth-century religious demagogue Kadızade Mehmet (1582–1635). As a provincial *vaiz* (born and raised in Balıkesir, south of the Marmara Sea), this figure had been trained in his home district and did not count as an ulema proper (Zilfi 1988: 163). However, as a talented *vaiz* – he marked himself out as an eloquent and emotive preacher, even attracting the interest of the palace – he managed to advance to positions as Friday preacher in the most prestigious cathedral mosques in the capital. Such appointments were made by the sultan, the sheikh ül-Islam or the grand vizier (Zilfi 1988: 165–6). Kadızade Mehmet's first such appointment was to the Sultan Selim I mosque, followed by an appointment to Beyazid in 1623, to Süleymaniye in 1631, and later the same year to Aya Sofya, which was the highest-ranking mosque in the Ottoman Empire. Consequently, he attained the highest position a Friday preacher could reach. There he stayed until his death, considered to be the most popular preacher of his time (Zilfi 1988: 132). Kadızade Mehmet's career trajectory also illustrates the then existing hierarchy among imperial mosques in Istanbul.

### Friday Prayer in Nineteenth-century Ottoman Cairo

Edward Lane's *Manners and Customs of the Modern Egyptians*, written between 1833 and 1835, is a rare ethnographic work about Friday sermons – however, from an Ottoman context at some distance from the capital. Lane's vigilant eyes and unceasing patience in narrating and drawing the details of all the walks of life have resulted in a lively description of Egypt at the time of Muhammad Ali (1769–1849, r. 1805–48). An Ottoman commander of Albanian origin, Muhammad Ali was appointed Ottoman governor (*vali*) of Egypt in 1805, a time of turmoil and power vacuum in the wake of the French occupation in 1798 under Napoleon Bonaparte. Muhammad Ali consolidated his power by mounting a bloody coup against Mamluk troops trapped in the Cairo Citadel in 1811. It was thanks to his efforts during the Ottoman–Wahhabi/Saudi war (1811–18) that the Egyptian army, under command of his son Ibrahim Pasha (1789–1848), was able to reclaim control over the Hijaz. Muhammad Ali also conquered the Sudan before turning against the Ottomans. After the Egyptian–Ottoman War (1831–3), Egypt took control of Syria and advanced as far as Adana, Konya and Kütahya, even threatening Istanbul. However, fearful that a collapse of the Ottoman Empire would serve Russia's interests, Britain, Austria and other European states came to the help of the Ottomans, who were able to win back Syria in the Second Egyptian–Ottoman War (1839–41). It should not be forgotten that the Greek War of Independence (1821–32) coincided with the Egyptian–Ottoman conflicts.

It was during these turbulent times that Edward Lane (1801–76) stayed in Egypt.[26] He was twenty-four when he arrived but had by then already acquired sufficient proficiency in Arabic to get on well with the local people and, dressed in native clothes, was generally 'mistaken' for a Turk (Lane 2003: xv). The division of chapters bears witness to the fact that he had achieved insightful understanding of Islam and Islamic culture. 'Personal characteristics and dress of the Muslim Egyptians' (Chapter I), and 'Infancy and early education' (Chapter II) was followed by 'Religion and laws' (Chapter III) and 'Government' (Chapter IV). From a European perspective, government and laws belonged together, rather than religion and laws, but Lane was obviously mindful of the meaning of canonical sharia law to make the appropriate pairing. The first few lines in 'Religion and laws' read as follows:

> As the most important branch of their education, and the main foundation of their manners and customs, the religion and laws of the people who are the subject of these pages must be well understood – not only in their general principles, but in many minor points – before we can proceed to consider their social conditions and habits in the state of manhood. (Lane 2003: 64)

Thus does Lane convey his impression of the role of religion in the daily life of 'modern Egyptians'. The general atmosphere of mosque services is described as both egalitarian – 'the rich and poor pray side by side' (Lane 2003: 81)[27] – and restrained – 'looks and behaviour in the mosque are not those of enthusiastic devotion, but of calm and modest piety' (Lane 2003: 84). After a detailed description (full of 'minor points') of the daily ritual prayers and the purification rituals coupled with them, he gives an equally copious account of the Friday noon prayer, including the *hutbe*, which is reproduced in full.

Of special interest in relation to the Friday noon prayers, are the larger, congregational mosques (*cami*). The personnel or retainers active in such a mosque would be the following:

- One supervisor or *nazır*
- Two imams, of which one would serve as *hatip* and the other as 'ordinary imam' or 'prayer leader'
- One or more muezzins
- One or more door-keepers (depending on the number of minarets and entrances)
- Other servants for cleaning and general maintenance (Lane 2003: 82)

These people would be paid by foundations (*vakıf*) connected with the mosque, but their wages were low, meaning they would have to have other occupations (usually as traders, schoolmasters or druggists and perfumers) to make ends meet. It was also possible to make a living by reciting the Koran on special occasions in private homes (Lane 2003: 83). Large mosques would be open all day, but Al-Azhar, the most celebrated, was open around the clock. Smaller mosques, on the other hand, would be closed between the morning and noon prayers (Lane 2003: 83).

The smaller mosques could get by with fewer staff, for example only one imam, who would also serve as *hatip* during the Friday noon prayer (Lane 2003: 82). From this, one deduces that *hutbe*s were held not only in large mosques, but also in smaller ones.

## Friday Preaching in Modern Turkey – Rural Perspectives

Since written culture flourished in urban centres, historical archives and manuscripts are also mostly related to such areas, while scholarship related to village life is extremely scarce. As mentioned, *hutbe* traditions and practices are underrepresented in academic research. In the case of preaching customs in rural areas the available material is even more limited. Therefore, contemporary ethnographic studies of villages before the onset of modern urbanisation, as well as biographies linked to the early republican period, offer valuable insights into religious life also in traditional contexts. In particular, two studies related to modern Turkey stand out: one representing an anti-clerical perspective; the other written from within a circle of pious believers.

*A Village in Anatolia* (1965) distinguishes itself through its frankness and detailed observations. The author, Mahmut Makal (1931–2018), himself of rural background, was a village teacher, educated in one of the Village Institutes (Köy Enstitüleri) founded in 1940, but closed in 1954 due to political radicalisation (allegedly communist leanings), among the students. Makal finished his education in 1947 and worked for six years as a village teacher in remote and poor villages in Kayseri province, south-east of Ankara. The book is based on notes from this period and was first published in two volumes in Turkish in 1950 and 1952 respectively. The editor of the English translation was the British social anthropologist Paul Stirling, also known for his fieldwork in two villages in similar areas during almost the same period. In his monograph *Turkish Village* (1965), Stirling describes a village mosque as follows:

> The village mosques . . . looked from the outside like larger versions of village houses, except that an outside staircase ran up to roof level, ending in a platform covered by a small pinnacle which constituted the minaret. Inside, the floor was covered with rugs, where the faithful came shoeless to perform their ritual prayers or to listen to the Holy Koran. (Stirling 1965: 20)

The image of such a mosque is reproduced in Makal's book, which reflects the generally impoverished conditions of the village (Makal 1965: 14). Stirling's description of a village imam (*hoca*) was that of a person known to be respectable. He got his appointment from the mufti, while the latter was appointed by the Directorate of Religious Affairs. Especially during Friday prayers, the imam stands at the centre of attention and the whole village must listen to his exposition. Otherwise, what renders the imam prestige and status is his personal learning and piety. However, the situation prevailing in the two villages studied by Stirling deviated somewhat from this largely affirmative description:

> In Elbaşı and Sakaltutan, during the years I knew these villages, a new imam was appointed each year, and none of them was satisfactory to the villagers, nor highly regarded. The men appointed were ordinary villagers from local villages, not conspicuously more learned than the rest. Their objective in seeking office seems to have been the attached income. (Stirling 1965: 229)

Makal's description of the village imam and other religious people linked to various dervish orders is more in tune with Stirling's somewhat negative assessment.

> The Mosque is the villager's centre of learning. One might say that the whole shape of the villagers' lives is influenced by the admonitions of the Hojas on Fridays, and by the sermon of the preacher. On certain Fridays and feast days still more important Hojas come to preach, and this gives the thing an additional novelty. 'O congregation of Moslems, God Almighty states in the Sacred Koran . . .' So they begin; and such sermons read by the preacher are often full of wise precepts. At the same time the sermon invariably ends by insulting the congregation and informing them that they will all burn in hell. Whatever the sentence pronounced by the Hoja, *that* the congregation is. It is not like a lesson at school – you can't raise objections![28] As there's no raising of objections in religion, you just listen, as though to a story; and when you come out there's just nothing anyone can do about it. The only thing everyone is thinking about is the prospect of his burning away in hell. And, of course, he regrets having come into the world at all! (Makal 1965: 150)

Makal describes one imam, Molla Sıddık,[29] who, especially on Fridays, held fire-and-brimstone sermons. He would emphasise the importance of ritual ablutions, 'till one begins to wonder whether Mohammedanism is a matter of ritual ablutions and nothing more' (Makal 1965: 150). In order to illustrate that no excuse is strong enough to neglect the *namaz* prayers, he brought up a scaring example of a woman being in the midst of her birth-pangs: 'if the hour of prayer comes before the child is fully born, perhaps while only its head has emerged, it is a religious duty that she must perform the divine service even in that predicament' (Makal 1965: 151). What surprises, and fills the narrator, alias teacher, with envy, are the warm feelings that the villagers expose in relation to any religious personality. As poor as they usually were, they were always willing and able to give/offer something. After three hours of *vaaz* and one hour of *hutbe* from the pulpit 'my head was all fuddled and my body felt as if it had just come out of hell'. 'On emerging from the mosque we found they had spread a carpet in front of the door. Out came their purses, and they threw the Hoja his due on to the carpet. There was no one who did not do this' (Makal 1965: 152). As a 'secular' teacher in this religion-imbued environment, Makal was treated as an outsider, often ignored, even humiliated by the villagers. His description of the religious events and ceremonies bears the marks of that trauma. Still, the image of what preaching could be like in many rural areas is not belied by other sources.

### A Turkish Village Imam during Modernisation

Another rare testimony about religious life in a village setting in early republican Turkey is found in *Kutuz Hoca'nın Hatıraları* (Kutuz Hoca's memories) (2015), a book based on the protagonist's recollections, edited by his son İsmail Kara (b. 1955), professor of theology at Marmara University in Istanbul. Mehmet Kara (1918–2011), known locally as Kutuz Hoca,[30] was from Rize province on the Black Sea coast.

Kutuz Hoca's father, Kutuz Hüseyin (1880–1958), was a *medrese* teacher (*müderris*) or mulla, a profession he inherited from his own father. However, being a village mulla did not relieve a person of the usual village or farming duties, and it also meant having to serve both as imam and preacher (*hatip*). In Ottoman times, and even as late as the 1950s and 1960s, many villages could not afford a permanent imam and would instead hire one for the winter months and/or Ramadan.[31] As educated imams, Kutuz Hoca, his father and grandfather therefore also provided their services to nearby villages or towns during the cold season or the month of fasting.[32]

Kutuz Hoca began to study the Koran at early age, which coincided with the first years of the Republic. By the age of twelve he knew the Koran by heart, thereby becoming *hafız*. It was only after he had completed this basic

Koranic education that he attended the then three-year-long compulsory primary school.

As *hafız*, Kutuz Hoca was considered learned enough to serve as imam in nearby towns and villages during Ramadan, which earned him new experiences as well as an extra income. A month-long absence from obligatory schooling seemed neither to bother him nor his father unduly. Initially, his father provided guidance for these 'Ramadan campaigns'. His first assignment was to Bafra, not far from the Black Sea port of Samsun, when he was only thirteen, 'not even old enough to fast during Ramadan' (Kara 2015: 95). Father and son stopped at a carefully selected coffee shop, where the father gave a *vaaz*, thereby advertising their recitation and sermonising skills, upon which connections for the upcoming holy month were made.

The following year they went to the provincial centre of Rize. Henceforth, and for many years thereafter, Kutuz Hoca continued to serve as imam and *hafız* during Ramadan,[33] a quite lucrative engagement. Such services could even earn a skilful imam or *hoca* enough cash for a whole year (Kara 2015: 95). Kutuz Hoca's last *Ramazanlık* was in 1946, the year after he returned from his three-and-a-half years of military service. His earnings were sufficient for him to repay a loan on his house (Kara 2015: 103). However, pursuing a *Ramazanlık* was not an easy way to make money. There was no guarantee a *hoca* could find a proper place to stay and during one Ramadan Kutuz Hoca had to take lodgings in a coffee shop. Nonetheless, the hardships were worth the effort, because apart from the extra income, the undertaking allowed the *hafız* to burnish his skills as Koran reciter. Without such performances, this skill could easily wither (Kara 2015: 105).

Upon Kutuz Hoca's and his father's return to the village after Ramadan of 1932 they realised the *ezan* was no longer being called, the reason being the law forbidding *ezan* in Arabic (see Chapter 3). In particular, elderly imams were uncomfortable with reading the *ezan* in Turkish, and preferred, out of shame and distress, to omit it altogether. Kutuz Hoca, however, was young enough to learn the new *ezan*, even finding it amusing (Kara 2015: 95). It was not until 1950, when the law was abolished and he noticed how people rejoiced at hearing the *ezan* in Arabic again, that he realised how deeply this issue had touched the souls of common believers (Kara 2015: 95).

For Kutuz Hoca, learning was a lifelong process. He had started his train-ing at the age of eight and remained in touch with older and more experienced imams until he was well over forty, in order to improve his knowledge. So, for him, education and professional practice went hand in hand. Nor should it be overlooked that while discharging his responsibilities as imam – leading prayers and providing Koranic and religious education to new generations – he continued to work as a farmer. He was busy with beekeeping, in some years producing as much as 200 kg of honey (Kara 2015: 194). In his youth he had also worked as a plasterer in cities such as Istanbul and Ankara. Dur-ing the Second World War he was exempted from military service in order to join the Medical Corps, which required six months of training. Thus, when the war was over, he became the 'doctor' of the village, charged with admin-istering injections, sewing and dressing wounds, recommending medicines. Later, Kutuz Hoca participated in government vaccination campaigns against typhus and diphtheria, sometimes administering as many as 200 vaccinations a day (Kara 2015: 130). For this purpose, he travelled extensively, and wher-ever he went he would also serve as imam, *hatip* and muezzin. In this way, he became a well-known figure in the surrounding areas.

Kutuz Hoca was first appointed village imam in 1939, but only for the winter season. Then the war intervened, and he secured his second position as imam only in 1947. That was in Kayabaşı, a nearby village, and the year after he became imam in the Büyük Cami (big mosque) of his own village (Kara 2015: 140–2). As village imam, he was paid by the villagers themselves, not the state, but in 1951 he was officially enrolled by Diyanet as imam, but not *hatip*, even if he carried out that task as well.

**Imam, but not *Hatip***

The relationship between imam and *hatip* requires further explanation. According to Ottoman traditions, the *hatip* was at the top of the hierarchy of the local mosque, above the imam. It was he who read the *hutbe* and led the Friday noon prayer. Without his consent, no one else could perform this service. Moreover, the *hatip*, but not the imam, was appointed by the provincial mufti. The imam, by contrast, was appointed by a local founda-tion or *vakıf* (Kara 2015: 143).[34] In addition, the *hatip* was exempt from military service.

In larger villages, the *hatip* served the state as its religious official. Concerning relations with the village community, however, it was the imam who was in charge. Kutuz Hoca's story aptly shows how a village imam could be involved in all kinds of activities. The imam stood at the centre of village life – economically, culturally (religion and education), socially and – in Kutuz Hoca's case – even medically (Kara 2015: 148f.). The *hatip*, however, had a more detached relation to the villagers, but enjoyed higher formal status.

In 1948, when Kutuz Hoca was appointed imam by his own village, there was no officially appointed *hatip*, which meant that the Friday noon service fell to him. At that time, he started to keep a notebook on his sermons – 'Hutbe Defteri'. About these sermons, he recalled:

> These *hutbe*s were certainly not mine. They were *hutbe*s I had borrowed from other imams, written in Arabic. Sometimes I added a verse from the Koran. In those days, there was usually no '*vaaz ü nasihat*' [exhortatory preaching] in Turkish in the Friday sermons. (Kara 2015: 142)

Kutuz Hoca's official appointment in 1951 included an exam before the provincial mufti. Thereafter, he was secured a stable income. In addition to the already numerous duties, he was now responsible for setting of the times for *sahur* and *iftar* (starting and breaking the fast during Ramadan) (Kara 2015: 147).[35] He also made it a habit to hold a *vaaz* for men on Fridays (before the noon service) and for women on Saturdays before noon (Kara 2015: 201). He retired in 1977 but did not want to accept his redundancy payment, since he did not consider it canonical (*helal*). Instead, he donated his rather decent severance package of TL120,000[36] to various public projects such as schools and roads, to the consternation of his sons, who, as university students, were struggling to make ends meet (Kara 2015: 159–61).

## Conclusions

The schematic review of selected milestones in the history of the Islamic *hutbe* offered in this chapter is concluded in a self-biographical story about what it was like to be a rural imam – and *hatip* – in mid-twentieth-century republican Turkey. Even if a single portrait does not allow for far-reaching generalisations, and even if this image is tinged with some idealisation, Kutuz Hoca's story brings to life the circumstances under which many imams and *hatip*s carried out their professions in the newly established secular order. For example, concerning religious education, especially Koranic studies, the old *medrese* system persisted. Strict regulation of the official education of religious personnel and the subsequent closure of such education (1932) increased, rather than eased, the pressure on local informal institutions to meet the need for religious training. This kind of traditional training brought anxiety and even feelings of guilt, since someone, usually one of the younger students, had to stand on guard to watch out for gendarmes. Such 'involuntary' disobedience would also accentuate distrust towards the central authorities. Still, the traditional *medrese* or other forms of informal training ensured that a certain level of religious learning was preserved. Thus, when official religious training regained momentum following the political liberalisation of the 1950s, there was a legacy to build upon.

Kutuz Hoca's story is also telling concerning the provision of personnel to the mosques. By no means did all mosques have an appointed imam or *hatip*. Many village mosques had to do without an imam, or could hire one only for the winter, the only season when imams from neighbouring villages could take off time from their own farming duties. Another common practice was hiring an imam for Ramadan. However, a permanent imam was not needed for daily prayers: any villager who knew the required prayers could lead the *namaz*. For Friday noon prayers, villagers would go to a larger village or town nearby and there join the congregation of a larger mosque. In other respects, however, the village mosque was also the centre for activities outside of worshipping and preaching, such as various forms of religious instruction, and 'conversation' (*sohbet*) meetings, that is, more informal gatherings.

The story also contributes insights into the professional hierarchy of a local mosque. The *hatip*, appointed by the mufti, was at the top. Regarded as the mufti's representative in the village, he was also exempted from military service. Close daily relations with villagers, however, fell to the imams.[37] And, of special significance for this study, the memories suggest what the preparation of a *hutbe* might be like in the rural areas of the time. As a fairly young (thirty years old in 1948), but presumably rather experienced imam, Kutuz Hoca still collected *hutbe*s from more qualified imams. He recalls adding one or two quotations from the Koran, but there was really no *vaaz* or sermonising part in Turkish. The *hutbe* was thus merely liturgical, consisting of familiar phrases in Arabic, the meaning of which were not understood by the villagers. This also corresponds with Makal's (1965) and Stirling's (1965) accounts of Friday preaching in 'their' villages in central Anatolia. Here was a field, waiting to be filled with ideas in tune with the times. How this potential was used, and what the challenges were in terms of organisation and negotiation between different political, national and religious interests, is the topic of the following chapters.

## Notes

1. Despite its importance in the perpetuation of the Islamic tradition, the Friday sermon is generally underrepresented in scholarly research (Wensinck 1986; Becker 2006; Halldén 2005; Jones 2012; Gaffney 1994). However, limited in number though they be, the following studies offer vital insights into a range of historical periods and geographical areas: early history (Qutbuddin 2019), eleventh–fifteenth-century Spain and North Africa (Berkey 1992; Jones 2012); seventeenth–eighteenth-century Ottoman society (Zilfi 1988); nineteenth-century Ottoman society (Lane 2003); twentieth century, especially post-war, Jordan (Antoun 1989), Egypt (Gaffney 1994) and Turkey of the early republican period (Makal 1965; Kara 2015).

2. The official character of the *hutbe* also explains why, especially in the past, it was predominantly performed in larger, impressive or majestic ('cathedral') mosques.

3. In Arabic: Eid al-Fitr (fast-breaking) and Eid al-Adha (sacrifice). It should be added that *hutbe*s also can be performed on rarer, special occasions such as a solar or lunar eclipse or severe drought.

4. The steps described here follow contemporary Turkish practice. However, with small variations the ritual is the same all over the Muslim world.

5. The number of prostrations performed during the daily prayers varies according to the time of the day: morning (*sabah*) – two *sünnet* (sunna), two *farz* (obligatory) prostrations; noon (öğlen) – four *sünnet*, four *farz*, four *sünnet*; early afternoon (*ikindi*) – four *sünnet*, four *farz*; evening (*akşam*) – three *farz*, two *sünnet* (reversed order); evening (*yatsı*) – four *sünnet*, four *farz*, two *sünnet*; and night (*vitir*) – three *vacip* (neither *sünnet* nor *farz*).

6. To the extent that women are present during the Friday *hutbe*, they pray in separate spaces partly out of sight of the male congregation, such as in the rear or on the balcony.

7. Islamic jurisprudence (*fıkıh*) contains certain principles for grading correct and sinful behaviour. Correct acts range from the most obligatory (*farz*, somewhat weaker *vacip*) to the commendable (sunna, Turkish: *sünnet*) to the permissible

(*müstehap*). Likewise, behaviour to be avoided ranges from the bad or dreadful (*mekruh*) to the absolutely forbidden (*haram*). In between the more-or-less commanded behaviour and the more-or-less forbidden stands behaviour that is irrelevant from a religious point of view (*mübah*). *Sünnet* is sometimes rendered as supererogatory in English.

8. In modern Turkey 'rulers' – president and government leaders – are not mentioned by title or name. Instead, the prayers are done for the motherland, and the state (*Allah vatanı ve devleti korusun*).

9. Sword (or spire) has not been used in modern Turkey, a practice that was, however, forsaken during two successive Friday prayers (24 July and 31 July 2020) in Aya Sofya (Hagia Sophia), occasioned by the historical museum being reverted to a mosque (2 July 2020). The *hutbe*s were led by Diyanet Director Ali Erbaş.

10. The *kamet* (lit. standing) can be interpreted as having a deeper devotional meaning than the *ezan*. While the *ezan* simply summons the congregation, the *kamet* expresses an intent or readiness to undertake the obligatory prostrations. The *kamet* seems to have been added to the liturgy after Muhammad's lifetime, supposedly during the Umayyad Caliphate (Becker 2006: 64).

11. Abu Hurayra means 'father of the kitten'. The tradition has it that Abu Hurayra kept a kitten while herding his people's goats (Robson 1986).

12. Washing the entire body.

13. Wensinck argued that the ritual had three foundations: the early Arabian oratory, Muhammad's sunna, and Jewish and Christian sermon practices (Wensinck 1986).

14. Such a change would have implied performing the sermon (Arabic: *khuṭba*) before the prayer (*ṣalāt*), preaching from a pulpit (minbar), and making the call to prayer (*adhān*) as long as in the Friday service (Becker 2006: 51).

15. It is also believed that the Prophet inserted a '*amma ba'du*' here, which literally means 'as of after'. A freer translation would be 'after this, let's come to our topic'. Taking the Prophet as an example, this phrase has been used to separate the liturgical (praise, blessings and testimony) from the sermonising part. The expression is widely used and has become a distinguishing mark of a valid *hutbe* (Wensinck 1986).

16. A companion of the Prophet.

17. An uncle of the Prophet.

18. Frequently used sources were Imam Muslim and Muhammad al-Bukhari's *hadis* collections, which since the tenth century have been recognised for their canonicity within Sunni Islam. Needless to say, the canonical status of existing corpuses of jurisprudence and other sources varied according to the predominant law school.

As an example, the Maliki and Shafii schools hold that the Friday communal prayer should only be held in one mosque in a given town, while the Hanefi school does not recognise this limitation (Jones 2012: 24–5).

19. Sharia is derived from the two most authoritative sources, the Koran and the *hadis* (Arabic: *hadith*). Muhammad is regarded as the lawgiver, but only in the sense that his life and conduct serve as a model of righteous living. As a result of academic discussion based on these sources, a complex corpus of jurisprudence (*fıkıh*) developed. The two recognised methods for such legal elaboration have been reasoning by analogy (*kiyas*) and decision by consensus of the learned (*icma*). The earliest large-scale and systematic compilations of the law date to the late eighth and early ninth centuries. It was during the first century of the Abbasid Caliphate (750–1258) that the four different Sunni law schools – Shafii, Maliki, Hanbali and Hanefi – emerged, in addition to the Shi'a law school (Hjärpe 2005: 143; Hodgson 1974: Vol 1, 333ff.).

20. Liturgical preachers were appointed by the ruler, or at least with his sanction. The position of *hatip* was therefore political (Jones 2012: 259). This necessitated extra caution of the preacher. He was looked upon as the mouthpiece of the ruler, which did not require total submission. A *hatip* could resign or turn down an invitation for office in an effort to distance himself from the power-holder. However, the position also afforded opportunities, and a popular *hatip* could gather a large following, where people would gather after the Friday sermon to kiss his hand. Appreciation by the congregation and dignitaries would augment his power and influence (Jones 2012: 217–18).

21. 'Islam has known few more faithful guardians of its rites and precepts than the Ottoman Empire at its height . . . For ruler and ruled, Islam, more than monarchy or the Ottoman house, ordered and gave meaning to Ottoman life,' writes Zilfi (1988: 23–4). Paraphrasing the chronicler Hezarfen Hüseyn (d. 1691), the author continues: 'Islam was for the Ottoman Empire the root, while the state grew only as a branch from it' (Zilfi 1988: 23). This devotion was especially visible in its architecture. As a result of various endowments (*vakıfs*), Istanbul could boast hundreds of mosques, learning institutions (*medreses*), mausoleums, dervish lodges (*tekke* and *zaviye*), fountains, orphanages, public refectories, hospitals, asylums, Koran schools (*mektep*) and hospices. And what gave life to these architectural expressions were the ulema, the 'living embodiment' of Ottoman Islam (Zilfi 1988: 24).

22. The holy places were captured during the reign of Selim I (r. 1512–20), who was succeeded by Süleyman the Magnificent (r. 1520–66).

23. Preachers (*vaizan*, pl. of *vaiz*) did not belong to the upper echelons of the religious hierarchy. Mostly trained in their home provinces; they did not count as

ulema proper. However, it was possible for a talented *vaiz* to advance to *hatip* in one of the major or 'cathedral' mosques in the capital or any other imperial city. Such appointments were made by the sultan, the sheikh ül-Islam, or the grand vizier (Zilfi 1988: 163, 165–6).

24. *Mescit*, from *masjid* (place of prostration), which in Arabic is used for any size of mosque.

25. With around 200 Friday, or cathedral, mosques in the capital at the end of the seventeenth century, one could hardly say that there was a scarcity of such abodes (Zilfi 1988: 130).

26. Lane commented on this tumultuous situation in the first paragraph of Chapter IV, entitled 'Government': 'Egypt has, of late years, experienced great political changes, and nearly ceased to be a province of the Turkish Empire. The present Básha (Mohmmad 'Alee), having exterminated . . . the Memlooks, who shared the government with his predecessors, has rendered himself almost an independent prince. He, however, professes allegiance to the Sultán, and remits the tribute according to former custom, to Constantinople; he is, however, under an obligation to respect the fundamental laws of the Kur-án and the Traditions; but he exercises a dominion otherwise unlimited. He may cause any one of his subjects to be put to death without the formality of a trial, or without assigning any cause: a simple horizontal motion of his hand is sufficient to imply the sentence of decapitation. But I must not be understood to insinuate that he is prone to shed blood without any reason. Severity is a characteristic of this prince rather than wanton of cruelty, and boundless ambition has prompted him to almost every act by which he has attracted either praise or censure' (Lane 2003: 110).

27. '[T]he man of rank or wealth enjoying no peculiar distinction or comfort, unless (which is sometimes the case) he have a prayer-carpet brought by his servant and spread for him' (Lane 2003: 81).

28. See Chapter 4 for a discussion of Maurice Bloch's (1975) theory of 'everyday speech acts' versus 'formalised speech acts'.

29. Stirling reports that in some villages there was a new imam every year (1965: 229).

30. *Kutuz* means bold and short in stature; *hoca* (*hodja*) means teacher, religious or otherwise.

31. During the rest of the year the mosque would be opened in the evening and any one among the villagers who was knowledgeable enough would lead the prayer (Kara 2015: 39).

32. An anecdotal detail: traditionally *medrese* students were exempt from military service. Nonetheless, Kutuz Hüseyin (Kutuz Hoca's father), despite his lack

of military training, was drafted in 1912 for the Balkan war. During the First World War he fought in the campaign against Russia. He subsequently escaped to his village – hiding under the roof of a house – only to be discovered and sent to Hopa, a town east of Rize on the Black Sea coast. Only in 1916, when the Russians occupied the region, did he return to the village (Kara 2015: 31).

33. It is commendable for a Muslim to read or have the Koran recited in full during the month of Ramadan.

34. This means that 'episcopal appointment' was applied for *hatip*s, while 'congregational appointment' was valid for imams. See Richard Antoun's study of Jordanian preacher Luqman (1989: 84).

35. Around the mid-1960s, this responsibility was assumed by Diyanet in Ankara and disseminated over the growing radio network.

36. Equal to approximately five years of income at that time.

37. Under deputy director Tayyar Altıkulaç, the duties of imam and *hatip* were merged, meaning that the previous privileged position of the *hatip*s (same salary as the prayer-leader/imam, but duty only during the Friday noon service) was abolished. Henceforth, the official title became Imam-Hatip (Altıkulaç 2011: 191). For more on reforms initiated by Altıkulaç, see Chapter 5.

# 2

## EARLY AUTHORISED *HUTBE* COLLECTIONS: A HOMILETIC TRADITION UNDER SECULAR STATE CONTROL

The War of National Independence (1919–22) paved the way for the establishment of Turkey as a secular republic. Paradoxically, however, the war itself was largely waged as a holy war – jihad. Mobilisation was undertaken in the name of Islam against the invasion of 'infidel' Greece, supported by Western 'imperialist' powers. That the struggle, with its suffering and sacrifice, but also feverish hopes, was deeply entrenched in religious faith is unmistakably conveyed in the Turkish national anthem from 1921. Emblematic expressions like 'martyr', 'glorious God', 'sacred temples', 'call to prayer' (*ezan*) and 'confession of faith' (*şehadet*) undoubtedly bespeaks an atmosphere of strong religious ardour.[1] Even as the republican leaders after the war steered towards a modernising and secularist profile, they also had to pay heed to Islamic traditions and institutions. How political and religious interests played into each other, especially concerning the Friday *hutbe*, is the topic of this chapter.

The chapter is divided into three sections and starts with a description of how religion step by step withered from official, but not necessarily all public contexts.[2] The second section deals with the modern, republican polity as a moral order and how that compares to the Ottoman imperial system, especially concerning notions of citizenship and cultural and/or national identities. The third, and major part, is an analysis of the homiletic discourse that emerged through a couple of authorised *hutbe* collections of the 1920s and

1930s. The early republican *hutbe*s are important, not only for what they conveyed in terms of the mood prevailing during the early Republic, but also because they set the standards for *hutbe*-writing for several decades to come.

## Dismantling of Religion in the Official and Public Spheres

When Turkey, after a decade of continuous warfare (1912–22), entered the road of Enlightenment-inspired reforms – the abrogation of the caliphate (3 March 1924), the abolition of the sultanate (1 November 1922), and the proclamation of the Republic (29 October 1923) – this caused strong reactions in the Muslim world.[3] These spectacular moves were bolstered by new legislation, fortifying the foundations for the future secular order. Most important was the Law of the Unification of Education (*Tevhid-i Tedrisat Kanunu*), through which religious colleges (*medrese*s) were closed and all education – religious and secular – was assembled under the Ministry of Education. Simultaneously, two new agencies, the Directorate of Religious Affairs (Diyanet İşleri Reisliği, after 1965 Diyanet İşleri Başkanlığı) and the Directorate-General for Pious Foundations (Evkaf Umum Müdürlüğü), were created and subordinated to the prime minister's office.[4] Other secularising reforms followed in rapid succession. The canonical law (sharia) was rescinded (April 1924) and replaced with an order adapted from the Swiss Civil Code (February 1926). Thereby the sharia courts with their *kadı*s (judges) and other personnel were dissolved. In addition, all Sufi brotherhoods, representing popular forms of worship, were banned (December 1925).

The effect of these reforms was the dispersal of a good deal of the ulema, especially specialists from the higher echelons. Former *medrese* teachers (*müderris*, Arabic: *mullā*) and *kadı*s had to adapt themselves to the new secular institutions or take up some other work in order to find an income. Imams, *hatip*s and muezzins, however, mostly remained in their positions out of need for personnel to conduct daily prayers, including the Friday sermons, funerals and the two annual religious festivities. Another conspicuous consequence was the disappearance of various abodes of worship. Only the mosques were left in the new religious landscape, while *medrese*s, *tekke*s and *zaviye*s (dervish lodges), *türbe*s (tombs) and sharia courts either were closed or used for other purposes. That some *medrese* training and Sufi/dervish activities de facto continued bespeaks the presence of a quiet resistance.[5]

How abrupt the transition between the old and the new order was is better understood when considering the amount of religious paraphernalia attached to the opening ceremony of the first Turkish parliament on 23 April 1920, only a handful of years apart from the secularising reforms. This occasion is described in detail in a document issued by Mustafa Kemal [Atatürk] and quoted by himself in his six-days-long speech (*Nutuk*) in parliament in 1927. Written in great haste, the circular was communicated to army corps cooperating with the nationalist resistance movement; to all provinces (*vilayets*), districts, central committees of the resistance organisation Union for the Defence of the Rights; and to all magistrates, and reads:

1. On Friday 23 April, after prayer, the Grand National Assembly, if God be willing, will be opened.

2. As the duties of the National Assembly will be of a vital description and of the utmost importance – such as, for instance, securing the independence of our country and the deliverance of the seat of the Caliphate and Sultanate from the hands of our enemies – and as it will be opened on a Friday, the solemn character of this day will be profited by offering solemn prayer, before the opening, in the Hacıbayram Mosque. All the honourable deputies will take part in this prayer, in the course of which the light of the Koran and the call to prayer will be poured forth over all the believers.

When the prayer is over, we shall move to the place of meeting specially decorated with the sacred flag and the holy relic. Before entering the building, a prayer of thanksgiving will be said and sheep will be sacrificed as an offering of thanks.

During this ceremony, the troops belonging to the Army Corps will line the road leading from the Mosque to the building and will take up special positions *en route*.

3. In order to emphasise the sacred character of this day, the reading of the whole of the Koran and Bukhari [*hadis* collection] containing the tradition of the Prophet will begin at the chief town in the province under supervision of the Vali of the Vilayet, and the last portions will be read for the devotion of the people in front of the building where the Assembly will meet when the Friday prayer is over.

4. In every part of our sacred, suffering country the reading of the Koran and Bukhari will begin from today onward, and before Friday prayer the solemn call to prayer is to be intoned from the minarets. When during the Hutbe the Imperial title of His Majesty our Sultan and Caliph is pronounced, special

prayers and petitions will be offered, begging that within a short space of time His Sublime Person, His Imperial States and all his oppressed subjects may regain freedom and happiness. The reading of the Koran being finished at the end of the Friday prayer, sermons will be delivered on the importance and sacred character of the national endeavours which aim at the liberation of the seat of the Caliph and Sultan and every part of our country. Sermons will also be delivered on the obligation of everyone to do his patriotic duty, which will be pointed out to him by the Grand National Assembly that comprises representatives of the whole nation. Prayers will then be said for the deliverance, salvation and independence of our Caliphate and Sultanate, of our Faith and our Empire, of our Country and our Nation.

After these religious and patriotic observances have terminated and having left the mosque, a solemn ceremony of congratulations will take place in all the Ottoman towns and seats of the highest authorities to commemorate the opening of the National Assembly. After Friday prayer the Mevlit (*) will be read everywhere.

5. You are requested to use every possible means to spread the foregoing communication without delay to the remotest villages, among the smallest units of troops, among all the organizations and institutions in the country. It is to be printed in heavy type and placarded publicly. In places where this is not possible, it is to be printed and distributed free.

6. We pray God to grant that we may be successful. (Atatürk 2008: 365–6)

(*) Hymn in verse in honour of Muhammad.

The next day (22 April 1920), the following communiqué was distributed:

As the Grand National Assembly will be opened and commence its duties, if God be willing, on Friday 23 April, you are informed hereby that from this day forward the National Assembly will be the lawful authority to which all civil and military authorities and entire nation must turn. (Atatürk 2008: 367)

This circular is cited in full, because it underlines the impact of religion during the War of Independence. It is also a reminder of the fact that the 'nationalist' war was fought within what was still an Ottoman social and political order. At the same time, the opening of the first Grand National Assembly in Ankara signified a decisive break with the Ottoman government in Istanbul. Thus, it marked the peak in the struggle for national independence. The fact that the celebrations were draped in religious garb added even more gravity and passion to the situation. Choosing Friday for the inauguration contained its own deep-seated symbolism. Thereby the seriousness of the event had been duly conveyed to the Muslim/Turkish population.

The scene put in place by the elaborate religious ceremony stands in sharp contrast to the formal character of the public performance represented by the Great Speech itself seven years later. The different textual contents – one a religious revelation (the Koran) and the other a narrative about a military victory and political revolution (*Nutuk*) – speak for themselves. In light of the new, secular context, the religious atmosphere of the opening ceremony already appeared anachronistic. This aptly illustrates how Islam was stripped of its official status, that is, how its political functions were redefined. This was not least true of the Friday sermons. As shown in the subsequent analysis, instead of engaging in political issues of nationwide concerns they came to display an accommodation to local and/or small-scale environments; a trivialisation of sermonising discourse that also had effects on the character of the public sphere.[6]

Another example of reduced visibility of religious symbols in official contexts is the ceremony carried out in connection to the transition to republic (29 October 1923, subsequently Turkey's National Day). After the decision was passed, the parliamentary session was closed with a simple intercession. Instead, the newly inaugurated Republic was celebrated throughout the country with a salute of 101 guns (Kinross 2001: 381). This time turban, mosque, pulpit and Koran were pushed into the background, while symbols for state and military power held the stage.

A last example of the waning of religion in the official sphere is taken from primary and secondary school education, where religion almost totally disappeared. Traditionally, primary education (*mektep*) had been based on Koran reading and other related topics. Higher education was provided for in *medreses*. However, as a part of the nineteenth-century modernising reforms, education had taken a more secular turn – at least in larger urban areas. Still, even in its reformed shaping, religion had remained part of the obligatory curriculum. With the Republic, religion was removed from the schedule. Even vocational training of religious personnel came to a stop in the early 1930s due to lack of students, itself an effect of the general repression (Jäschke 1972: 75).

To sum up: two effects of the secularisation process should be emphasised. The first is related to the decrease in the number and diversity of places, where people could practise their religion and discuss issues of common interests.[7] Secondly, this trend had some leverage on the relative importance of the mosques, since they represented the only sacred abodes left for worship and religious gatherings – a development that promoted the overall standing of mainstream Sunni Islam at the cost of the other, especially Alevi and Sufi forms of worship. Thus, two tendencies were at work: a narrowing down of the space allowed for religious practices, and a transformation in the direction of greater homogeneity and uniformity concerning religious practices. Both trends undoubtedly facilitated official secular control.

## A New Social Contract

The legal reforms were part of a broader transformation affecting the underlying social contract, the principles of which were laid down in the 1924 constitution, a statute that remained in force until the military coup in 1960. However, before commenting on the 1924 charter, the principles of legitimacy underlying the previous order will be summarised.

The Ottoman Empire cannot easily be brushed aside as a form of Oriental despotism. According to time-honoured custom, the sultan had the right to dismiss or execute any of his subjects. This did not mean that his power was unlimited. As a matter of fact, the sharia was valid for the ruler as well, that is, the sultan did not stand above the canonical law. However, in force of their power as sovereigns, sultans also enacted laws of their own, *kanunname*s. This practice increased especially during the reign of Süleyman the Magnificent (r. 1520–66), therefore the epithet 'law-giver' (*kanuni*). Even if these practices brought restrictions, they never overturned the spirit of the sharia-based judicial system.[8] The special status of the canonical law appears from the fact that it was the religious scholars, who, as *kadı*s, were authorised to interpret and pass opinions on legal matters, including *kanunname*s. The *kadı* courts addressed cases concerning Islamic as well as sultanic laws. Therefore, despite its legal complexity, even disarray, and autocratic legacy, a kind of limited rule of law was practised within the Ottoman polity (Berkes 1998: 14–16).

A long-standing doctrine provided the philosophical underpinnings of this rule, named the 'circle of equity'. The hub of this doctrine lay in its proposition that the polity represented a functional equilibrium. The desired stability of the state (royal authority) was preserved as long as the three orders (or estates) – the military, the producers (farmers and traders) and the men of knowledge (those enjoined to interpret and administer justice – the sacred law) – fulfilled their respective functions/duties (Itzkowitz 1972: 88).[9] It was incumbent upon the ruler to uphold this balance, that is, to see to it that everyone remained within his own estate or area of activity and responsibility.[10] The legitimate or good ruler, who deserved obedience, was the one who succeeded in preserving order and stability. The good subject, on the other hand, was the one who fulfilled his duties within the given order of functional divisions. This was a kind of 'paternalist conception of authority' (Moore 1978: 23), representing a Hobbesian type of social contract, according to which individuals (the subjects) 'agree' among themselves to collectively submit their natural freedom to the all-powerful sovereign, who secures peace, safety and property rights (Hall and Gieben 1992: 106–7, 122). The social contract, on which the newly established Republic was built, was different. Sovereignty did not belong to the sultan, but to the people or the nation; the laws were not given by God and therefore immutable or issued by the sovereign (*kanunname*s) but enacted through an assembly elected by the people; and the individual, as citizen, was granted certain individual rights and freedoms.

Transition from the traditional Ottoman to the modern Turkish polity did not occur all at once. In fact, it was the outcome of more than a century of reform efforts, mixed with setbacks. Citizenship rights had been granted to all Ottoman subjects through the Tanzimat reforms of 1839. Thereby the 'slave' (*kul*) system, which had given the sultan the right to confiscate the property of, or even execute, his subjects at his own discretion, was abolished. The right to life and property and the rule of law was to be applied equally to all, including non-Muslims.[11] A parliamentary system, as part of a constitutional monarchy, had already been put to test during the last decades of the Ottoman Empire (1876–8 and 1908–18), albeit with varying degrees of success. The political turmoil that had surrounded earlier Ottoman constitutional reform efforts constituted an important background to the decisions taken by republican leaders. Presumably functioning as warnings, the 1924 constitution was not modelled so much on the two previous constitutions, as it was a product of developments during the War of Independence. The foundation of the 1924 constitution was laid in connection to the first national assembly. This urgently summoned assembly (see above) had been convened at the request of being endowed with 'extraordinary powers', meaning a fusion of the legislative and executive powers. Such an all-powerful assembly stood in contrast to the earlier Ottoman constitutional applications, where the legislature had been separated from and subordinated to the executive power, headed by the sultan (Özbudun and Gençkaya 2009: 8). The constitution of 1924 was based on the following principles:

- National sovereignty: The Grand National Assembly was the sole representative of the nation on whose behalf it exercises the rights of sovereignty (Article 4).
- All-powerful assembly: Both legislative and executive powers were concentrated in the Assembly (Article 5).
- Presidency: The Assembly was to exercise its executive authority through the President of the Republic, who was elected by the Assembly and the Council of Minsters appointed by the President (Article 7).
- The Assembly was empowered to supervise and dismiss the Council of Ministers at any time, while the Council had no power to dissolve the assembly and to hold new elections. (Özbudun and Gençkaya 2009: 11)

According to Özbudun and Gençkaya, the 1924 constitution was democratic 'in spirit'. 'However, this was a "majoritarian" or "Rousseauist" conception of democracy, rather than a liberal or pluralistic democracy based on an intricate system of checks and balances' (Özbudun and Gençkaya 2009: 12). There were, however, good reasons for the Turkish leaders to favour a strong 'all-powerful' assembly, since the establishment of such a forum represented the finale of a long struggle against the sultans.

> It was not surprising, therefore, that the only perceived threat to national interests was that which could come from the sultans; once this threat was removed, the revolutionaries thought, there would be no need to protect the nation against its own true representatives. Evidently, the framers of the Constitution of 1924 were not sufficiently aware that the tyranny of a majority was just as possible, and as dangerous, as a personal tyranny. (Özbudun and Gençkaya 2009: 13)

What the authors warn against is the possible despotic outcome of a constitutional law based on what comes close to Rousseau's theory of the 'general will'. According to such a majoritarian concept of democracy, sovereignty is absolute, indivisible and infallible, since the legislature represents the will of the nation. There is no place for special interests or demands, neither individual nor group based. Any challenge would be regarded as a threat to the sovereignty of the people. In practice, the theory may easily turn into the opposite of its intentions. The executive body – the president and the council of ministers – is tighter and therefore more prone to exercise power, while the legislature is numerically larger, diverse and therefore weaker. Thus, an all-powerful assembly easily works in favour of the executive body, which turns into the supreme and commanding power.

This confirms the tendency towards authoritarianism in post-revolutionary Turkish politics. Both during the single-party (1925–46) and the multi-party period (1946–60) the main executives and strong party cadres drove the assembly into a secondary position (Özbudun and Gençkaya 2009: 13). Another serious problem was the want of sufficient formal restraints on the legislative power, especially the lack of a judicial mechanism to control the constitutionality of enacted laws,[12] deficiencies that added to authoritarian tendencies. In sum: the 1924 constitution was democratic in spirit, but it lacked the legal checks and balances needed to curb tendencies towards authoritarianism and/or dictatorship.

Concerning the development of a democratic notion of citizenship, the above discussion reveals that demands for civil, political and social rights on an individual basis were not high on the agenda in early republican politics. Instead, the will of the nation stood in focus. Citizens were imagined as bound to the state, not as independent individuals, but as members of a closely unified national community. The strength of the nation was conditional upon its cohesion, but such unity was not supported by a common concern for individual rights and liberties. It was largely through membership of a culturally, rather than politically, defined community that citizens were bound to each other and to the state.

How did such a discourse resonate in the Friday sermons? Mustafa Kemal had advocated a national community built on shared political, linguistic, territorial, ethnic/racial, historical and ethical/moral identities (Afet İnan 1969: 22). There was no explicit reference to Islam here. However, inside the mosques Muslim identities ruled. Here it was not only the religious messages articulated through the *hutbe*s that held the fort. The symbolisms conveyed by the Friday sermons and other worship practices bolstered an already incipient sense of 'national' belonging based on Islam. When now turning to the *hutbe*s, the questions to be asked are: 'who was according to this homiletic discourse a good citizen?' In other words, 'what went into good citizenship?' and 'what distinguished a Turkish national in the existing context?'

## Muslim Identities in the Service of a Secular Nation State: *Hutbe* Collections of the Early Republican Era

The fact that common people gather for the Friday prayer every week certainly renders this medium an attractive arena for anyone who wants to reach out to the masses. The agency enjoined to organise these performances was Diyanet, but with an agenda restricted to 'belief and worship' (*itikadat ve ibadat*) (Law Number 429, Article 1). As will be discussed further in Chapter 5, Diyanet remained a modest institution during the mid-war period. It was not until 1965 that it was rendered a firmer administrative structure.

So, during the early decades of the Republic, how did the regime deal with the Friday *hutbe*s? The technical means for reaching out on a week-to-week basis were not available. Radio broadcast and telephone networks did not reach the villages until the 1950s, and not even then on an all-inclusive basis. Periodical journals and other printed material reaching out to all imams was not realised until the second half of the 1960s. *Hutbe* collections, however, offered a feasible alternative under the prevailing conditions. Islam had a long tradition of such publications, available also in the Ottoman book markets. In that perspective the problem boiled down to producing new (contemporary – *çağdaş*) *hutbe* collections that suited the times and purposes of the new regime. Particularly significant were two collections published by Diyanet. The first was *Türkçe Hutbe* in Ottoman script with two editions, 1927 and 1928 (fifty-one sermons). The second was a widely extended, two-volume collection (151 sermons), published in 1936 and 1937 in modern Turkish as *Yeni Hut-belerim* (My new sermons) (see Appendix II). Even though the author's name is only on the latter publication, both collections were written by Ahmed Hamdi Akseki (b. 1887), head of Diyanet from 1947 until his death in 1951.[13] Below follows a screening of these two collections. Since Akseki's *hutbe*s were used as templates for many decades to come, they are dealt with at some length.

### 'Turkish Sermon'

In the 1925 Estimates a special allowance was earmarked for the publication of a collection of *hutbe*s in Turkish. A competition was announced by Diyanet, encouraging religious staff around the country to submit contributions. What in fact happened to this initiative is unknown, but in 1927 the first edition of *Türkçe Hutbe* was published (Bulut 2006: 48; Bulut 2019a: 36) The topics, depicted below, spanned from economic and sociopolitical to religious and moral issues:

**Table 2.1** Topics of *hutbe*s (in Turkish and English)

| Topics of *hutbe*s (in Turkish) | Topics of *hutbe*s (in English) |
|---|---|
| 1. *Calışan mükafatını görür* | 1. He who works gets the reward |
| 2. *Vatan müdafaası* | 2. Defence of the homeland |
| 3. *Tayyare Cemiyeti'ne yardım* | 3. Aiding the Aeroplane Association |
| 4. *Temizlik* | 4. Cleanliness |
| 5. *Sağlığın başı temizliktir* | 5. Cleanliness as the beginning of health |
| 6. *Temizlik* | 6. Cleanliness |
| 7. *İman ve amel* | 7. Faith and good deeds |
| 8. *Kamil mümin* | 8. The ideal believer |
| 9. *Namazın hikmeti* | 9. Wisdom/inner meaning of *namaz* |
| 10. *Namaz ve hikmeti* | 10. *Namaz* and its wisdom |
| 11. *Peygamberimizin ahlakı* | 11. Our Prophet's ethics |
| 12. *Anaya babaya itaat* | 12. Obedience of mother and father |
| 13. *Anaya babaya hürmet* | 13. Respect of mother and father |
| 14. *Evlenmek ve evlat yetiştirmek* | 14. Marriage and raising children |
| 15. *Herkes kazancına bağlıdır* | 15. Everyone is tied to his earnings |
| 16. *İslam dininde çalışmanın değeri* | 16. The value of work in Islam |
| 17. *Çalışma ve uygulama* | 17. To work and put it into practice |
| 18. *Ticaret* | 18. Trade |
| 19. *Ticaret* | 19. Trade |
| 20. *Sanat* | 20. Crafts |
| 21. *Ziraat* | 21. Agriculture |
| 22. *Saygı ve yardımlaşma* | 22. To help each other with respect |
| 23. *Öksüzlere yardım* | 23. Helping orphans |
| 24. *Öksüzlere himaye etmek* | 24. Protecting orphans |
| 25. *Allah'ın ve Peygamber'in hayat verecek emirleri* | 25. Commands of Allah and the Prophet that give life |
| 26. *Allah'ı sevmek ve peygamberlerine uymak* | 26. Loving Allah and living according to the prophets |
| 27. *Ramazan ve oruç* | 27. Ramadan and fasting |
| 28. *Oruç ve önemi* | 28. Fasting and its importance |
| 29. *Kötü huylardan sakındırma* | 29. Staying away from bad habits |
| 30. *Suizan, tecessüs, gıybet* | 30. Bad thoughts, prying, and slandering |
| 31. *İstihza, kötü söz, kötü lakap* | 31. Mocking, bad words, bad monikers |
| 32. *Eksik ölçenler, yanlış tartanlar* | 32. Those who use deficient measures and incorrect weights |

| Topics of *hutbes* (in Turkish) | Topics of *hutbes* (in English) |
|---|---|
| 33. *Dünya ve ahiret için çalışmak, fesat çıkarmamak* | 33. Working for this world and the afterlife, not causing trouble |
| 34. *Nifak ve haset* | 34. Dissension and jealousy |
| 35. *Allah'tan korkmak, insanlarla hoş geçinmek* | 35. God-fearing, getting along well with people |
| 36. *Emanete riayet* | 36. Upholding trust |
| 37. *İçkinin kötülüğü* | 37. The malignancy of alcohol |
| 38. *İçkinin kötülüğü* | 38. The malignancy of alcohol |
| 39. *İçkinin toplumsal zararları* | 39. The malignancy of alcohol for society |
| 40. *Kumarın kötülüğü* | 40. The malignancy of gambling |
| 41. *Hekim, ilaç, hastalık* | 41. Doctors, medicine and sickness |
| 42. *Herkes yaptığının cezasını bulacaktır* | 42. Everyone will receive the punishment of their actions |
| 43. *Kardeşlik dargınlık* | 43. Resentment between siblings |
| 44. *Tevazu ve kibir* | 44. Humility and arrogance |
| 45. *Mevlid* | 45. *Mevlid* (birthday of the Prophet Muhammad and its celebration) |
| 46. *Miraç* | 46. *Miraç* (heavenly ascension) |
| 47. *Kadir gecesi* | 47. The Night of *Kadir* (first verses of the Koran revealed) |
| 48. *Ramazan Bayramı* | 48. The religious holiday of Ramadan |
| 49. *Kurban Bayramı* | 49. The feast of the sacrifice |
| 50. *Bayram haftası* | 50. The week of the religious holiday |
| 51. *Askerliğin şerefi* | 51. The honour of military service |

Examples of topics from the 'worldly' sphere are the importance of military service and defence of the fatherland; hard and orderly work, especially within trade, agriculture and manufacture; importance of getting married, thus of forming and protecting the family; respect and honour for parents and the elderly; solidarity with other fellow beings, treating them as brothers; concern and care for poor people and orphaned children. Among the issues related to more explicitly religious questions are the daily prayers and the importance of ritual cleanliness; love and fear of God; reverence of the Prophet and efforts to live like him; fasting during Ramadan; sacrificing during the *Kurban Bayramı* (feast of sacrifice); remembrance and celebration of the sacred evenings of *mevlid* (the birth of the Prophet), *miraç* (the Prophet Muhammad's ascent to heaven) and *kadir* (revelation of the Koran). In addition, there are also *hutbes* issuing warnings against particularly corrupt behaviour, such as cheating with false measurements in trade; drinking of alcohol; gambling; enviousness; slander and backbiting.

## The Good Citizen Is a True Believer

Judging from these *hutbes*, what does the ideal or good citizen look like? The chief characteristic appears to reside in being a true believer. However, the relationship between being a true believer and a good citizen is not straightforward. If being a good citizen is put on par with being a law-abiding citizen, the faithful may run into difficulties, when existing laws do not harmonise with their sense of a higher, Islamic justice. The protracted headscarf controversy of the 1980s and 1990s is an example of an issue that caused much anxiety and indignation. Another deeply disturbing issue was the ban against chanting the *ezan* in Arabic during the 1940s (see Chapter 3). Less concerning issues have been related to monogamy, interest rates and religion in secondary school education. However, controversial issues have usually been glossed over in official oratory. And, as long as they are not brought up to the surface, the discourse that stands out from the *hutbes* is that of overlap: the good citizen equals the true believer and vice versa – a leading theme in the sermons examined below.

### In the footsteps of the Prophet

The paragon of a true believer was the Prophet Muhammad. In particular, three areas are emphasised in the *hutbes*: his high moral standing, and as a result of that his civilised behaviour; his scrupulous dealings in daily affairs; and his exemplary manners during religious ceremonies.

His praiseworthy morality and civilised behaviour are reported in the following way:

[1][14] In order to be happy in this world and the afterlife, we must take our master as an example for ourselves, to live ethically by his morals, and in every matter to abide by him. Know that the ethics of the noble Prophet are made out of the Koran. Now listen carefully and I will explain to you all about our master: first of all, every action of our Prophet was wise and true. Never in his life did he tell a lie. He never mocked or slandered anyone, and he never

became jealous of anyone. He disapproved of slandering and sleuthing, and he forbade such ill habits. He didn't waste any time with words not useful in this world or the afterlife. He didn't get angry with anyone, and he didn't like those who remained angry. (*hutbe* 11)

The Prophet's work ethic is also raised to the skies. This is rendered through the following short narrative about the Prophet:

[2] Bestower of grace, mercy, kindness and benevolence to his servants, the almighty Allah created night-time suitable for our rest, and daytime correspondingly for all types of our works. Thus, every morning while he invites with light to happiness, sitting lazily under the sun and walking around aimlessly is not appropriate behaviours for Muslims. In Islam, work has great importance. Work and labour are more favourable than and superior to idle worship.

One morning while speaking with his honorable companions, the Prophet saw a strong and virile youth passing by. As some of the companions were about to say, 'What a pity! Had only this youth, youthfulness, strength and virility been used towards Allah's path, what could have been?' Our Prophet stated thus: 'Don't speak like this, if that youth has begun to work in the morning in order to support himself or his small children, or even his aged mother and father, then his actions are in the way of Allah. But if he is doing this in vain or for showing off to the world, then it is not in the way of Allah.'

The venerable Ömer states that: 'Do not abandon working for daily sustenance and say that Allah will provide for me. You know that neither gold, nor silver rains from the sky. Seek your daily sustenance by working.' (*hutbe* 16)

Another work-related aspect is honesty and trustworthiness. The Prophet was a tradesman, but he would never cheat or defraud anyone. In addition, honour was also rendered through decent family relationships. This included being respectful to the elderly and loving and caring to children. Even animals came under the Prophet's special protection. He would never force an animal to carry loads if it was not strong enough to do so. The Prophet was also known for his generosity and humbleness.

[3] Our master was generous. He offered help to everyone and he commanded us to do as such as well. He was at once humble, serious and earnest. Whenever he wanted to enter anyone's home or room, he would first knock

on the door and ask permission, and then he would enter. He would never sit without greeting those present. He would greet those he saw and shake their hands. Whenever he entered a gathering, he immediately sat wherever there was an empty space. For those present at the gathering, he would set an example in every way. He never offended anyone. He knew the manners of gatherings quite well and he avoided acting in ways that would cause others harm . . . Our master spoke softly and smiled at everyone. Never did he say bad words to anyone, nor treat them poorly. He never interrupted anyone. He didn't reveal anyone's secrets or faults, and he regarded this as a profoundly wrong behaviour. He treated his servants immensely well and never offended them. Whatever he ate, he also fed to his servants. Whatever he wore, he also provided to his servants. (*hutbe* 11)

Cleanliness was a very important part of his appearance.

[4] Our master was extremely clean and immaculate. He strongly recommended cleanliness. He said that those who do not keep themselves clean are deficient in faith. He gave much importance to frequently washing his teeth with a *misvak* [tooth-cleaning stick]. He also firmly commanded his followers to act this way. Even if ablution was not needed, he said that once a week it was necessary. He always washed and shaved his hair and beard, and perfumed himself. He did not like bad smells, dirt and mildew. (*hutbe* 11)

On ceremonial occasions cleanliness was pointed out even more emphatically, as in a *hutbe* written for celebrations held on the Prophet's birthday (*mevlid kandili*). Here the portrayal is rendered in even greater detail. The congregation is encouraged to listen very carefully:

[5] Oh Muslim community!
Make sure to know your Prophet well. Strive to increase your love for our Prophet both in this world and the next. Listen now and I will explain to you our Prophet.
Our master the Prophet kept himself quite clean, he was extremely careful in cleanliness in every situation. He never went about dishevelled. He cut his moustache well such that the red of his upper lip could be seen and sometimes he shaved his head. Other times he grew it until it just barely passed over his ears. But he never grew his beard longer than a handful's worth.

Not only in normal times, but also in times of war, he never left behind his cleaning items such as a comb, scissors, *misvak* and water tin. He always kept his hair and beard clean; looking in the mirror he combed himself. Even if bad smells crept in with blessed sweat, he smelled of musk. Even in that state, he always smelled lovely. While in this world he said one of his most beloved things was a beautiful scent.

Our master the Prophet was a lovely person in this world to whom an equal doesn't exist.

Allah blessed and created him this way, his stature always in place. He had no deficiencies. Our Prophet emitted light from his beautiful and loveable pinkish white face. He also had beautiful teeth while talking, and when he smiled, they shined like pearls. This was a gift from God; however beautiful his body was his ethics were as virtuous as well. With a smiling face and sweet words never did a bad word leave his mouth. He never broke anyone's heart or lost his temper. He treated his servants well. He was never arrogant and he never showed off. He always maintained his dignity. No one who ever saw our Prophet grew fearful. Rather, after seeing and speaking with him awhile, everyone gave him their hearts. (*hutbe* 45)

These imaginative images render a strong sense of presence, as if the purpose is to evoke the impression that the Prophet stands in the midst of the congregation or that he is the person speaking from the pulpit.

*God-fearing*

Apart from making an example of the Prophet, the most distinguishing quality of a true believer is his devoutness or god-fearing. Without a sense of fear and anxiety human beings would easily turn away from the right path.

[6] Oh Muslim community!

The almighty Allah, in the verse that I read now, commands 'Oh Believers! Fear Allah. Every soul should prepare for tomorrow and beware of Allah, because Allah knows all things you do.'

Yes, Allah the almighty knows all. People should always fear Allah in their hearts, because the beginning of wisdom is the fear of Allah. Those who do not fear Allah tempt evil. In this way a person cannot see the good. No light or virtue can be found in their hearts.

Allah the almighty commands us that we examine the deeds we do in this world while preparing ourselves for the afterlife.

Thus, how do we pass our lives? How do we waste our precious time? Do we find good works that will provide for our happiness in the afterlife? What have we done up to now? What have we prepared for the future? We must think about all of these things. Final regrets are useless. (*hutbe* 35)

### Thankfulness

A good believer is also grateful. God has created everything from 'soil and a drop of water'. But God's bounty should not be taken for granted. The true believer must be able to appreciate what he gets for nothing and turn this consciousness into gratitude and humbleness before God.

[7] Oh Muslim community!

All of the worlds, the seen and unseen, the known and unknown, all varieties of creation are solely Allah's. Allah the almighty brought the prophets and us into a human form from the soil and a drop of water. He gave us reason and thought, ability and will; he bestowed us with innumerable blessings like eyes, ears, hands and feet. He gave these to good people and also to unbelievers. He didn't discriminate against anyone when bestowing these blessings. (*hutbe* 1)

### Worship and consciousness in worship

The true Muslim is also characterised by performing his daily prayers with great awareness. Evil or wickedness occurs when the believer stops being mindful about God; that is when his thoughts are distanced from God. The ritual prayer – *namaz* – is the best guarantee against falling into such predicaments.

[8] Thus, in order for people not to come to this state, and so that they don't forget Allah, it is necessary to place a gatekeeper near everyone's chest. This can only be realised with *namaz*. It is only *namaz* that can prevent the doing of bad deeds. *Namaz* makes a person never forget his master. *Namaz* takes man and changes him. It makes him contemplate and come to himself. *Namaz* places man within the court of Allah the almighty. Moreover, it continuously helps him to remember that he is in the presence of Allah. In twenty-four hours, dropping your work in the world and pausing in the presence of Allah at least five times is not a small thing.

In this way, anyone who never forgets his master would never do a bad deed. Thus, even if all treasures of the whole world were entrusted to someone like this, he would never betray this trust by lying hands on these treasures. That is because he is in the presence of the almighty. He always sees himself with Allah. From then onwards would anyone like this, or anyone who has reached this state even once, long to possess the goods, chastity, life and honour of this world? Would this person descend to such sinful things? How could he ever associate himself with such vileness?

Have you thus seen, oh Muslims, the greatness of *namaz*? This informs people of the reliability of this rational religion. If this were an empty thing would Allah command us, 'Perform *namaz*'? Those who do not know what *namaz* is, or those who do not know its taste well, suppose that *namaz* only consists of prostrating and rising. They do not know that *namaz* transforms the person into an angel. *Namaz* allows man to be with Allah. In this world there is not a greater form of worship than this. In this world there is not a greater pleasure of heart. Thus, you too should know *namaz* in this way. You too should revel in *namaz* this way. When the muezzin says 'Allahu akbar', quickly come to your senses. Take leave from this world. At that moment don't talk about work, sleep, hot or cold weather, and rise to prayer. Make an effort to never let the time of *namaz* pass by you. Do your best in caring for *namaz*. Do not perform *namaz* negligently. Do not prostrate your bodies and allow your thoughts to wander about. Do not only pray with your bodies, but also with your hearts. Those who perform *namaz* without their hearts find no value in it. This type of *namaz* can never carry someone into the presence of Allah.

Thus, if someone performs *namaz* this way, even if it is for forty years, his heart does not soften and his morals do not become straight, and his spirit does not take pleasure from it. For this reason, keep the *namaz* by knowing what you are doing and thinking of whose presence you are seeking. If you do like this, and perform the *namaz* like this, do not doubt that you will go beyond the heavens and surpass the angels. At the very least you will be with Allah and forget yourselves for a moment. Thus, this is your *miraç* [ascension to heaven]. How happy is he who knows *namaz* in this way, and performs it thus. What a shame for those who do not prostrate before the Merciful and forget Allah. (*hutbe* 9)

The true believer is thus a person who performs his prayers and other ritual obligations with a sincere disposition (*ihlas*, *samimiyet*). Worship should not be performed out of routine. Presence of mind is required during every step of the religious performances. Otherwise, it loses its value and is done in vain.

### Faith (*İman*) and Deed (*Amel*)

In the previous section the focus was on devoutness, that is, duties concerning the practising Muslim's relation to God. However, even if the exhortations appear under headings separating the worldly from the other-worldly (see above), the basic message of the *hutbe*s is that the two spheres are firmly linked to each other. Obligations and duties regarding beliefs and ritual practices should not be fulfilled only with an eye to the afterlife. Worship also has to leave imprints on daily life. Otherwise, these efforts have been carried out in vain. Religious rituals do not exist in isolation. Likewise, daily dealings should always be carried out with God and the next life in mind. Concern for life in this world and the next go hand in hand. They are nourished and flourish through each other. In this sense the *hutbe*s bespeak a holistic worldview.

> [9] Faith without practice is like a lamp burning in the open. With just a light wind it would be put out. If that lamp were placed inside a nice lantern, then no danger would remain. If you preserve belief thus continuously with worship and good deeds, then no one can snatch your faith and take it from you. If you do not possess faith and swim night and day in sin, not only will you not be doing good deeds, but gradually your hearts will blacken and your faith weaken. One day that godsend will fly from your heads and you will not be aware. At that time all your confessions (*şehadet*) will be to no avail. What is the benefit of such an empty Muslim way? (*hutbe* 7)

In another *hutbe* the organic connection between *iman* (faith) and *amel* (deed) is expressed in the following way:

> [10] Oh Muslim community!
> Are you attentive to what the venerable Prophet states? In order to be a complete Muslim it is necessary to not escape from the world or the afterlife. Those who abandon the world and only work for the afterlife are not good Muslims. Those who abandon the afterlife and only work for this world are also not good Muslims. A good Muslim is someone who doesn't give up his afterlife for this world and who doesn't give up this world for the afterlife and he is someone who works for both and does not burden people. One should cling to the world like he will never die and prepare for the afterlife like he will die tomorrow. (*hutbe* 33)

Every act carried out in our daily life is an expression for worship. They should all be carried out with the same sincerity and urgency as a religious duty (*farz*). Everyday pursuits are not for the moment only, but for the next world as well.

> [11] Trade and agriculture, earning money with the skills in hand and making a livelihood is the religious obligation of every Muslim. Additionally, it is a great form of worship. In order to prosper in this world and the afterlife, working is our individual duty. (*hutbe* 33)

Thus, concern for the next life permeates every single act. This world and the next are conflated, two faces of the same God-given reality. This state of things also confirms the impression that the good citizen equals the true believer.

## Duties towards the State

That the good citizen fulfils his obligations towards the state without hesitation is a matter of course, especially if it concerns the defence of the country. The last *hutbe* in the 1927–8 collection is exclusively reserved for the military service and carries the title 'The Honour of Military Service'. This obligation, which so clearly links the individual as a citizen to the state, is justified in religious terms, that is, as a sacred duty. This is illustrated in the following excerpt:

> [12] Oh Muslim community!
>
> Oh, servants of Allah! Preparing forces for fighting the enemy is our religious duty. Without a doubt, one of the most important elements of these forces is the soldier. The soldier is an actively armed force that saves our religion, our homelands, our honour and virtue from the enemies. For this reason, military service is a great and sacred duty. Every person who loves Allah, the Prophet, the homeland and home, everyone who knows the value of honour and virtue, should do their military service with pleasure.
>
> The position of the military service is very high in our religion. If a soldier dies, he is a martyr (*şehit*), if he survives a warrior/war-veteran [in the faith of Islam] (*gazi*). After the rank of prophethood, the next highest position is martyrdom. These two titles are such great and honourable titles for any human

being. Thus, when one is called to do his military service, it is necessary to go with eagerness and pleasure.

Our Prophet ordered, 'Whenever you are invited to take up arms, accept at once.' (*hutbe* 51)

Readiness to sacrifice oneself in defence of the fatherland (*vatan*) constitutes the strongest pledge or obligation of the individual towards the state. This is, together with tax-paying, the only instance in which the individual citizen's partaking in public affairs is mentioned.

### Duties towards the Larger Society

Hard work is especially emphasised throughout the 1927–8 *hutbe*s. God renders his bounty to all, but it is up to the individual believer to manage what he gets according to his own will, comprehension and capabilities. Everything is rendered by God, but . . .

[13] know that people are not created with intelligence, will, or need and then given blessings. The blessings that will be given to them are bestowed according to their effort and labour. In the world, the worker earns and takes the equivalent to what he has worked for. Those who don't work will surely receive the punishment for laziness. For this reason, Allah the almighty will give the prophets the blessings he will give them in the afterlife and everyone as well according to their effort and labour. He will grant to his servants as a reward in the afterlife the thing they have used their will on, according to the strength of their faith and quality of their work. In the world, those who work for prosperity and spend their time on good deeds will obtain Allah's blessing in the afterlife, and they will receive their rewards. For those who do not take up good deeds there is no blessing in the afterlife. (*hutbe* 1)

The efforts spent by the individual are not primarily for his own benefit, but for the good of the wider society. The individual sacrifices himself for the improvement of all, a civic virtue bolstered by sacred values.

[14] Every Muslim should work to make both his world and his afterlife prosper. It is the religious duty of every Muslim to work and earn money for his own livelihood, the livelihood of his family, and to be useful to his religion, people and homeland. Working with this intention is a great form of worship.

Earning a living with this intention in a lawful way is as good as fighting on behalf of Allah. However much a person works with this intent, however rich he becomes, he increases in worth to that degree near Allah and the Prophet. For good and virtuous people money and property is a very good thing. A virtuous, rich person can do all types of good things, for both himself and his family, as well as for his country. He becomes helpful in raising up his people. What can a poor person do? What other work can he contribute besides being a burden to others? At this time, a person cannot do anything without money. During a period with no money, a person cannot preserve his religion, his honour, or even his world! All of these good things are possible with money and faith. As our Prophet has commanded, 'It is necessary to work as if we will never die and worship as if we will die tomorrow.' (*hutbe* 15)

Here, the *hutbe* admonishes the believers to contribute to the building of the country and the nation through hard work. To obtain a good income from work increases one's prospects to make a difference. However, without an honest and charitable disposition that work falls on barren ground with respect to the hereafter.

[15] Muslims!

Therefore, do not withhold from making effort in a legitimate way. Busy yourselves in any craft or trade or even agriculture. Direct your sons and grandsons to those useful jobs as well. Our people's welfare and our country's progress can only be realised by these means. Believing servants that work in this way also pleases Allah the almighty.

Our forefathers as well as our religion have continuously informed us that laziness is not suitable to humanity. (*hutbe* 17)

**Duties towards the Family**

The good citizen also protects and honours his family. This means respect for the mother, the father and the elderly, and responsibility for the upbringing and welfare of children and minors.

[16] Oh Muslim community!

Know that after the worship of Allah, our next greatest obligation is submission to our mothers and fathers. We should be respectful and obedient towards them. This is such an important thing that Allah the almighty mentions it several times in the Koran. In fact, in some of the verses Allah, immediately after commanding us not to see ourselves as his equal, states that we should treat our mothers and fathers well. Then he orders that we not treat them poorly, and even forbids us from saying, 'Ugh, but . . .' to them. Our Prophet also gives many commands for treating mothers and fathers well. He states that it is a pity that those who do not treat their elderly mothers and fathers well will not enter heaven because of that. (*hutbe* 12)

To fulfil these duties is also an expression for worship.

[17] Yes, obeying the rights of mothers and fathers is a very great form of worship. (*hutbe* 13)

Respect for and duties towards parents do not end with death. The offspring must also continue to care for their elderly after they are deceased.

[18] Oh Muslim community!

You should give prayers and supplications for your mothers and fathers after their deaths, just as you should be obedient to them when they are alive. By doing this and giving offerings to their relatives and friends, you will have fulfilled your duties. One person coming into the presence of the Prophet, peace be upon him, asked, 'Oh Messenger of Allah! After my mother and father die, would there be anything else I could do to please them?' Our Prophet said, 'Yes, after your mother and father die then the duties of praying and giving supplications for them, fulfilling their wills, giving offerings to their friends, and giving gifts and goodness to relatives and close ones remains. That is your responsibility.' Our Prophet has ordered thus with this *hadis* to preserve the brotherhood among Muslims and national cohesion of the people. Thus, whenever one dies, the desired oneness and togetherness between Muslims is strengthened through protecting the occupation of his father, preserving the rights of his friends, and fulfilling the social and religious duties. (*hutbe* 13)

## Obedience

The good citizen is the obedient citizen. The *hutbe*s convey strong expressions for a 'culture of obedience' (*biat kültürü*). Commands and exhortations of worldly activities as well as religious and moral rituals and practices are presented within an order manifested by God as the absolute, impeccable authority over his 'slaves' (*kuls*). Hierarchical social and political structures (state, parties, economic enterprises, civil associations, family, and so on) can hardly feature in the God–slave relationship, since the latter is based on an egalitarian understanding of the individuals vis-à-vis each other, but total submission to God's authority. However, the fact that worldly authorities cannot easily invoke the divine rule exercised by Allah through the Koran and the Prophet does not mean that the sermonised admonitions cannot be interpreted in that way. It seems the obedience culture expounded within the mosque contributed to the justification of a political order based on a centralised and authoritarian power structure. This should not be taken as an indication that *hutbe*s breathe of bitter austerity. On the contrary, the general intonation is not particularly harsh, rather benevolent and paternal. The texts evoke the image of a shepherd guiding his herd, which goes well with a basically egalitarian spirit within the flock.

## Social Solidarity

The alleged rationale behind the demand for obedience is the fear of split or discord within the community of Muslims. Division arises from many sources, external as well as internal. Threats from external enemies are described in the following way:

> [19] Oh Muslim community!
>
> There is no one in the world without enemies. By the time a person has one friend, it is said, he also has a thousand enemies. These are not empty words. There are open and hidden, known and unknown, large and small enemies. But they are enemies, and as such they are all watching for an opportunity, waiting for the right time. For that reason, one must always remain alert, alert and strong enough to frighten the enemy and not allow him to assault. One should not say that an enemy is small or big, even if an enemy is the size of an ant one should still give him importance and work to defeat him. One should be using all one's force and always be in a strong and prepared condition. There isn't another way that one can live comfortably in the world and let others live as well. (*hutbe* 51)

Muslims must constantly be prepared to defend themselves against any kind of assault:

[20] Oh Muslim community!

Allah the Almighty commands thus in this verse from the Koran: And prepare against them whatever you are able of power and strength by which you may terrify your enemies!

This verse reminds us Muslims that it is always necessary to be prepared. It shows how country, independence, honour and virtue can be preserved. In order to preserve property, consider not only against the enemy but also against those who are not openly enemies, those who seem to be friends in the open but inside are enemies; this verse says to prepare strength to frighten all of them, to suppress all of them and to discourage all of them. Thus, for this purpose, it is our duty to use all our strength and might that we have. In this respect, however much we work and take pains then to that proportion we will receive a benefit. Our efforts will certainly not go to waste. (*hutbe* 2)

Dissension can also be sown from inside the community itself. Therefore, the believer must avoid everything that may cause split:

[21] Allah commands us to 'Work to make the world and the afterlife prosper, do not seek to possess each other's property, honour or life, and prepare strength to save the homeland and to frighten enemies. Work with all your strength to do these things.' He commands us to not abandon justice, to uphold the trust of others, to help one another, to know the truth, and to be aware of unrest and separation. (*hutbe* 25)

Dissension weakens the community and makes it more vulnerable against external threats as expressed in the following *hutbe*:

[22] Oh Muslim community!

Allah the almighty commands in the Koran: 'Be obedient to Allah and to his Prophet; do not grapple with one another, otherwise you would lose your trust, you would fall from strength, and your grandeur would be taken from your hands too. Also do not ever give up the strength to resist any danger or enemy. It is no doubt that Allah is with those who are patient.'

Oh Believers, oh dear servants of Allah!

If we don't want to be miserable in this world and contemptible in the afterlife, we should follow the path this verse shows. Yes, an Islamic people that is obedient to Allah, that follows the path of the Prophet, that is one and together with its individuals is not deprived of greatness and grandeur. But a people that are not obedient to Allah, that do not listen to the commands of the Prophet, that cannot stick together and struggles between itself becomes weak and is cut off from strength and power. It does not have the materials or time to prepare strength to store against external enemies nor can it find faith. Then cowardice comes to them, their financial strength is broken, and they roll off a cliff. This is the reason that Allah the almighty invites us to sub-mission to him and to the Prophet, and prohibits us from disputing amongst ourselves and to be patient with one another. (*hutbe* 34)

The believers must avoid anything that may lead to splits and instead work for the strengthening of the community by suppressing all kinds of con-ceited and self-centred behaviour, resist leanings to envy and back-biting. All kinds of pernicious behaviour like gambling and the drinking of alcohol is condemned. The justification for controlled, civilised and ethically good behaviour is the unity and harmony of the community itself. Certainly, this kind of praiseworthy behaviour is also remunerated in the next life, but in an in-worldly perspective it is the unity and harmony of the wider community of believers that counts. In the name of solidarity, it is also a duty to support poor and ailing people. Orphans have a special place in the Muslim tradition. That the question of unity and harmony is untiringly repeated all through the *hutbe*s may be related to the special charismatic status rendered religious communities in Islam, a question further elaborated upon in Chapter 3.

## National Unity

The social imagery evoked by the *hutbe*s is the local community. Rarely does it extend beyond family, kinship, village or small-town relations, where produc-tion is based on small-scale agriculture, trade or manufacture. The believer is addressed as an individual involved in face-to-face or personal relationships. References to membership in larger, anonymous contexts are rare. Where it happens, Muslim identity ranks first. Muslim believers constitute a nation of their own – the 'Islamic nation' (*İslam milleti*) – which, in this situation, is identified with the national community of the Turkish republic. It is in the capacity of being Muslim that an individual is a national or citizen. As such, the citizens, cum Muslim believers, owe each other brotherly love. This fervently solidaristic attitude is described in the following:

[23] Oh servants of Allah, become brothers! Any Muslim is another Muslim's brother. Thus, do not oppress a Muslim when he is in need of help, do not leave him by himself, and do not lie and cheat him. Do not look at him with insulting eyes. Piety is in man's heart. If anyone looks at their Muslim brothers insultingly, then that should be more than enough sin for the perpetrator. For a Muslim to covet anything – life, property, honour – from another Muslim is forbidden (*haram*). (*hutbe* 31)

To stand up in solidarity for one's Muslim brothers – for the sake of unity – is an important duty enjoined on the believers.

[24] Performing *namaz*, fasting and giving alms are our religious duties. It is also our duty to work for the prosperity of the Islamic peoples, and to provide the necessary material and moral strengths to help our nation to continue to exist. (*hutbe* 35)

The image of family solidarity is used in order to explain the importance of national solidarity.

[25] Think about a family, a household, where the individuals are angry at one another. In such a family, in such a house, can there be peace, calm, comfort? Between the members of such a family does any security or trust remain? Is there harmony in such a house? Can this family be strong against the outside? Can it save itself from attacks that can come from the outside? Never. Thus, a people are also like this. A people, where individuals are not sincere with one another cannot be strong within itself or against the outside. A people's members are brothers to each other. Thus, all things that loosen the bond of brotherhood among Muslims is banned. (*hutbe* 31)

That Muslim identities should be emphasised in an Islamic religious context is a matter of course. Still, under the new republican regime 'nation' (*millet*) takes on a meaning different from that of imperial Ottoman times. In that multicultural context, Muslims had constituted but one among other non-Muslim *millet*s. True, Muslims held a position of special sublimity, but the other *millet*s were recognised as religious communities in their own right. In the new, nation-state context, all Turkish citizens, Muslims as well as non-Muslims, were meant to be part of one and the same Turkish 'millet' or nation. In the name of secularism religion was in theory erased from the notion of republican Turkish citizenship, but in practice Islam retained its cultural hegemony. A homiletic discourse, where Muslim brotherhood was conflated with national belonging, rendered new strength to Islam as the basic matrix of Turkish nationhood. What was preached from the *minber*s easily carried over into society outside of the mosques, especially considering the fact that the number of non-Muslims had been drastically reduced during the convulsions leading up to the final collapse of the old empire. The strings that the Ottoman administrations had played on in their dealings with non-Muslim communities more or less lost their *raison d'être*. Thereby, that part of the secularist doctrine which promised the state's equal distance to different religious communities was drained of meaning. Concerning national identities, the authority of Islam could hardly be overruled by secularism, a paradox that has rendered modern Turkey its special character.

### 'My New *Hutbes*'

As already mentioned, the collection of *hutbes* published in 1936–7 contained about three times as many *hutbes* as the 1927–8 publication. Does that also imply a difference in content between the two publications? According to the findings of this study the overall discourse did not change markedly. Concerning topics, style and content, nothing striking separates the two collections from each other. Still, a change in emphasis did take place, most probably affected by the overall reformist atmosphere of the early republican period.[15]

The first change is related to the arrangement of topics, where the 1936–7 collection[16] is more thematic compared to the 1927–8 edition. Thus, the larger collection follows a kind of sacrosanct hierarchy and starts with a sermon describing God as the creator of the entire existence (universe). The reader/listener is instructed that human beings owe everything to His creation. Life and property are indiscriminately rendered to everyone and human beings are therefore indebted to Him for His kindness and blessings. This is followed by a sermon about *mevlid*, the celebration of the birth of the Prophet. Thereby, the two fundamentals of confession or 'witnessing' (*şehadet*) are presented: the oneness or unity of God and the belief that Muhammad is his messenger, the last prophet.

The third sermon is about Turkey's aviation industry and the importance of keeping up with the latest technology of warfare in order to defend the independence of the country, alias nation and fatherland. Thereby, the confessional order of topics is broken, undoubtedly a concession to military and governmental interests. However, when pointing this out, I have been reminded by forthcoming Turkish theologians that one should not overlook that defence of the nation is a sacred duty.

The fourth sermon starts with a reminder that confession is at the very foundation of being a Muslim. To testify about the existence of the Creator and His messenger, is both the 'foundation and the entrance door of the house of Muslimhood' (Akseki 1936: 43–9). The important thing, however, is not only to get on the true path, but to remain on that course until the end of life. The confession must be followed by ritual ablution (*abdest/gusül*)[17] and ritual prayer (*namaz*) five times a day; fasting during Ramadan; almsgiving; if one can afford it, making a pilgrimage; and fighting the enemy. The believer also has responsibility to pass on this learning to the new generations. The fifth sermon is on the Koran, Allah's own words constituting the basic source of learning for any Muslim. The road laid out in the Koran is the road of justice and the rule of (canonical) law. This is followed by a sermon on god-fearing (*takva*) – the key to happiness. 'Beware of those who do not fear God!' – a frequently heard exhortation.

After having elaborated on these aspects of belief (*itikat*), Akseki turns in the seventh sermon to worship (*ibadet*). The first command given by Allah to human beings is that they should worship him. The first and foremost duty of each individual is to believe and worship – '*iman ve ibadet etmektir*' (Akseki 1936: 59–63). God supplies us with everything; thus, as human beings we owe Him our devotion and worship. The basic forms of worship are ritual prayer (*namaz*); fasting (*oruç*); almsgiving (*zekat*); pilgrimage (*hac*); and holy war (*cihad*) (Akseki 1936: 61–2). In order to be valid, worship necessitates a clean body. Cleanliness is the topic of the two following sermons, eighth and ninth. Spiritual and corporal cleanliness are equally important, the latter also incorporating the outfit. It is also disgraceful to take part in the prayer if you have eaten onion or garlic. If that is the case you should stay at home for your prayer. Cleanliness is always important, but for the Friday *hutbe* it is even more binding (Akseki 1936: 64–7, 68–72).

The three main pillars of Akseki's sermon collection are belief (*itikat*), worship (*ibadet*) and ethics (*ahlak*).[18] After the introductory sermons dealing with the basic elements of belief and worship, the major part of the subsequent sermons is related to ethics. However, before elaborating on specific ethics-related topics like slandering (Akseki 1936: 82–6), or lying (Akseki 1936: 102–7), the author expounds on more general dimensions of ethics. Thus, in the tenth sermon Akseki draws out the lines to the very beginnings of Islam and explains why ethics has always been very important. 'Muslimhood equals ethics', but – or just because of that – we have to be vigilant against forces pushing in the opposite direction. Beware of your circle of friends, warns the author. Human beings are easily moved in this or that direction. Therefore, the believer is urged to choose his associates very carefully (Akseki 1936: 74–7). The afore-mentioned kind of introductory explanations are inserted here and there all through the collection, as, for example, in the sermons on 'confession' (Akseki 1936: 44–7) and 'worship' (Akseki 1936: 59–63). This technique bears witness to a more didactic and forward-looking discourse in the 1936–7 compared to the 1927–8 publication.

A more lucid arrangement is not only true for the overall disposition, but also for sermons taken separately. One example is provided by the sermon on aviation industry, the third in both collections. In the 1927–8 version the sermon starts by saying that no state exists that does not have an enemy, that is, a hostile foreign power that it has to protect itself against. In the 1936–7 version, however, there is a lengthy explanation as to why there are such rival states. Power ambition (*hırs*) is in the nature of human beings. It is thanks to this ambition that people are impelled to live, work and advance. However, when this ambition is driven too far it leads to oppression and injustice. Those kinds of power-hungry people and organisations are always 'adversaries to a just, God-given order' (*hak düşmanları*). Such oppressors do not recognise the rights of others. The only thing they are after is power. Nobody, neither an individual human being, nor a nation, can rid itself from such an enemy. These kinds of reflections are new for the 1936–7 collection. Similarly, the sermon on cleanliness is almost the same in the two collections (*hutbe* 4 and *hutbe* 9 respectively). Still, in the 1936–7 version stricter arguments are added, emphasising how accommodating these commands are, not only in promoting a proper appearance, but also good manners and civilised behaviour. Both preacher and audience are reminded of Islam's civilising mission. Thereby both depth and breadth are added, expositions the *hatip* could reflect upon dependent on interests. The 1936–7 version therefore offers more food for thought for audience as well as preachers.

The following points sum up some of the differences between the 1927–8 and 1936–7 *hutbe* collections:

- The 1936–7 collection is thematically better arranged, both concerning single *hutbe*s and the collection of *hutbe*s, as a whole. An organising principle is constituted by belief, worship and ethics as in Akseki's manual from 1933 (Akseki 2014).
- There is a special urge to bring about 'improvements'[19] of religious life. Such developments were parts of a wider reform process, including material as well as cultural achievements (civilisation). Emphasis on modernisation (social, economic and cultural) is stronger in the 1936–7 than the 1927–8 publication.
- National consciousness is more articulated in the later publication, where improvement of social and religious life is more clearly linked to nation-building.
- The language is more embellished, meaning that more attention is paid to rhetorical eloquence in the 1936–7 publication. Along the same lines, the book contains an address to *hatip*s about the importance of feeling and empathy in oratory.
- There are closer connections to the daily affairs of the common, labouring people, whereby attention is drawn to the importance of rhetorical zeal.

In contrast, themes that more or less remain the same are as follows:

- A culture of obedience, above all in relation to the official authorities
- An outlook on military service and defence as a sacred duty

- Fear of division, discord and schisms, mirrored against a scenario that speaks of total collapse, or the loss of the motherland (*vatan*) and the nation all together
- A social imagery, where the provincial, small-scale society dominates over references to macro-structures, such as state and nation
- A holistic worldview, where this world (*dünya*) and the next (*ahiret*) are inseparable

## Conclusions

A striking feature of Akseki's *hutbe* collections is the concern for a stronger society. When admonishing the believers to live like good Muslims, emphasis is on economic improvements (agriculture, manufacture, trade and infrastructure), strengthening of community ties (social solidarity) and improvement of moral standards. The exhortations to hard work have to be seen against the background of the destruction and sufferings caused by ten years of continuous warfare (1912–22). In addition to the material wreckage and geographical losses, the non-Muslim population, who for centuries had dominated trade and manufacture, were also radically reduced. Turkey's economy was therefore worse off in the 1920s than it had been at the brink of the Balkan Wars (Owen and Pamuk 1998: 10–12). However, the acute need for material reconstruction did not overshadow duties related to worship, especially daily prayers. In fact, worship and responsibility for the wider society go hand in hand, hence the strong connection between being a good believer and a good citizen. The sermonising discourse called for active participation by the individual believer for the best of the surrounding community. A sense of civic virtue therefore permeates the sermons, but within the boundaries of a 'culture of obedience' (*biat kültürü*). They speak almost exclusively of duties or obligations, not rights.

Concerning social imagery, the *hutbe*s convey the image of a small-scale society. The sermons are markedly detached from the social and political transformations occupying contemporary decision-makers: on the one hand, the loud reverberations of the struggle for a new republican order, including resistance, rebellions and severe repression; on the other, a religious discourse speaking at length about cleanliness; of gratefulness to the all-mighty, who rules over life and death; of hard work and honesty; of hospitality, compassion and charity; of behaving the way the Prophet did and keeping his character as a model; of daily prayers and sacred holidays. With the exception of advocating special support for the domestic aircraft industry (*hutbe* 3), it is as if all the social turmoil is erupting without leaving any traces at all. Rather than elaborating on events and developments of relevance for the nation as a whole, the sermons steer the minds of the congregations into largely local, household or sacrosanct, esoteric issues. Religion is not reduced to the private sphere only, but the topics addressed are to a large extent screened off from what is happening on the macro levels.

During Ottoman times, Friday *hutbe*s of large imperial mosques had, from time to time, addressed topics related to the state, both domestic and international.[20] When religion fell under stricter secular control, the difference between *hutbe*s held in local and centrally situated grand mosques faded. Over the following decades, *hutbe*s were geared to the same, often parochial issues. Thus, under secular, republican rule a small-scale social imagery was conveyed to audiences of large urban mosques, as well as those of smaller towns and villages. The effects of this all-encompassing, provincial discourse on the national consciousness will be further elaborated upon in later chapters.

With its provincialism, *hutbe*s confirmed the ranking of the new, secular order. Religion was subordinated to the state, or, as it were, transferred backstage. This rendered both the sermonising act and its admonitions a loss of prestige; it also affected the status of the sacred space, the mosque and the congregation. However, one should not disregard that other, counteracting dynamics were at work. Even if the state dominated over religion, it was not the kind of active interference materialising during the later stages of modern state development. As already mentioned, Diyanet was not rendered a viable administrative structure until the 1960s. Instead, during the early republican period it led a rather obscure life. Consequently, the mosques could function as a protected space, a sanctuary, where an atmosphere of familiarity and continuity with the past could serve as a counterweight to the future oriented rationalism of the secularist regime. From the point of view of the republican leadership, the existence of such a refuge did not at least harm or prevent the development of the official reform projects, especially as the sermons urged order and obedience.

Thanks to this sheltered status of the mosques, a sense of self-sufficiency could be maintained around the daily and weekly sacred gatherings. With the exception of a few grand mosques of the former imperial centre Istanbul, every mosque was marginal, or situated in the periphery. Or, rather, as Patrick Gaffney has pointed out, all mosques were, in fact, peripheral in relation to the sacred abodes of Mecca and Medina. '[Every] mosque is . . . peripheral, for no ruler nor capital city corresponds to the triumphant community of believers in Mecca and Medina in the Prophet's own lifetime' (Gaffney 1994: 25). However, every mosque was also built to enclose and protect the two most important objects of worship, the prayer niche (*mihrap*) and the pulpit (*minber*). Therefore, since these two artefacts represented the highest sacred authority, every mosque was also a symbolic manifestation of the centre (Gaffney 1994: 25). By virtue of this symbolism every mosque represented a universe in its own right. Within this abode, the traditional cosmology of Islam was allowed to thrive. As such it represented a contrast to the moral order of the Republic, which, through the separation of state and religion, was dualistic in character. Nourished by Akseki's sermons, symbolic mini-universes were maintained within each and every mosque, through which the vision of a holistic cosmology could be preserved and restored. Such a unitary or all-inclusive worldview helped in perpetuating the sense of closely integrated congregations. One should be reminded that in Islam communities of believers, not individual leaders, are the potential carriers of salvation-bringing charisma.[21]

Apart from contributing to the creation of such a 'sacred community', mosque attendance was a manifestation of a civic duty. The disciplined way in which Turkish men usually participate in the Friday prayer is in itself a manifestation of a commitment of the believers, cum citizens, in the constitution of the public sphere. This involvement is no less significant than casting a vote in the general elections. Mosque attendance understood as a civic duty merges with mosque attendance understood as a sacred duty (to join the collective worship). It is through such imaginations that the spell of the tightly knit and solidaristic community – national and religious – is manifested.

The *hutbe*s contributed to the formation of an ideology, where being *milli* (national) and Muslim overlapped or became almost synonymous. The importance of Islam as a fundamental element of modern Turkish national identity found fertile ground in the mosque environment. In that context it was natural to refer to the larger national community as a community of believers, something that easily carried over into society at large. In the development of modern Turkish nationalism, an increasingly restricted discourse takes form, where Islam narrows down to Sunni Islam and eventually mainly comes to mean the Hanefi law school (*mezhep*, Arabic: *madhhab*).[22] The seeds of such a restrained understanding of Turkish Islamic identity are sown in the *hutbe*s of the early Republic.

The secularisation reforms of the 1920s meant that the number and variety of sacred abodes decreased. With *medrese*s and Sufi lodges closed, the only places allowed for religious gatherings were the mosques.[23] Thereby the relative importance of the mosques increased. So did the possibility for the state to exercise control. However, the mass-mediatic means available for supervision and guidance were limited. The authorised *hutbe* collections analysed in this chapter represented a rare channel, by means of which the authorities could reach local congregations. In spite of their limited scope, however, the Akseki collections set the direction for the subsequent development of official Friday preaching in two respects: standardisation through centralisation, and, as a paradoxical effect, provincialism.

The republican order was based on a separation between the secular, which ruled on the official, national level, and the religious, which retained its hold over provincial towns and villages. As long as state interference was limited to the *hutbe*s, mediated through a limited number of *hutbe* collections, civilian peace was maintained. However, the Kemalist leaders had more far-reaching projects in mind. One was their Turkification programme, which, when interfering into the Koranic liturgy and the call for prayer (*ezan*), touched sensitive strings. Such challenges are approached in the next chapter.

## Notes

1. See, for example, verses 7–8 (ten in all) of 'Independence march' (*İstiklal marşı*)
   (7) What man would not die for this heavenly piece of land?
   Martyrs would gush out if you just squeeze the soil! Martyrs!
   May God take all my loved ones and possessions from me if he will,
   But may he not deprive me of my one true homeland for the world.

(8) O Lord, the sole wish of my heart is that,
No infidel's hand should touch the bosom of my temple.
These *adhan*s, the *shahadah* of which is the base of the religion,
Shall sound loud over my eternal homeland (available at: <http://umich.edu/~turkish/links/manuscripts/anthem/english.htm> (last accessed 6 January 2021)).

The author Mehmet Akif Ersoy (1873–1936), a deeply religious nationalist, was active in the War of Independence. Even if Ersoy's Islamic fervour clashed with the secularist regime, he remained the most celebrated national poet, quoted more often than any other lyricist in the Friday sermons. See also Chapter 6.

2. The terminology used here is taken from Hoexter et al. (2002), which, following Habermas, separates three domains: the official (state), public and private spheres. 'While both the official and public spheres work for the common good, the public sphere recruits its personnel from the private sphere, not from the ruler's domain. The public sphere is thus autonomous from the political order, and its "influence rests on interpretations of the common good vis-á-vis the ruler, on the one hand, and the private sphere, on the other"' (Hoexter et al. 2002: 9 [from Eisenstadt and Schluchter 1998: 10]).

3. In that context, Turkey, for centuries the leading power of the Muslim world, but now champion of secularism, stands out as a unique and contradictory case. A related paradox has been brought forward by Kushner (1977): 'It is one of the peculiarities of Turkish history that the people who were the first Muslims in our century to proclaim their adherence to the idea of a secular national state had in the past gone furthest in submerging their identity in the wider Islamic one, embodied in the principle of the Umma – the all-embracing community of believers – recognizing no political or ethnic barriers between them' (p. 1).

4. These two institutions substituted the venerated office of sheikh ül-Islam, the highest religious office in the Ottoman Empire, until 1834 enjoying the same status in the *divan* or council of state as the grand vizier, *sadrazam* (Berkes 1998: 98), and the Ministry of Religious Affairs and Pious Foundations (Act 429) (Zürcher 1994: 195).

5. See Kutuz Hoca's story in Chapter 1 (Kara 2015).

6. Before leaving the circumstances surrounding the inauguration, Mustafa Kemal's comment on the circular is a telling expression of his leadership: 'I think I ought to quote the contents of the circular sent out by me on 21 April [1920] . . ., because it constitutes a document that will show *how far we were obliged to adapt ourselves* to the sentiments and views prevailing at this time' (Atatürk 2008: 365,

my emphasis). Here he presents himself as the statesman, who from the beginning had been the determined republican and secular-minded reformist he was only later recognised to be. Thus, tactical considerations had prompted him to keep a low profile concerning his future revolutionary aims. Looking back, there was no longer room or need for the 'old-fashioned' celebrations of 23 April 1920, and he was the architect behind that alleged progress.

7. Interaction between different Muslim and non-Muslim communities (*millet*s), especially on occasions of religious festivities, was an important manifestation of a public sphere. Doumanis (2013) offers a rich and variegated material on Muslim–Christian coexistence during the decade preceding the Balkan Wars and the First World War.

8. From a strict sharia perspective these sultanic law-giving practices were looked upon as 'non-constitutional'. Liberal intellectuals of the late nineteenth century like Namık Kemal (1840–88) would use this as an argument in their criticism of the autocratic sultans, especially Sultan Abdülhamid II (r. 1876–1909) (Mardin 1962: 102–6).

9. A more detailed discussion of the doctrine and its pre-Ottoman origins is provided by Mardin (1962: 94–102). From the *Kabus Name* (1082) originating in Central Asia: 'Make it your constant endeavour to improve cultivation and to govern well, for understand this truth, *good government is secured by armed troops, armed troops are maintained with gold, gold is acquired through cultivation and cultivation sustained through payment of what is due to the peasantry, by just dealing and fairness: be just and equitable therefore*' (Mardin 1962: 97–8, author's emphasis).

10. Tendencies in the direction of transgressing the established functional divisions, like having military personnel or ulema going into trade, were seen as threats to the established equilibrium. Such tendencies were therefore frequently brought up among the learned people as possible causes behind imperial decline in times of setbacks (Itzkowitz 1972: 89–91).

11. With the Tanzimat reform programme, also known by the name of the charter, Edict of the Rose Chamber, 1839, which guaranteed the life and property for all subjects, including non-Muslims, the *millet* system was also eliminated, by which Jewish and Christian communities had been granted certain autonomy.

12. This lack of constitutional checks and balances did not cause remarkable difficulties during the one-party period, which in itself implied heavy concentration of governmental authority. Neither could the reform programme have been carried out, had power been divided and dispersed. The problems started during the multi-party system of the 1950s, eventually leading to the military coup of 1960 (Özbudun and Gençkaya 2009: 13).

13. There is no official author for the 1927–8 collection, only an introduction signed by the then director Rıfat [Börekçi]. Still, in the introduction to the 1936 edition, Akseki notifies that he was also the author of the previous publication (therefore, 'My new *hutbes*' in 1936) (Akseki 1936: 6; Bulut 2006: 49; Bulut 2019b: 31). The only available printed edition of *Türkçe Hutbe* in modern, Latinised Turkish is a volume transcribed and edited by Emine Şeyma Usta as *Atatürk'ün Hazırlattığı Cuma Hutbeleri* (translated as Friday sermons initiated by Atatürk) (Istanbul: İleri Yayınları, 2005). *Türkçe Hutbe* is recorded under Ahmet Hamdi Akseki's name in this book's bibliography.

14. See Appendix I for the texts in Turkish. The quotations follow the numbers in square parenthesis. The translation to English has been done by Allison Kanner-Botan (PhD candidate in the Divinity School and the Department of Near Eastern Languages and Civilizations, University of Chicago).

15. The author himself was of the opinion that 'important changes' indeed had been made. In fact, that was the very purpose of the 1936–7 publication (Akseki 1936: 6). What is meant by 'important' is of course relative. Needless to say, the following analysis is that of an outsider.

16. The *hutbe* topics of the 1936–7 collection are reproduced in Turkish and English in Appendix II.

17. *Gusül* – ritual ablution of the whole body.

18. Akseki was a prolific writer and one of those ulema who contributed to an understanding of Islam in line with the new secular order. Significant in this context is his handbook of Islam for imams and *hatips*, *İslam Dini. İtikat, İbadet, Ahlak* (Islamic Religion. Belief, worship and ethics), published in 1933 and meant as a manual to the sermon collections (Akseki 2014). The Turkish secularist order required clerics not to pass judgements on anything other than purely religious topics. '*Muamelat*', related to *amel* (deed), traditionally associated with rules related to worldly affairs (business transactions, including interest rates; family relations; inheritance and political action) was absent in this publication. The subtitle – 'Belief, worship and ethics' – bore witness to this restriction.

19. Better here to use 'improve', not 'reform'. The latter is generally avoided among Muslims, since it is suggestive of the 'Protestant reformation', a doctrinal reinterpretation with far-reaching divisions within Christianity. When calling for 'improvement', the aim is revival, rather than change. This terminological issue also touched a sensitive string in the relationship between religious circles and Mustafa Kemal, who wanted to push for a more extensive 'reform' of Islam, a question to be further discussed in Chapter 3.

20. Historian Hans-Lukas Kieser remarks in passing in his biography of Union and Progress leader Talaat Pasha (1874–1921) how Louis Rampart, director of one of the agencies of the international administration of the Ottoman debts, frequented the public prayers from which he was able to divine governmental strategies: 'For connoisseur of political Istanbul Rambert, *who also listened to public prayers*, three things appeared clear in August 1914 . . .', (Kieser 2018: 191, my emphasis).

21. 'It also appears to be a fact that other men look for salvation not to a leader but to a community possessing certain charismata. By being a member of such a community (and by doing nothing to forfeit one's membership) a man attains salvation' (Watt 1987: 3). More on the sacred nature of the worshipping congregation in Chapter 3.

22. A majority of the Kurdish population belongs to the Shafii *mezhep*. The Hanbali, which is dominant in Saudi Arabia, is almost non-existent in Turkey. The Maliki *mezhep* is dominant in North Africa.

23. This is the opposite to what Patrick Gaffney observed about the Egyptian Muslim Brotherhood, who took worship beyond the mosques, to all sorts of places – a 'loss of borders' – 'the boundaries of the mosque were eliminated, as it were' (Gaffney 1994: 25).

# 3

## THE SIGNIFICANCE OF RITUAL: LITURGICAL TURKIFICATION CONTESTED

Religion could hardly remain unaffected by the modernising reforms of the nineteenth century. Consequently, the changing role of sacred institutions and traditions became the subject of debate among Muslim as well as non-Muslim Ottoman intellectuals. For non-Muslims, especially with a background in the Balkans, such discussions often merged with the struggle for national independence. For Muslims, on the other hand, the increased meddling of religious identities into politics, in hindsight epitomised as the 'politicization of Islam' (Karpat 2001), blended with efforts to keep the disintegrating empire together. This became especially apparent during the reign of Abdülhamid II (r. 1876–1909), who promoted pan-Islamist leanings in an effort to summon Turks, Arabs, Kurds and other Muslim groups under an Ottoman umbrella. In spite of the fact that the Young Turks, who forced Abdülhamid II from the throne in 1909, distanced themselves from the sultan's pan-Islamic policies in favour of an emphasis on Turkish identities, the fervour for Islamic values (jihad) resurged with the Balkan Wars, followed by the First World War and the War of Independence.[1]

As already mentioned, the Kemalist leadership that emerged from the War of Independence was determinedly secularist in orientation. It was not only that the high tide of jihadist-influenced patriotic feelings receded when the wars were over; the leaders also pursued a highly insistent, modernist political agenda. However, as already mentioned, the de-politicisation of

Islam in combination with the secularising reforms were not aimed at doing away with religion, but to confining it to the private sphere and the mosques, the only abodes of worship left after the closure of *medrese*s, *zaviye*s (dervish lodges) and *türbe*s (shrines).

Late Ottoman pan-Islamism as a form of proto-nationalism was now a long distance off. With most Arab provinces gone and large sections of the non-Muslim population put to flight or deported, the ethnic composition of the new Republic had markedly changed in the direction of greater ethnic and religious homogeneity, with an overwhelming majority of Muslim Turks. Concerning the two basic components, Muslim and Turk, there was no obvious incompatibility. Contrary to Arabs, Turks are almost unexceptionally Muslims. Therefore, unlike 'Christian Arab', the epithet 'Christian Turk' almost appears as a contradiction in terms.[2] Leaving the imperial order behind, language distinguished itself as the key characteristic of Turkish identity, a circumstance that also called for modernising linguistic reforms. With the exception of limited groups of academics and intellectuals, Latinisation of the alphabet and Turkification of the vocabulary were never seriously questioned.[3] Nevertheless, a limit was reached when Turkification efforts interfered with the rituals of religious worship. The translation of the Koran and the sacred/liturgical texts struck a sensitive chord, not only among the educated ulema, but also the common people. How such grievances were played out and what they expressed concerning the significance of the liturgical aspects of worship, especially in a national identity perspective, is the topic of this chapter. But first, the wider context of identity politics during the late Ottoman and mid-war period will be briefly delineated.

## Turkism in the Late Ottoman Period

For the Ottoman Empire, the nineteenth century was a period of loss of territory and decline, as well as reconstruction and modernisation. The power and authority of the dynasty was weakening, but at the same time official institutions like the army, judiciary and education were reorganised based on modern, European standards. This was also a time of large-scale state-sponsored infrastructure projects like railways and postal services. In addition, vital parts of the state bureaucracy gradually steered clear of religion. Partly side-lined, religion took on a relatively static character

(Berkes 1998: 480). New citizenship rights (after 1856) partly wiped out the judicial and political significance of the previous barriers between religious communities (*millets*). It was in the midst of these shifting developments that the quest was raised for new collective, proto-national identities. In the wake of the loss of territories, the response shifted from emphasis on Ottomanism to pan-Islamism, and finally Turkism. Ottomanism belonged to the earlier reform period, while pan-Islamism loomed after the Russo-Turkish war of 1877–8, when Turkey lost Bulgaria, Serbia, Rumania and Montenegro in the west and Kars, Ardahan, Batum in the north-east – areas dominated by non-Muslims. Turkish sentiments rose in connection to the Young Turk revolution in 1908, and even more so after the First World War and the loss of the Arab provinces.

A prominent figure in the development of modern Turkish nationalism was Ziya Gökalp (1876–1924). Born and raised in Diyarbakır he yearned to go to Istanbul, and, after a turbulent adolescence he ended up studying French philosophy, psychology and sociology in the imperial capital. This is how he, also as an active member of the Committee of Union and Progress (CUP),[4] became the first professor of sociology at the Dar-ül Fünun (Istanbul University) in 1915, and emblematic promoter of Durkheimianism in modern Turkey.

As a CUP member, Ziya Gökalp had been at the centre of the Turkist movement. At that time the linguistic question was not new. On the contrary, it had been on the agenda since the middle of the nineteenth century. Ottoman Turkish,[5] heavily influenced by Arabic and Persian, was different from the language spoken among the common people. As the political and economic Tanzimat reforms evolved and the old elite structure yielded, the idea of Turkification won adherents among the reform-minded intelligentsia. Şinasi (1826–71), a leading figure of the Young Ottomans, a group of intellectuals active during the later period of the Tanzimat (1867–78), devoted much of his life as poet, publisher and journalist to the modernisation of the Turkish/Ottoman language. Having spent several years in Paris – as a student, and later as an émigré – he initiated translations of French literature to Turkish and the writing of an Ottoman dictionary (Mardin 1962: 252–5, 262–3). Mention must also be made of Namık Kemal (1840–88), who 'went further in the use of the vernacular than his predecessors such as Şinasi . . . and thereby reached an even wider audience than these precursors of the simplification of the Turkish language' (Mardin 1962: 283). Another prominent figure was Yusuf Akçura (1876–1935), a Tatar émigré from Kazan in Russia. He favoured a radical pan-Turkist or Turanist profile,[6] a position he brought forward in *Türk Yurdu*, a periodical founded on his initiative (Poulton 1997: 82). Ziya Gökalp, on the other hand, who had made Türk Ocağı 'his' association, promoted an interpretation of Turkism which was more Anatolia/Balkan-oriented, putting more emphasis on Islam. One reason behind Gökalp's dissociation from far-reaching Turanic visions, was that he saw the nation as a cultural community, not a fellowship defined by race or wide-ranging geographies. Neither should the nation be looked upon as a voluntary association. It existed naturally, without deliberate efforts. A national community was based on language, culture and faith, so to stretch the borders as far as Central Asia in the east and the Balkans in the west would not constitute stable ground for the kind of tightly knit community Gökalp had in mind (Karpat 2001: 378–9). Different nations could be part of the same civilisation, like European modernity, but compared to the depth, intensity and natural character of the national community, the wider order, or 'civilisation', was artificial and superficial.

**Turkism, Islamism and Modernity**

Ziya Gökalp is known for his triple notion of Turkish national identity, that is, being Turkish, Islamic and modern. Thereby he expressed a belief in progress, which meant that Turkey had to catch up with Western, modern civilisation, but without therefore overruling Islam. As much as he endorsed the social and economic progress of the Tanzimat period, Gökalp deplored how, in the name of liberal constitutionalism, new legal councils, courts and law codes were introduced. These innovations, mainly concerned with administrative, civil, criminal and mercantile law threatened the traditional sharia institutions. Gökalp wanted to preserve the integrity of Islamic law. That said, he was also aware of its need for revisions, when brought face to face with fundamental political and socio-economic transformations (Dressler 2015: 513).

Gökalp built his reformist ideas on the distinction between Islamic rituals and Islamic legal rules. 'Religious rites' and 'religious laws' were two branches of Islamic jurisprudence (*fıkıh*). This distinction was similar to the one between *ibadet* (worship, which concerned the relation between human beings and God) and *muamelat* (ethical/legal rules, which concerned relations between human beings) brought forward by well-known reformers like Muhammad Abduh (1849–1905).[7] According to Abduh, only *ibadet* can be firmly fixed on the basis of the Koran and the Sunna. With regard to *muamelat* it was different. Here Koran and Sunna only provided general guidance, since that domain was subject to the forces or changes of history. Therefore, according to Abduh, *ijtihad* (independent reasoning), alongside the classical methods of Islamic jurisprudence based on *icma* (consensus) and *kiyas* (analogy), was a necessary tool to be used in developing legal judgements related to *muamelat* (Dressler 2015: 515).

Gökalp followed a similar line of reasoning but added the idea of *örf* (local custom), which, together with *nas* (Koranic revelation), represented a legitimate source of *fıkıh* (Islamic jurisprudence). *Örf*, according to Durkheimian sociologist Gökalp, was an expression of social consciousness. As such it was infallible – and sacred. Just as the laws of nature have been regarded as a product of divine revelations, so God reveals himself through the laws or norms determining social life. This link between social consciousness and the sacred law of Islam did not, according to Gökalp, challenge or threaten the religious sentiments of the believers (Heyd 1950: 87).[8] Sharia was both *ilahi* (divine) and *içtimai* (social). The textual tradition (Koranic revelation) was regarded as absolute and unchangeable; the social tradition, *örf*, on the other hand, was attuned to the particular circumstances of time and place. In various articles in *İslam Mecmuası*, Gökalp made extensive use of *ijtihad*, in a way similar to another famous figure of the time, Jamal al-Din al-Afghani (Dressler 2015: 515–16).

Gökalp's deliberations on the role of Islamic law in modern society, based on a more sharia-friendly discourse, were abruptly superseded by the secularising reforms of the newly established Republic. Sharia was not only substituted by laws copied from France and Italy; legal sanctions were even imposed on merely speaking in favour of that system. The space allowed for discussions of the relation between the political institutions and Islam under modernity thereby shrank considerably. Due to the fact that he died in 1924, only a year into the Republic, Gökalp was never confronted with its authoritarian and stringently secularist course of development.

### Religion under the Spell of 'Scientific Reform'

The fundamental steps on the road to a secular republic were laid with the abolition of the caliphate (1924), unification of all educational institutions under the Ministry of Education (same year), and the reform of legal institutions modelled on Western law codes (1926). Religious institutions were thereby duly cut off from the political realm. Still, the ambitions of the Kemalist leadership went beyond that, including also alleged ameliorations of religious worship itself.[9]

In 1924, the Faculty of Theology at Istanbul University appointed a committee assigned to investigate how to bring about a 'scientific reform' of Islam. A report was submitted in 1928 with clear marks of Gökalp's ideas, proposing the use of Turkish in prayers, sermons and readings from the Koran. The importance of cleanliness, both of visitors and sanctuaries, was also emphasised.[10] Besides, sermons should be more expressive, so as to increase the enthusiasm and elation of the audiences, but emphasis should be on purely religious values. In the name of implementing a kind of 'aesthetic reformism' suggestions were made to use musical instruments.[11] Even the abolition of prostration was ventured. It was also pointed out that the implementation of reforms was dependent on adequate education of muezzins, imams and *hatip*s (Berkes 1998: 493–4; Heyd 1950: 103; Jäschke 1972: 40–1). However, most of this Enlightenment-inspired programme was never implemented. Berkes comments that Mustafa Kemal's interest in religious reform slowed down after 1928. '[He] came to the conclusion that the course of development of the religious consciousness of the people could not and should not be led by the state or by secular personalities' (Berkes 1998: 495–6). The year 1928 was also when the clause 'The religion of the Turkish state is Islam' was eliminated from the second article of the 1924 constitution. Thereby the secular basis of the regime was safeguarded. Eventually, after many turnabouts, the 'scientific reform of Islam' boiled down to a drive for Turkification of worship.

### Linguistic Reforms

What first comes to mind with respect to language reform in Turkey is the Latinisation of the alphabet, legislated in November 1928. Its impact was manifold. Linguistically, the Latin alphabet represented a more suitable

orthography for the Turkish language. Written Turkish became highly pho-
netic, making reading and spelling easier. In this way it represented an important step forward in the government's alphabetisation campaign. Literacy was
at a low 13 per cent in 1927. As for its impact on the formation of a modern national identity, Latinisation clearly put Turkey at a distance from the
Arab world, while drawing it closer to Europe. Similarly, the linkage to the
Ottoman legacy grew thinner, which facilitated the search for an alternative
Turkic-oriented historical heritage. And, not least, it resulted in the building
of a new orthographic wall between the Koran and the Turkish readership, all
in tune with the other secularising reforms.

The setting up of the Language Council[12] in March 1926, marked the
beginning of a media campaign in support of Latinisation, shored up by
Mustafa Kemal [Atatürk] (Aytürk 2008: 279). Besides the script, the Language Council was entrusted with simplification and purification of the
Turkish language. This is not the place to go into details of language reform;
let it just be mentioned that out of the linguistic debates initiated by European scholars in the middle of the nineteenth century, and further advanced
by a handful of Turkish intellectuals and academics, arose the idea that the
Turkish language was not only a given part of the Indo-European linguistic
family; it also constituted the most original source of all Indo-European languages. The source of such far-fetched ideas was the problem encountered by
European Orientalists concerning the classification of Turkic languages, since
they were considered neither Indo-European, nor Semitic. Scholars would
dispute whether they should be identified as Finno-Tataric, Scythian, Altaic,
Ural-Altaic, Ugro-Japanese or Turanian (Aytürk 2004: 4).

For patriotic intellectuals of the early Republic, it was of great importance
to determine a classification that rendered both language and nation world-
wide recognition and prestige. Among international linguists, the ancient
Sumer language had also been evaluated as being neither Semitic, nor Indo-
European. Ahmet Cevdet Emre, a self-taught linguist, called attention to
alleged similarities between the Sumer and the Turkic languages (Aytürk
2004: 10). This eventually led to the notorious Sun Language Theory, which
claimed that all languages literally 'radiated' from Turkish like beams from
the sun. However, this theory suffered an incommodious collapse at the Third
Turkish Language Congress in 1936 (Aytürk 2004: 16). The Sun Language

Theory was clearly not sustainable, but the language purification campaign continued until it also suffered a backlash in 1941, three years after Atatürk's demise. The resistance then came from academics inside the ruling party. The purification efforts had gone too far, which did not favour, but rather hampered the national cause. To this controversy should also be added the dispute around the Turkification of the call to prayer, an issue that not only touched a small group of academics, but sowed bitterness among the common people.

### Turkification of Religious Worship

As mentioned above, initiatives on the road to Turkism were taken already during the Tanzimat reform period. The firebrand[13] among the Young Ottomans, teacher and journalist Ali Suavi (1839–78), was early out and urged – in the name of spreading education to the masses – for a simplification of the language. He also demanded that the codification of Islamic law should be translated to Turkish (Mardin 1962: 371–2).[14] As teacher, Suavi worked for the Ministry of Education, but was dismissed, accused of inciting the people to revolt during his weekly sermons (Mardin 1962: 361).[15] However, the person who most systematically followed up on these early attempts to use the vernacular in religious contexts was Ziya Gökalp, who meant that the Koran, which is at the foundation of all worship, should be translated to Turkish. Consequently, all ritual ceremonies should be held in the vernacular – *ezan, hutbe, vaaz, dua* (prayer) – everything, except the fixed recitations from the Koran (*tilavet*), performed according to specific tunes or *makam*s (Gökalp 2014: 195–6; Heyd 1950: 102–3; Jäschke 1972: 42–3).[16]

The reasons for promoting 'Religious Turkism' (*Dini Türkçülük*) were many. Firstly, the use of the vernacular or 'national language' (*milli lisan*) had already been suggested by the medieval Islamic scholar Ebu Hanife (d. 767), founder of the Hanefi *mezhep* that dominates among Turkish Muslims. Thus, the idea of using the vernacular was neither new nor alien to Turkish Islamic culture. This idea was linked to a second argument, which maintained that certain less formal ceremonial practices common among Ottoman/Turkish Muslims were held in vernacular Turkish. The most well known is the *teravih namazı*, a long evening session of prayers, poems and hymns performed during Ramadan, in which women participate to a much larger extent than in usual, daily *namaz* prayers; the performance of *Mevlid*, a long poem written by Süleyman Çelebi (d. 1422) about and in memory of the Prophet Muhammad, also recited in private homes or mosques in connection to circumcision ceremonies or to commemorate a relative's death; and *zikir*, special prayer sessions, often combined with rhythmic movements, performed in mosques or various dervish lodges, of which the most renowned are the 'whirling dervishes' (*semazen*s) of the Mevlevi order. Turkish was consequently not a language alien to religious ceremonies. Gökalp maintained that the folksier ceremonies, performed in vernacular Turkish, also represented more popular and well-attended gatherings. One would therefore expect that extending the use of the vernacular to all forms of religious worship would result in greater attendance and stronger emotional attachment (Gökalp 2014: 195–6).

A third incentive was related to the intelligibility of the recited texts. No one should leave the mosque or any other religious service without having understood the meaning of prayers and sermons. In addition, people should not only learn more about religion, they should also be able to better appreciate the excitement involved in worship. Thus, by using the vernacular the ordinary worshipper would be raised spiritually, that is, 'Muslims should be able to leave the mosque with great excitement and belief' (Gökalp 2014: 195). An implicit outcome would be a stronger community of believers – and nationals.

In terms of purification of the Turkish language, Gökalp was not a radical purist. Concerning Turkification of worship, on the other hand, his reform proposals were among the most far-reaching, encompassing everything except Koranic *tilavet*. Even if Gökalp's ideas constituted a source of inspiration, the Kemalist leaders had to watch their step when confronting the sentiments of the ordinary people. Therefore, some of Gökalp's visions were shelved or handled with caution, as is shown in the following discussion.

## The Friday Sermon

It is one thing to target a reform, quite another to implement it. In the case of the Turkification of the Friday noon service, the reason for impediment was that the *hutbe* consists of several, in terms of their symbolic meaning, different sections, such as invocation of God (*tekbir*), confession or witnessing (*şehadet*), praise to God's messenger (*salat ü selam*), quotations from the

Koran and the *hadis*, preaching (*vaaz*) and intercessions (*dua*). The least ceremonious part is the *vaaz*, while *tekbir* and *şehadet* are pregnant with liturgical devoutness. With respect to preaching, it seems likely that even in Ottoman times, imams, *hatip*s or governors, or whoever mounted the pulpit, would speak in their own language when addressing the congregations on political or social issues. That the sermon was often filled with citations from the Koran and *hadis*, which means that it in practice constituted a kind of prolongation of the liturgical parts, does not mean that the sermons at other times and/or places could be held in the vernacular (Jäschke 1972: 43–4). On the other hand, it would not be unwarranted to assume that the dominant *hutbe* practices at the time of the opposition movements of the Young Ottomans and later the Young Turks were marked by a high degree of formalisation and ritualisation. Only against the background of such an assumption do Gökalp's and later the Kemalists' demands for Turkification make sense.[17] According to Jäschke, the first *hutbe* in Turkish was performed right after the election by the parliament (TBMM) of Abdülmecid Efendi (of the Ottoman dynasty) as caliph on 24 November 1922 – preceded a few weeks earlier by the abolition of the sultanate (1 November). Such occasional events were followed up by petitions in parliament (23 February 1925) in favour of making that practice permanent. New proposals were added demanding that the intercessions should also be in Turkish, that is in both Arabic and Turkish (Jäschke 1972: 44).

Soon enough, a standard was set for the language regime of the *hutbe*s. In the missive attached to the mailing in 1927 to imams and *hatip*s around the country of the authorised collection *Türkçe Hutbe* (see Chapter 2), the head of Diyanet, Rıfat [Börekçi], added instructions saying that the Koranic and *hadis* texts should be read in both Arabic and Turkish, while the exhortation (*vaaz* or *nasihat*) should be only in Turkish (Jäschke 1972: 44). Sermonising in Turkish, yes, but concerning the liturgical parts, Arabic should not be abandoned.

Still, this ruling did not put an end to disagreements, especially in learned circles. While professors at Istanbul University were pressing for a complete Turkification of the *hutbe*,[18] Diyanet played a decelerating role as custodians of the preservation of the rooted traditions of Arabic liturgy. New efforts to launch seamless *hutbe*s in Turkish were carried out several years later in

Istanbul during the Ramadan of early 1932 under the personal initiative and supervision of Atatürk. However, these experiments were not followed up by any new regulation from Diyanet. Neither did the parliament issue any prohibition against using Arabic during the *hutbe*s. Diyanet's ordinance from 1927, which called upon the use of both Arabic and Turkish[19] for the Koranic and *hadis* sections, and Turkish only for the sermonising (*vaaz*) part, remained in force (Jäschke 1972: 44–5). Thus, readings from the Koran and *hadis* remained in Arabic, while the sermonising part and the intercessions (*dua*) were held in Turkish. This is the order still valid today (Qutbuddin 2019: 469–72).

### Son Inkilab: Towards a Turkish Ezan

Concerning the *ezan*, the outward manifestation of daily worship, Turkification became a more hard-fought issue – a controversy, which resulted in a law (Article 526 in the penal code accepted in 1933) forbidding the call to prayer in Arabic, punishing any muezzin who flouted the rule. The law was further aggravated through an addendum in 1941, which ruled three months of imprisonment for reciting the *ezan* in Arabic, even if it was done by someone other than the muezzin (Jäschke 1972: 46).[20]

The various turnabouts in what became known as 'the last reform' (*son inkilab*),[21] the Turkification of the *ezan* is worthy of a story of its own. Turkish scholar Dücane Cündioğlu has meticulously recorded how these changes, in an experimental fashion, were ushered in (Cündioğlu 1998: 135–60). The time chosen was Ramadan of 1932, starting on 9 January. Atatürk arrived in Istanbul on the fourth day of the fasting month and established his headquarters in the Ottoman Dolmabahçe Palace by the Bosphorous. There, he gathered nine specially chosen *hafız*s, together with whom he tried out various translations and tunes (*makam*s). Towards the end of Ramadan some recitals were enacted in a selection of mosques – performances that were carefully announced in the press. Special preparations were made for the twenty-seventh night of Ramadan, *Kadir Gecesi* (the Night of *Kadir* [Power]), which commemorates the revelation of the first Koranic verses. Marked out as the great breakthrough, this was set in the imperial Aya Sofya mosque. On this occasion a *mevlid*[22] was performed by thirty *hafız*s. Several suras from the Koran were recited in Turkish. In addition, the Arabic '*Allahu ekber*' (God is greater) was substituted by the Turkish '*Tanrı uludur*' (God is great).[23] These performances were also broadcasted nationwide on radio. A few days later, on the first day of the end of Ramadan festivities, the *ezan* was called out in Turkish in several mosques in Istanbul and elsewhere (Cündioğlu 1998: 140–60). However, at the end of these rounds, Atatürk decided that more time was needed for an all-embracing enactment of the 'Turkish *ezan*'. In the meantime, performance continued in Arabic. About a year later, 6 March 1933, Rıfat Börekçi issued a communiqué to all muftis stating that henceforth, 'in harmony with the nation's politics', the *ezan* should be called out in Turkish (Jäschke 1972: 45).

### Ritual Prayer (*Namaz*)

Atatürk's visions for the 'last [*inkilab*] reform'[24] had also included the Koran, and, with regard to worship, especially those suras which are recited during the daily ritual prayers. Atatürk had thus engaged himself in also having the daily *namaz* performed in the vernacular. However, on that issue he had to concede. Leading ulema such as the head of Diyanet, Rıfat Börekçi, and his successor Ahmet Hamdi Akseki, had expressed serious doubts concerning the use of Turkish in the *namaz* liturgy, since it is exclusively based on the Koran. So, while the *hutbe* was partly, and the *ezan* eventually fully vernacularised, the *namaz* remained untouched by such reform efforts. Translation of the Koran was no problem, as long as the purpose was to reproduce its meaning (*meal*). However, when used for ritual purposes the question was different. The fact that the renowned national poet Mehmet Akif Ersoy had his translations of the Koran burnt before he died was linked to an alleged apprehension that in the hands of the Kemalist leadership the text could be used for ritual purposes – in his eyes apparently a sacrilege.

### Vernacularised Worship Contested

To interfere with ingrained liturgical traditions obviously constituted a challenge, but what were the arguments? The most fundamental objection was related to the character of the Koran itself, the foundation of most liturgical worship. The Koran is thought to be a direct manifestation of God's words, which implies that the expressions are not reproduced or rephrased by an intermediary. The Prophet Muhammad, who first pronounced them, was simply a receiver. Therefore, any rendition into another language can at most be an approximate interpretation of the original text with no guarantee against skews or imperfections.

Another argument is related to linguistic and idiomatic difficulties. The text builds on a poetic and rhythmic structure, which it is difficult to do justice to in another language.[25] In addition, the various suras are performed or chanted in various *makam*s. It is unlikely that the *makam* used for the original Arabic would also be suitable for a Turkish translation. Old *makam*s would have to be re-arranged or new ones created. This kind of difficulties were encountered during the experimental sessions at Dolmabahçe Palace during the Ramadan of 1932.[26]

In addition to the afore-mentioned challenges, a significant amount of anxiety was also involved in engaging in such allegedly dubious experiments. In his memoirs, Hafız Yaşar Okur, the leading reciter in Atatürk's Dolmabahçe team, described the procedure in more detail. Tendentious announcements in the newspapers, addressing the ruling secular, rather than the religious audiences, had made the *hafız* tense and nervous, since announcements about 'reciting the Koran in Turkish' easily could stir fanatic groups, deeply distrustful about having the Koran recited in any language other than Arabic. According to his own narrative about a trial performance realised at the very beginning of the critical Ramadan of 1932, he had first recited Yasin (Sura 36) in Arabic.[27] Only after that had he – very cautiously and humbly in order not to stir feelings – turned to the audience telling them that now he would 'read' (not recite or chant)[28] a translation of that sura in Turkish, followed by an intercession (*dua*) in Turkish. The arrangement, in the form it was reproduced by Hafız Yaşar, could hardly be described as 'reciting the Koran in Turkish'. The *hafız* was eager to emphasise the difference between the impression rendered by the official announcement, which held out the prospect that Turkish was substitutable for Arabic, and the actual performance carried out by himself, since his reputation as a serious, trustworthy and responsible imam and preacher otherwise would be in peril (Cündioğlu 1998: 208–12).

**Silent Resistance**

During these years, open discontent against Turkish *ezan* was limited to a few incidents. The first dates back to November 1932, when complaints were lodged during a sermon held in the Great Mosque (Ulu Camii) in Bursa (Jäschke 1972: 45). A few months later (March 1933) the same mosque became the scene of two members from the congregation reciting – in the absence of the muezzin – both the *ezan* and *kamet* in Arabic. When the police intervened the two protesters appealed to the Directorate of Pious Foundations (Evkaf Müdürlüğü), requesting that the *ezan* – and *kamet* – be held in Arabic. The turmoil was reported to Ankara and ended in several arrests, including the provincial mufti, who had insisted that reading the *ezan* in Turkish was against sharia (Jäschke 1972: 45, Azak 2010: 58–9). A handful of additional cases of muezzins arrested immediately after having read the *ezan* in Arabic have been reported, among them from Istanbul. However, both reporting and implementation of sanctions were arbitrary (Azak 2010: 59–60) and hardly indications of a strong opposition. Still, the resistance was reported and dismissed as religious fanaticism (*irtica*). To exhibit any appearance of resistance as an effort to set the clock back to the old sharia-ruled order was part of the hegemonic Kemalist discourse. That is also how it has been etched into the collective memory of later periods.[29] However, as will be deliberated in the following section, there was more to the *ezan* event than fits into an alleged controversy between official secularism and pro-sharia conservatism.

### Liturgical Sensitivities

The exposition now takes a step back to an event that occurred before the Turkification campaign of the early 1930s. On two subsequent occasions during the Ramadan of 1926, Fridays 15 and 22 March, an imam in Göztepe (Istanbul), held the whole *hutbe*, including the recited Koranic *ayet*s, or verses, in Turkish. When reported to Ankara the imam was removed from his position (Jäschke 1972: 44; Kaplan 2014: 404).

In order to evaluate the religio-political dynamics of this event, which seemingly went against the modernising trends of the current regime, one needs to look closer into its protagonist, Rıfat [Börekçi]. Rıfat, who remained chief of Diyanet from 1924 until his death in 1941, belonged to a wealthy ulema family from Ankara with roots in Konya (Kaplan 2014: 37). He was appointed mufti for Ankara in 1908, a position he held at the time of the beginning of the War of Independence. Before that he had been a member of the Ankara Court of Appeal (İstinaf Mahkemesi) (1896–1907). As mufti he temporarily served (1911) as district governor (*kaymakam*) for Eskişehir and Sivrihisar, indicating that he was well acquainted with inner Anatolia. Based on his family and professional networks in Ankara he was active in mobilising its residents for the national cause, before Mustafa Kemal arrived there. Active on many fronts, he contributed to putting Ankara on the map during the resistance movement (Kaplan 2014: 37–8; 62–3; 111f.).

Support of authoritative religious leaders was of vital importance, since, after all, the War of Independence was defined as jihad in defence of Islam against Greece and its Western allies. A *fetva* issued by the Ottoman sheikh ül-Islam in Istanbul condemning the activities of the 'nationalists' in Ankara was counteracted by a *fetva* delivered by Rıfat and other ulema in Ankara. While the Istanbul *fetva* had been written under foreign pressure, the Ankara *fetva* was presented as genuinely Muslim – and Turkish – signed by 153 ulema (*kadıs*, muftis, *müderris*). It was launched into the press on 19–22 April 1920, followed by the opening on 23 April of the Ankara 'national' parliament, accompanied by greatly adorned religious ceremonies (see Chapter 2), whereby the break with the Istanbul government – but not the sultanic authority – was a fact (Kaplan 2014: 172–81). These were critical steps on the road to national independence, with confidence-inspiring effects on the relationship between Rıfat and Mustafa Kemal. Rıfat could hardly have remained chief of Diyanet for seventeen years had it not been for a good working relation with the Kemalist leadership, above all Mustafa Kemal himself.

Rıfat was an *alim* (sing. of ulema) with long experience of service both in the Ottoman and the republican state administration. He had also since the beginning been active in the resistance movement, which meant that his political sympathies were clearly in favour of the nationalists against the sultanic regime. His achievements in the struggle for the new order were such that his loyalties for the Republic and the modernising reforms could hardly be questioned. It is for this reason that it is especially telling to follow where and for which reasons he drew the lines concerning how far the Turkification of religious worship could reasonably be stretched.

In relation to the episode in Göktepe (Istanbul), when the imam reading the whole Friday *hutbe* in Turkish lost his position, Rıfat's bold reaction could hardly have passed unnoticed. Ahmet Ağaoğlu,[30] a well-known nationalist and writer, commented in the daily *Milliyyet*, 'How could it be that the director (*reis*) of Diyanet punishes a reformist (*inkilapçı*) hodja?' Rıfat's response in *Cumhuriyet* was:

> Reformism (*inkilapçılık*) is one thing; *namaz* is something else. It is absurd to maintain that our religion would improve by having the *namaz* performed in Turkish and that, as a consequence, such worship would contribute to the further development of the wider reform project. To claim such a thing also means one has not understood the meaning of reform (*inkilap*). *Namaz* cannot be performed in Turkish and the Koranic verses and chapters should be read in their original Arabic.[31]

As mentioned above, the ritual prayer, *namaz*, was never vernacularised (Jäschke 1972: 47).

Concerning the Turkish *ezan*, however, Rıfat had to yield. On this issue the political leadership was more intransigent than for other forms of worship.[32] One reason for this may be that the *ezan* represented religion's face towards the outside, while other forms of worship took place within the mosque or the privacy of the home. While the open, public sphere had to be vigilantly guarded, the same sensitivity was not valid for private and semi-closed or semi-public spheres. Looked upon from the perspective of those pious circles who defended the traditional Arabic *ezan*, the question was equally contentious since the *ezan* contains the venerated liturgical expressions *tekbir* (God is greater), *şehadet* (witnessing or confessing) and *salat ü selam* (greeting and blessing of the Prophet), which are all parts of *fatiha*, the opening sura of the Koran.

On 6 March 1933 a notification was sent to all *müftülük*s, signed by Rıfat [Börekçi], requesting that from now on the whole *ezan* should be read in Turkish. The Turkish text was attached, including three options for the *salat ü selam*. The justification offered was linguistic consistency, referring to the need for harmony with overall 'national politics' (*milli politika*) (Jäschke 1972: 45–6). Having to stand behind this circular was based on a concession that caused Rıfat some remorse, especially as disobedience on part of any muezzin involved legal sanctions (Jäschke 1972: 46). However, Rıfat's doubts can hardly have been ruled by a political agenda fundamentally different from that of the republican leadership. It is therefore questionable that his hesitation was a manifestation of *irtica*, that is hostility to the regime in the name of religious fanaticism. For him, as for many others – imams, *hatip*s, muezzins and common believers – this was rather a matter of sacredness, religious enchantment and peace of mind. Worship in Arabic was defended in terms of its alleged 'magic force' (*sihirli güç*) (Jäschke 1972: 43). Dislike of the enforcement of the Turkish *ezan* triggered qualms of conscience or remorse and was voiced as grievances of 'moral anxiety' (*manevi huzursuzluk*) and a quest for 'freedom of conscience' (*vicdan hürriyeti*). Something different from regime-related political concerns was at stake, even if the demands for freedom of conscience and freedom of religion merged into the wider political opposition against the CHP's single-party regime in the freer atmosphere of the post-war years. 'Moral anxiety' and 'pangs of conscience' are subjective notions. Against these self-declared concerns, some more tangible but also subtler, issues may be outlined.

### A Sacred Community

The key to the urge for correct liturgy lies in the importance attributed to the act of gathering itself. The *ezan* is a call to Muslims to summon, but it is not an appeal to any kind of 'getting together'. It is summoning with the purpose to pray, and to pray collectively as a community. This is especially important for the Friday *hutbe*, because unlike the daily *namaz*, *cuma* is obligatory for Muslim men. Moreover, in order to be valid as prayer a certain number of followers have to be present (see Chapter 1). It is by participating in correctly summoned and constituted prayers that man attains salvation (Watt 1987: 3). Thus, the congregated participants do not just form an audience of bystanders but represent an active partaker or agent in a sacred performance along with other sacred artefacts, like the pulpit, the praying niche, the Koran and its traditional (Arabic) liturgy. Unlike ordained priests, imams do not possess any status separate or elevated from that of the ordinary believers. It is the praying community itself that is loaded with such features. In order to understand the social dynamics involved in these ritual gatherings, anthropologist Victor Turner's theory of 'liminality' and 'communitas' offers useful clues (Turner 2008).

The concepts 'liminality' and 'communitas' belong to the theory of transition rites. Turner's predecessor and source of inspiration, Arnold van Gennep (2004 [1960]), had counted upon three stages: separation, margin (or limen signifying threshold) and aggregation. Turner himself especially elaborated on the transitory stage.

> During the intervening 'liminal' period, the characteristics of the ritual subject (the 'passenger') are ambiguous; he passes through a cultural realm that has few or none of the attributes of the past or coming state. (Turner 2008: 94)

Liminality is characterised by ambiguity, of being in between otherwise valid institutions, laws, customs, conventions and ceremonials.

When passing from childhood to adolescence, that is from a state of being single into one of being married, men and women pass through a transition zone of different length and depth depending on issue and cultural context. During this interlude, the ordinary laws and customs of the previous and subsequent periods are suspended. Such liminality also affects the character of social interrelatedness during that interim, which brings what Turner called 'communitas', a social intercourse based on egalitarian, instead of hierarchical values; homogeneity, rather than heterogeneity; unselfishness, rather than selfishness; humility, rather than pride or conceit; and sacredness, rather than secularity (Turner 2008: 106). Periods of liminality and communitas are not limited to primitive societies. Also in modern contexts, shifts occur between 'structure' and 'anti-structure', that is, between states of hierarchical, law-regulated orders, on the one hand, and states of egalitarianism and openness, on the other. As a matter of fact, these two states depend on each other.

> [For] individuals and groups, social life is a type of dialectic process that involves successive experience of high and low, communitas and structure, homogeneity and differentiation, equality and inequality. The passage from lower to higher status is through a limbo of statuslessness. In such a process, the opposites, as it were, constitute one another and are mutually indispensable. (Turner 2008: 97)

The congregation summoned for a Friday *hutbe* carries traits of a communitas. The obligatory ablutions, leaving shoes at the entrance, putting on a headscarf (for women not already wearing one) mark the transition from a normal, to a separate and transitory state, which is marked by humbleness and equality. Not even the imam or the *hatip* represents a status above any of the other members of the congregation. As partaker in the ritual prayer the individual is stripped of distinctions of wealth and status. During the ceremony, obedience and silence are mandatory for everyone. The congregation is united through an absence of rank, that is in shared lowliness. The relief or sense of having experienced something edifying comes after the end of the ceremony, when members of the congregation leave the praying room for the outside courtyard, where they greet and congratulate each other (see Chapter 6).

Turner's theory of liminality and communitas highlights the liturgical aspects of the Friday sermon – a concrete manifestation of unity and togetherness based on egalitarianism. The theory corroborates the assumption ventured in this book that the ritual gathering should be seen as the leading part of the sermon. It is through the liturgical passages that the congregation experiences itself as a community with enhanced status and authority. Understood in this way, the praying community can be seen as a ritual manifestation of Benedict Anderson's notion of the nation as an 'imagined community'. 'It is *imagined* because the members . . . will never know most of their fellow-members, meet them, or even hear of them, yet in the minds of each lives the image of their communion.' And, 'it is imagined as a *community*, because, regardless of the actual inequality and exploitation that may prevail in each, the nation is always conceived as a deep, horizontal comradeship' (Anderson 1983: 15–16).

## Arabic Liturgy in the Service of Turkish Congregational Unity

The prohibition against Arabic *ezan* touched sensitive strings. But which were the challenges? Firstly, Turkification was experienced as a threat against the seriousness, solemnity and sacredness of worship, that is, it signified a step towards desacralisation and disenchantment of long-cherished traditions. Thereby, it touched a deeply entrenched order of social and moral authority. A second challenge was related to the potential splits (*fitne*) involved in translation itself. Any translation can be questioned concerning authoritativeness and correct wording, meaning it opens the door to linguistic controversies, not least when considering that a vernacular is continuously subject to change.

A third point is related to the fact that in worship Arabic was everybody's language, while Turkish was only that of the country's majority, a situation that could stir feelings of discontent, not least among the country's Kurdish-speaking minority. So, in this particular context, the situation built on the paradox that Arabic – a foreign language – could have more unifying effects on the congregations than Turkish – the national language.

## Back to Arabic *Ezan*

The most vociferous outbursts of emotion came when the ban against Arabic *ezan* was lifted. This was right after the parliamentary elections in May 1950 and became the first legislation enacted by the new Democrat Party government, implemented just in time for the upcoming Ramadan. The stories about people running to the mosques, weeping out of joy, and demanding the chanting of the *ezan* over and over again are legion. The relief was great. 'Something, that had been taken away from the people, was now given back' (Armağan 2015: 107); expressions testifying that identity-related concerns stretching beyond the *ezan* itself had been at stake.

The feelings of humiliation following the obligation to read the *ezan* in Turkish have been expressed in different ways. One imam/muezzin speaks of 'looking down' out of shame before the congregation; others speak about skipping the *ezan* altogether (Armağan 2015: 61). A village imam already mentioned (Chapter 1), Kutuz Hoca, recalls in his memoirs how he as a young boy was summoned to read the *ezan* in order to spare the elder imams the trouble or predicament of either trespassing the law, or going against the rule of sacred traditions and their own conscience (Kara 2015: 95). In other places the village fool had been engaged for the purpose (Armağan 2015: 42–3). Another way to get around it was to read it silently in Arabic, after first having read it aloud in Turkish (Armağan 2015: 82). Yet another muezzin would read the Arabic *ezan* silently, declaring the end of it with a loud 'Bitti!' (finished). In those places, where the imam and muezzin could trust their congregation, children could be put on guard to issue warnings if the gendarmerie showed up. Other stories tell about people distrusting whether the Turkish call to prayer was in fact a real (valid) *ezan* or not, or warning others that the consequence of reading the *ezan* in Turkish would signify a loss of faith (Armağan 2015: 95–6). A general understanding was that the congregations shrank during this period (Armağan 2015: 76, 125). Similar observations included the opinion that the Turkish state was losing prestige, that the country came to suffer from 'moral poverty' (*maneviyat yoksulluğu*), or that a whole cultural heritage was in peril (Armağan 2015: 49, 61, 106). Many people, especially from religious circles, would agree with Armağan's verdict that seldom has a religious issue touched such broad sections of the people, so deeply (Armağan 2015: 44).

### Conclusion: Ritual Worship, Traditional Authority and Nationhood

In summarising this chapter's deliberations on liturgy and language, three issues will be emphasised. First, the mainly quiet struggle for maintaining parts of the liturgy in Arabic was not primarily an expression of 'reactionary tendencies' (*irtica*). Rather than wanting to restore a sharia-ruled past, resistance was based on a concern for the sacredness embedded in the symbolic universe of the *namaz* rituals, including the sanctity of the praying congregation itself. A frequently overlooked effect of such piety-related conservatism was that holding on to the traditional liturgical forms rendered honour, status and authority to rituals and performers alike. This was accomplished through the power inherent in retaining Arabic as the liturgical language.

Second, by rendering respect and esteem, holding on to the traditional Arabic liturgy also had a strengthening effect on the coherence of the believers, and, as a consequence of that, the larger social community. Looked upon from the point of view of the formation of national identities, two, seemingly contradictory, processes were at work. On the front stage the official establishment appeared in its efforts to form a national community built on secular values and Turkish identities; however, backstage local forces were at work guarding traditional religious values and identities. One operated through modern institutions such as the reformed educational system, the ruling political party and the state institutions (bureaucracy); the other through local networks (villages, townships) manifested in mosque communities. In spite of the fact that they pulled in different directions in terms of values and objectives, both promoted, in their different ways, the formation of national consensus building.

The third conclusion is that the sermonising part of the *hutbe* only comes second in relation to the act of gathering itself, conducted through the liturgical rituals. A sermon may emphasise the importance of social, political and national unity very, very much. Solidarity, brotherhood, consensus, obedience and allegiance to authority are indeed the most recurrent themes of the official sermons. However, what really counts in the constitution of the nation as a community is the ceremonial act of gathering itself. It is the liturgical rituals that have bearings on the message conveyed through the preaching act, not the other way around. This observation is crucial for the analyses of subsequent chapters, since it puts the official Friday sermons – the key issue of this study – into due perspective.

## Notes

1. A powerful promoter of an Islamist – in combination with a Turkist/Turanist – agenda was the Union and Progress leader Talaat Pasha (1874–1921) (Kieser 2018).
2. According to Bernard Lewis: 'For the Ottoman Turk, his Empire, containing all the heartlands of early Islam, was Islam itself. In the Ottoman chronicles the territories of the Empire are referred to as "the lands of Islam", its sovereign as "the Padishah of Islam", its armies as "the soldiers of Islam", its religious head as "the şeyh of Islam"; its people thought of themselves first and foremost as Muslims. Both Ottoman and Turk are . . . terms of comparatively recent usage, and the Ottoman Turks had identified themselves with Islam – submerged their identity in Islam – to a greater extent than perhaps any other Islamic people' (Lewis 1968: 13). That the situation on the local level, where communitarian cross-bordering, especially before the Balkan Wars (1912–13), was not too infrequent, expressions such as 'Muslim Christian' could be used for a Christian girl married to a Muslim boy. Recent works, scholarly as well as fictional, bear witness to the fact that inter-communitarian relationships in late Ottoman society were more flexible and unprejudiced than those of the subsequent nationalist period (Bernières 2005; Clark 2006; Doumanis 2013).
3. The situation was different concerning the Kurdish and Arabic minorities, the latter living in the Hatay province (Antioch), which through a referendum was annexed to Turkey in 1936.
4. Ziya Gökalp was a permanent member of the CUP Central Committee from 1909 until the dissolution of the party in 1918. Leader of the CUP 'triumvirate' was Talaat Pasha. For Gökalp's relation to Talaat, but especially the latter's role in the Armenian massacres of 1915 – 'architect of genocide' – see Kieser (2018). For extensive analyses of the Young Turk movement and CUP, see Hanioğlu (1995; 2001).

5. The 'classical' definition of Ottoman according to Turkish literary historian Fahir Iz: 'Ottoman was a hybrid language, composed of Turkish, Arabic and Persian sharing the vocabulary and grammatical rules of these three languages, and was developed in the Ottoman court and the *medrese* and became increasingly "more so" during the sixteenth century onwards, reaching its "ceiling," in the seventeenth century, in the hands of writers like Veysi (d. 1628) and Nergisi (d. 1635) (whose over-quoted names have become proverbial for "Ottomanization" of Turkish). This hybrid language was the official jargon of the empire for centuries and could only be handled by a highly trained elite and was a "Chinese puzzle" for the rest of the people. This state of affairs lasted until the middle of the nineteenth century, when Şinasi (1826–1871) arrived. He and his associates of the *Tanzimat* literary movement, carried out a drastic reform in the language and style and thus achieved the simplification and Turkification of the Ottoman language' (Iz 1976: 118–19). Iz added, that this hybrid language did not encompass all, only Divan literature. Folk and dervish poetry and prose were never 'Ottomanised' in that sense.

6. Turanism, the idea that all Turkic peoples from the Balkans to China should be united in one country called 'Turan', gained momentum after the Young Turk revolution (1908), and was, in émigré Akçura's version, 'avowedly pan-Turkist and non-Ottoman' (Poulton 1997: 82). There were indications that CUP leaders in their dealings with Germany before the First World War nourished plans for a 'Great Turanian Empire' (Hanioğlu 2008: 179).

7. The conceptual distinctions are reminiscent of an earlier Ottoman institutional practice based on the distinction between *kaza* (issuing of legal judgements) and *ifta* (issuing of *fetva*s). Both fell under the jurisdiction of the sharia but were separated so that the first applied to 'worldly' affairs, while the second applied to more narrowly defined religious issues. The first was under the authority of the *kazasker* (or *kadıasker*, chief judges – one for Anatolia and one for Rumeli) and the second under the authority of the sheikh ül-Islam. Traditionally the rank of sheikh ül-Islam stood above that of the *kazasker*s, but in practice they were independent from the sheikh ül-Islam and responsible to the central Ottoman administration. This changed in 1836 (in connection to the Tanzimat reforms of 1839), when, in an effort to centralise the administration, the offices of the major *kazasker*s were moved to the *fetvahane*, the seat of the sheikh ül-Islam, who, after another two years became the supreme authority over *kaza* as well and thus had the power to oversee all major aspects of sharia affairs (Dressler 2015: 513).

8. Local custom, *örf*, could not be dismissed as completely secular in origin, according to Gökalp. 'If social consciousness, moral customs, legal practices, and general political opinions of tribes and peoples are subject to natural laws

that are independent of individual will yet govern it, can then the power that establishes these sunna and laws be anything other than the eternal will? Therefore, does not örf in the same way as the revealed text (*nass*), not in a direct and positive, but in an implicit and figurative sense, have a divine nature?' ('İçtimai Usul-i Fıkıh,' *Islam Mecmuası*, quoted in Dressler 2015: 516).

9. 'Had the new regime merely desired the persecution of religion, it would have abandoned such projects after these two major changes ["promulgation of the Republic and abolition of the Caliphate"]' (Berkes 1998: 484). However, the idea behind the Turkish reform programme was that it should cover all aspects of social life (language, moral, law and economics). All social institutions should be recast according to rational/scientific and national principles. This meant that also religious life should be improved with scientific methods (Jäschke 1972: 40).

10. See Chapter 2 and the emphasis on cleanliness in authorised *hutbe*s.

11. The person behind this interest in adornment was İsmail Hakkı Baltacıoğlu (1886–1978), president of Istanbul University (Berkes 1998: 494).

12. *Dil Heyeti* or *Dil Encümeni*, both names used (Aytürk 2008: 276, n. 2)

13. For example, Ali Suavi was different from Namık Kemal, another Young Ottoman intellectual, in that he defended the right to civil disobedience (Mardin 1962: 377).

14. Thanks to these initiatives there would even be reason to name Suavi the 'First Turkist', according to Mardin. However, this would still not be appropriate, because for Suavi, Islam represented a stronger unifying force than Turkish linguistic or ethnic identities (Mardin 1962: 371).

15. Speaking in Turkish, Ali Suavi stood out as a rare exception to the dominant practice of keeping exclusively to Arabic in the Friday *hutbe*s (Azak 2010: 47).

16. Vernacularisation of *namaz* was not part of Gökalp's programme. Jäschke comments that Mustafa Kemal went further than Gökalp, because he advocated that it should be performed in Turkish (Jäschke 1972: 48).

17. Professor Bünyamin Erul maintains that in Ottoman times *hutbe*s were exclusively held in Arabic (see interview in Chapter 6).

18. This was a demand they later took back.

19. Turkish only as interpretations of the Arabic original. The Koran cannot be translated, only interpreted by providing its meaning (Turkish: *meal*).

20. In 1947 the Minister of Justice declared that twenty-nine people had been arrested for violating that law (Jäschke 1972: 46). In order to avoid punishment children had been used for the *ezan*. See Kara (2015).

21. The term *inkilab* translates both as reform and revolution. In the Kemalist vocabulary of the mid-war period it was used for a radical or revolutionary reform, implemented with strong determination.
22. The *Mevlid* is usually performed in Turkish.
23. Various alternative translations were suggested, but the final version was the following:

> Tanrı uludur (x4)
> Şüphesiz bilirim bildiririm Tanrı'dan başka yoktur tapacak (x2)
> Şüphesiz bilirim bildiririm Tanrı'nın elçisidir Muhammed (x2)
> Haydi namaza (x2)
> Haydi felaha (x2)
> Namaz uykudan hayırlıdır (only morning prayer) (x2)
> Tanrı uludur (x2)
> Tanrı'dan başka yoktur tapacak. (Jäschke 1972: 45)

*Tekbir* in Arabic translates as 'God is greater' (in the comparative), while the Turkish form translates as 'God is great' (in the positive).

24. 'You will be the ones to carry out the last revolutionary reform [*son inkilab*], Mr Hafızs,' Atatürk had incited the Koran reciters at Dolmabahçe Palace during the Ramadan of January/February 1932 (Cündioğlu 1998: 216).
25. The difficulties encountered in translations of Homeros' and Dante's classical works may give an idea.
26. Atatürk had wished for a 'full-fledged' translation, but those in religious circles were sceptical as to whether this was at all possible. Hafız Sadettin Kaynak: 'the translations are in prose; and not in good prose either, for that part' (Cündioğlu 1998: 213).
27. This was on the second day of Ramadan in the Yerebatan Mosque (in the vicinity of Sultan Ahmet), where Hafız Yaşar Okur served as imam.
28. Another *hafız* described his way of 'reading' the Turkish translation as '*hitabet tarzı*' – a sermonising, prose-like style (Cündioğlu 1998: 214).
29. For a well-documented study of events and narratives feeding into the spectre of *irtica* (reactionary Islam) such as the 'March 31 incident' (1909), the 'Menemen incident' (1930), the 'Turkish *ezan*' (1930s/1940s), the 'Malatya incident' (1952), and the 'Said Nursi (1877–1960) movement', see Azak (2010).
30. For an extensive biography on Ahmet Ağaoğlu, see Shissler (2003).
31. *Milliyyet*, 11 April 1926 and *Cumhuriyet*, 3 May 1926, quoted in Kaplan (2014: 404).

32. An indication of sometimes strained relations between Diyanet and the government was the decision in 1931 to transfer the control over personnel assignments of the country's approximately 28,700 mosques from Diyanet to the Ministry of Education (Jäschke 1972: 59, 66).

# 4

# PREACHING BROTHERHOOD TO AN
# UNRULY NATION

This chapter concentrates on official *hutbe* texts from the 1970s. There are two reasons for choosing that decade. Firstly, it marks the beginning of the fortnightly *Diyanet Gazetesi*. Starting from 1968, when this periodical first appeared, it becomes possible for the first time to follow the religious authorities' responses to various challenges to national unity. This means that from now on *hutbe*s can be matched to or interpreted in relation to a more tangible social and political reality. The second reason is that this was a very unruly decade politically, a question expounded below. How did Diyanet deal with these problems in its sermonising discourses? Was it trying to enlighten their audiences about their responsibilities as citizens, or was it mostly admonishing their congregations to stay calm and refrain from meddling in social and political affairs? In other words, was the emphasis on fostering more civic-minded citizens, or on discouraging the audiences from engaging in common, public issues, safeguarding their loyalty by relying on religious exhortations? The 1970s is also a particularly interesting period from the point of view of what Diyanet achieved in terms of institution-building and relative autonomy vis-à-vis the state. That is, however, the topic of Chapter 5.

## Free Enterprise and Parliamentary Democracy: New Social Dynamics

The new world order that emerged after the Second World War with the USA as the leading Western power meant a marked upswing for Turkey. In contrast to the First World War, which had caused the Ottoman Empire severe damage and final disintegration, modern Turkey managed to stay outside of the military hostilities of the Second World War. However, Turkey was, after more than two decades of reform efforts, still a poor and basically agricultural country. The Truman doctrine and the following Marshall Aid (March and June 1947 respectively) gave the country a needed push forward. The number of tractors increased rapidly,[1] a mechanisation that in a few years' time triggered mass migration, especially to the bigger cities. Generous foreign loans and investments generated economic growth, on average 6 per cent between 1950 and 1955.[2] Also, the political landscape changed radically in that the one-party state gave way to a multi-party system. In the first democratically held elections in 1950, the opposition, represented by the Democrat Party (Demokrat Parti, DP), won 408 seats, while Atatürk's Republican People's Party (Cumhuriyet Halk Partisi, CHP) shrank drastically to a meagre sixty-nine seats.[3] The demands for economic improvements and political and religious space of action became louder. However, popular mobilisation was not matched by sustainable formal organisation, neither with respect to labour unions nor voluntary associations. The political parties continued to be ruled from the top and popular manifestations remained unrehearsed and chaotic. The seeds of the subsequent unruly decades were sown during the sudden and overpowering acquaintance with the world markets of the early 1950s.

## Turkey in the 1970s

The 1970s represent an unusually turbulent time in the country's modern history. This decade-long commotion should be seen against the background of the military coup of 1960, which had put a tragic end to the 'roaring fifties'. In the aftermath of this event, which, in spite of the violence displayed during the military takeover itself,[4] rendered the country a new, relatively liberal constitution (1961). The monopoly-like position of the majority party (be it CHP or DP) inherited from the 1924 constitution, was now exchanged for a system allowing more space of action for a greater variety of political actors, including labour unions and student associations, and more autonomy to institutions like the Constitutional Court, the National Security Council and the universities. Once the wheels of the new order got moving, a certain amount of stability presented itself, bolstered by economic growth and an average increase in real income of 20 per cent in the years 1963–9 (Zürcher 1994: 263).

It was not long, however, before a political radicalism emerged heralding that of the 1970s. On the left, debating societies appeared, flanked by Marxist–Leninist or Maoist revolutionary groups, some of which advocated armed guerrilla warfare. On the right various anti-communist and ultra-nationalist groups were receiving paramilitary training in order to conquer the streets and university campuses. Things turned violent during the spring and summer of 1968. In June, Istanbul University was occupied by radical leftists, followed in July by protests against the US sixth fleet, whence American soldiers were sensationally thrown into the Straits of Bosporus. The unrest escalated. In February 1969, a march heading towards Taksim Square gathering 30,000 people was attacked by counter-revolutionary groups, equipped with knives and sticks – a confrontation leaving two people dead. Another spectacular event took place in early March 1971, when five leftist militants kidnapped four US military personnel in Ankara; however, they were released after four days. Just a few days later, on 12 March, a temporary end to the violent clashes was brought about by the second military intervention in post-war Turkey. A brutal repression followed, especially hitting leftist organisations. This kept the streets relatively calm for a few years, but towards the end of the decade violent clashes between different political fractions resurged, escalating to unbearable levels.[5] To this was added increasing tensions between religious communities, especially Sunni and Alevi (see below), in various places in Anatolia.

An important reason behind the renewed street violence was political instability and lack of due leadership and authority. Neither of the two general elections, 1973 and 1977, led to a majority government. Instead, the period was marked by shaky coalition governments (seven governments in seven years, 1973–80), more or less inapt to shoulder governmental responsibilities. New parties, especially the pro-Islamic National Salvation Party (Milli Selamet Partisi, MSP), had a fragmenting effect on the overall party structure. As a matter of fact, it was this unpredictable and capricious actor that held the balance of power until the military coup of 1980.

Below is a selection of events that especially highlight the quandaries of the turbulent 1970s. This abridged 'timeline' starts already in 1968, because the antagonism between left-wing and right-wing groups, so characteristic of the 1970s, flared up during that year – as did the periodical publication of official sermons. The editorial of the first issue of *Diyanet Gazetesi* sets the tone: 'the development of a society, and its chance to achieve peace and harmony is dependent on the strength of its faith [in God]' (*Diyanet Gazetesi*, 22 November 1968). Such statements give the impression that the basic mission of the *hutbe*s was to heal the nation by responding to and counteracting discord and fragmentation.

A selection of events that attracted special attention:

- Student unrest and opposition starting with the occupation of Istanbul University and demonstrations against the US sixth fleet during the summer of 1968; continuing with repeated clashes between right- and left-wing groups around the country; and culminating in the kidnapping of four American military servicemen in Ankara in early March 1971.
- The military intervention of 12 March 1971 and the persecution of particularly leftist groups and organisations.
- The execution by hanging on the night of 5–6 May 1972 of three leftist militants, Deniz Gezmiş (b. 1947), Yusuf Arslan (b. 1947), and Hüseyin İnan (b. 1949), whereby the repression of the military regime reached its peak.
- General elections on 14 October 1973: the CHP, under its new democratic left leader Bülent Ecevit, became the first party with 33.3 per cent of the votes; the newcomer in Turkish politics, the pro-Islamic National Salvation Party, scored 11.8 per cent.
- The pro-enosis (Greek irredentist) *coup d'état* of 15 July 1974 against the president of Cyprus, Archbishop Makarios, staged by the Cypriot National Guard and the Greek military junta (1967–74). When Great Britain, in the capacity of one of three guarantor states – Great Britain, Greece and Turkey – declined to intervene against the coup-makers, Turkey invaded the island on 20 July. Nationalist sentiments rose sharply and Ecevit turned into a national hero (Zürcher 1994: 289–90).
- The formation on 31 March 1975 of a coalition government, 'First Nationalist Front', preceded by a long governmental crisis with negative effects on democratic institutions and leadership. Without a viable government more divisions were expected along social class, ethnic and communal lines, and renewed pressures from the military.

- As a response to the unilaterally declared Turkish Federated State of Cyprus on 13 February 1975, the US government announced a three-year arms embargo on Turkey. The 'Nationalist Front' government under Süleyman Demirel countered by bringing all American bases (except for Incirlik in Adana) and other establishments on Turkish soil under domestic control. This decision was taken 25 July 1975, causing headlines in the press, and was seen as a manifestation of strength vis-à-vis the great power.[6]

- The massacre on Taksim Square on May Day 1977. The rally, gathering some 500,000 people, was organised by DİSK, the leftist labour confederation, which had commissioned around 20,000 functionaries for the occasion. When the meeting was about to end, unidentified snipers – suspicion fell on the 'deep state' and associated right-wing organisations – opened fire from atop one of the surrounding buildings, resulting in uncontrolled shooting and pandemonium, and leaving thirty-nine dead and hundreds injured.[7]

- General elections 5 June 1977. The CHP under Ecevit's leadership, promoting a democratic left agenda, increased its vote share to 41.4 per cent. However, a representation of 213 out of 450 seats was thirteen seats short of forming a government with full majority. The political stalemate of the previous term of office continued.

- The assassination of seven university students, all members of the Labour Party of Turkey (Türkiye İşçi Partisi, TİP), in Bahçelievler, Ankara in October 1978. Five were killed in their apartment, two taken away and executed in a place nearby, and one seriously wounded and taken to hospital, where he died eight days later. The perpetrators were leading members of the ultra-nationalist organisation Grey Wolves.[8]

- The massacre in Kahramanmaraş in December 1978. This outrage, which has gone down in history as the 'Maraş massacre' (*Maraş katliamı*), lasted for several days (23–6 December). It was triggered by the bombing by an allegedly leftist militant of a cinema showing a nationalist or anti-communist film and resulted in more than 100 people killed, mainly Alevi (Kurdish and Turkish), and the burning and destruction of more than 200 houses and 100 workplaces or shops. The reason for the massive casualties was that local right-wing nationalists had mobilised support from other parts of the country, while the government was slow in responding to the local governor's request for military reinforcement (Sayarı 2010: 204, Birand et al.1999: 79–87).

## Homiletic Discourses

With this chapter we have arrived at a period where it is possible to follow more directly the religious authorities' responses to societal events and developments. From now on sermons therefore differ from those of the earlier *hutbe* collections (1927–8 and 1936–7), which could not be associated with specific, current events. The early *hutbe*s were instead projected against the background of the wider panorama of transition from empire and caliphate to a modern, secular republic. The fact that the sermons by the end of the 1960s began to be written in closer relation to the ongoing course of events does not mean, however, that the addresses were particularly explicit in relation to the underlying realities. Quite the contrary, both secularist principles and long-standing homiletic traditions – each in their own ways – set limits, implying the use of sometimes thick filters or buffers between what occurred in daily political affairs and the exposition of *hutbe* texts.

As a constitutional principle, laicism held that religion must not meddle in state affairs and politics. Religion should stay detached from daily politics, as in the dealings of political parties, governmental policies, political debates and ideologies, election campaigns, and any issue related to class antagonisms or ethnic conflict. Warnings against utilising the walls of the mosques for advertisement during election campaigns were expressions of such a ban against involvement in anything political (*Diyanet Gazetesi*, 1 October 1975). This, as a matter of fact, coincided with the concerns of those responsible for religious traditions, because second only to *tevhid* – the principle of monotheism – the uppermost aim of Islam is to promote unity among believers – the *umma* (Turkish: *ümmet*). This applies not only to political rivalry and conflict, but to all social and communal rifts. However, before elaborating further on this complex of problems, eight selected sermons, which illustrate Diyanet's responses to perils threatening the Turkish nation, are reproduced in whole. The aim is to confront the texts with what was going on in the wider society at the time, that is, what was on the agenda in political circles, newspapers and other media.

With respect to the increasing social and political unrest and the deepening economic crisis, one can distinguish two overarching sources of anxiety. The first relates to internal splits; threatening to tear up society from within (*fitne*), such as deep socio-economic inequalities; political conflicts; and ethno-religious antagonisms. The second concerns external threats, prompting a call for jihad. The Turkish people may face external threats on two fronts: from alien cultural (particularly Western) influences, which allegedly poison and harm the authentic Turkish and Muslim traditions, an intrusion made possible because some groups fall prey to thoughtless imitation (*taklit*); and from military assaults, which pose a threat to territorial integrity and independence. The first five of the following *hutbe*s are responses to threats originating from internal splits or disturbances (*fitne*). The remaining three are related to external threats, demanding defence and struggle – jihad. Each calls attention to special dimensions of the overall challenge to unity and independence.

## Official *Hutbe*s Related to Internal Social and Political Strife[9]

*ONE: Diyanet Gazetesi, 15 March 1971*

Event: Military intervention of 12 March 1971

### *Islam is a Life-sustaining Religion*

Preamble: O mankind, there has to come to you instruction from your Lord and healing for what is in the breasts and guidance and mercy for the believers (The Koran [SI], Jonah 10: 57).[10]

Islam as a religion sent down to earth by Allah as a source of life in itself for guiding wise people to reality, beauty and truth. Most glorious Allah created this source, and every living creature in the world according to its appropriate form, so too it governs the laws of the world in the best and most true manner. During the time an individual or a society exist in the world, the provisions to maintain their lives are their rights and these rights are reserved. To endanger a harmless living creature's life, to prevent someone from earning his livelihood through legitimate means, and to stop rightful owners from exercising their rights over their belongings have been strictly forbidden by God, and are considered to be some of the biggest sins. As it can be understood from these divine principles, Islam speaks completely to reason by causing belief in the existence of one true existence and saving the humanity from a variety of disputes, and it does not approve of anything that remains exterior to reason or logic.

Islam as a religion states and forbids in numerous commands that there will be an ultimate consequence to catastrophic division, ignorance, darkness, laziness and misery.

Islam as a religion centres upon its members treating one another as brothers in order to preserve honour and virtue, establish peace and tranquillity and conserve freedom and independence. It has legalised science and knowledge for the development of intelligence, hardworking for the development of the economy, and marriage for individual and societal needs.

Islam as a religion makes freedom as a right known to every individual from birth and harshly condemns captivity and slavery, hatred and lethargy, and greed and plotting. Morals, virtues, correct guidance, generosity and bravery are conducive to Islam and to perfected faith. Islam brings into balance social life by giving preference to national gains over personal gains.

Islam as a religion recalls the importance of helping relatives and neighbours by calling upon all types of self-sacrifice, be they religious, national or for the homeland, from its members. It also encourages obedience to mother and father, which is necessary for the continuation of generations and lineage that is second only to obedience to Allah.

Islam as a religion promotes cleanliness, the foundation of health and welfare, as half of belief as it gives esteem to the health of the individual and community and it has harshly forbidden libation, gambling and other games that resemble gambling as they are the reasons for material and moral sickness in society. For the continued health of the community, Islam has commanded and recommended to not enter upon places where communicable diseases are found. Anyone who has caught sickness should not leave the place from which they caught it, and by virtue of the important dangers that exist in communicable diseases anyone else should escape those places like one who is escaping from a lion. Thus, for us as a people, our master Muhammad (Peace be upon Him), who is more merciful than the most humane father, explains in a succinct manner the value and importance of life, health, and wealth: Know the value of life before death, health before sickness, wealth before poverty, leisure before business and youth before old age.

Islam as a religion promotes necessary societal and individual functions such as agriculture, crafts and trade from a point of view that would benefit the public as a whole. Additionally, by explicating that the most permissible nourishment that a person could put in their stomach is the morsel that he worked for with his labour. Islam decidedly forbids begging and indicts with the heaviest tongue not working oneself and taking daily sustenance off the backs of others.

By containing these principles, Islam is enough for the procurement of every aspect of the happiness of mankind, and it gives the most prosperous life to its followers for it is a life-sustaining religion. (Author: Fikri Duman, Mufti of Şarkışla)[11]

## Comment

The above *hutbe* appeared just a few days after the military intervention of 12 March 1971. This stirring event is not explicitly mentioned. Still, it is hardly possible to read the sermon without paying due attention to the social and political context, given that the military had just seized command of the country.

To start with, the tone is largely defensive. Here, the representatives of religion feel the pressure from the armed forces, the most powerful segment of the state elite that is utterly secularist, sometimes even hostile to religion. Therefore, the *hutbe* is designed as a kind of lecture that summarises what Islam represents in the most concentrated, and, from a secular point of view, most acceptable way. It reassures the military and the other guardians of the secular state that Islam is a religion that speaks to reason, logic and scientific knowledge, meaning that Islam, as described here, does not degenerate into religious fanaticism or emotional over-indulgences. In addition, the rhetorical form of the *hutbe* is highly didactic. After a first introductory prologue, each paragraph starts with 'Islam as a religion . . .'

However, this text would not be a proper *hutbe* were it not for the concern for the common people. The message conveyed to the congregational audiences is that as long as they obey the laws, avoid divisions and conflicts, and are loyal to the state and the larger society (nation), nobody will touch or interfere in their rightful economic enterprises or other professional dealings, that is, it will be business as usual. In the same spirit, the sermon also contains an indirect warning to the military not to go too far, since, in essence, there is nothing to fear from Islam and the pious people defined as hard-working, intelligent and loyal citizens. Thus, the *hutbe* contains a double message: it speaks to the military authority (state) as well as to the popular masses, that is, it speaks of reconciliation. In this way, both Islam and the Muslim population, on the one hand, and the state, especially the military, on the other, are described in soothing terms, so as to contribute as much as possible to a peaceful resolution of the prevailing political tensions. The author writes in the name of a higher, sublime or transcendent authority that stands above all the involved actors. Concerning how to achieve balance in social life, worthy of the harmony represented by Islam and the sacred cosmos, the national gains must rule over personal gains.

TWO: *Diyanet Gazetesi*, 15 May 1972

Event: Execution of three leftist militants on the night of 5–6 May 1972 (see above timeline)

*Entrustment and Betraying Entrustment*

Honourable Muslims,

In the verse that I read, Allah the exalted states as follows, 'O you who have believed, do not betray Allah and the Messenger or betray your trusts while you know [the consequence]' (The Koran [SI], The Spoils of War 8: 27).[12]

Preserving entrustment is a right given to us. Such entrustment either belongs to Allah or to the people, it can be material or spiritual – it is composed of all of these things. Spiritual entrustments are Allah's commands and offers that come with our worship. Our bodies, our health, our wealth and our children are all entrustments. The duties we take up, the honour and virtue entrusted to each of us, personal and societal secrets, and every single inch of the soil that the nation has are our important entrustments. All of these have been handed over to us so that we know them as entrustments and that one day we will be obligated to account for them in the presence of Allah the Almighty, Lord of the worlds, without an intercessor and thus we should act accordingly. Our noble Prophet reminds us of this responsibility by stating:

All of you are shepherds and all of you are responsible for shepherding. The imam (chief) is a shepherd and is responsible for shepherding. A person is the protector of his family and is responsible for those under his protection. A woman is her spouse's and home's protector, and she is responsible for all that is related to this. A servant is protector of his masters' possessions and he is responsible for all things related to this.[13]

Honourable Muslims,

Unconditionally protecting the entrustments that are given to us is our duty. Not observing them is betrayal. For example, carrying out forbidden acts or not complying with the commands of Allah, who created us and gave us life and innumerable blessings, and his beloved Prophet is a betrayal of entrustment. Not ruling with justice, not giving importance to entrustments, not doing the duties taken up or using your authority malevolently betrays entrustment. For a religious official not giving good advice to people, and not working to show the true path to them and the duties of religion with Allah's book and the traditions of the Prophet is betrayal of entrustment. One who is entrusted with the education and nurturing of children and does not do it well is a teacher who betrays entrustment of pure and clean hearts with perverted doctrines and harmful ideas. A merchant, who cheats people and tells lies and profiteers from them, betrays entrustment. A craftsman who uses his craft poorly, a worker who does not do his work properly betrays entrustment. One who reveals a national secret that was entrusted to him, extorts the property that was left for preservation, and abuses the honour and virtue entrusted to him has betrayed entrustment.

Honourable Muslims,

Our noble Prophet informs that those who betray entrustment are lacking in mature belief and are counted amongst the hypocrites. Betrayal of societal and national entrustments is a reason for the coming forth of great disasters and the unravelling of societal order. Thus, a man came up to our master the Prophet and asked: 'Oh, Messenger of God, when will the Last Day be?' Our noble Prophet stated: 'Wait for the Last Day when all entrustments have been lost.' The man asked: 'How are entrustments lost?' The noble Prophet responded: 'Wait for the Last Day, when necessary work has been entrusted to incompetents.'[14]

From this reliable *hadis* we learn that it is possible to avoid the loss of national and societal entrustments by giving every work to people who are competent in their field. Once entrustments are not given to competent people, works will go astray, patrons will become uneasy, and chaos will arise. For this reason, Allah the Almighty shows us the true path and states: 'Indeed, Allah commands you to render trusts to whom they are due and when you judge between people to judge with justice. Excellent is that which Allah instructs you. Indeed, Allah is ever Hearing and Seeing.'[15]

In that case beloved Muslims, entrustments should be given importance and we should observe these entrustments. Only then will we find what we have been searching for and the tranquillity that we have missed will be attained. (Author: Lütfi Şentürk, Mufti of Ankara)

Comment

We do not know whether the Ankara mufti had the afore-mentioned executions especially in mind when writing the above *hutbe*. However, it is very unlikely that such a disturbing event would not have left deep scars and doubts on the minds of many congregational listeners during these early weeks of May 1972. Here, the state had acted in the role of executioner (*cellat*), but who would dare to speak out in front of the hangman? Not even the highest religious authority gave a hint about where it stood concerning a higher justice and human rights on this troublesome issue. Who was, in fact, responsible for what had happened? Was it the rebellious students themselves and their organisations, or was it the ruthless state, and the hegemonic groups and institutions supporting it? But, instead of nailing down any specific person, group or institution, responsibility was transferred to the whole community and turned into a question of securing communal survival, based on the notion of entrustment, or rather the lack of, or threat against entrustment.

Trust and entrustment are depicted here as constituting the basic conditions for the survival of any integrated social unit or community. God is the main source of trust. Modelled on that, however, every individual is a source of trust. Human beings (believers) are entrusted with and therefore responsible for their bodies, their health, their wealth, their offspring and their nation. These are things or manifestations entrusted to believers, meaning that as good Muslims they must do all that is humanly possible to protect and preserve those assets. The idea that everyone is equally entrusted with responsibility is conveyed in the notion of the shepherd. It is not only that individual believers turn to God in order to be protected and guided by him, but that everyone in fact is a shepherd: the imam for his congregation; the father/patriarch for his family; the woman for her husband and their home; the servant for the possessions of his/her master. The examples are extended to teachers, merchants, craftsmen, workers and national leaders.

The reverse of entrustment is betrayal. Not living up to entrustments means split, disunion, and in the end total disaster or the apocalypse. Implicitly alluding to the tragic fate of the executed leftist militants and their sympathisers and companions, one is reminded that a teacher who has induced 'perverted doctrines' into 'pure and clean hearts' has betrayed his entrustments, which are the students. The utmost cause behind a final breakdown of inner peace and order is incompetence, that is, when entrustments are given to incompetent people. As to the question of who represents incompetence, that is left to the individual listener to imagine. The key message holds that chaos must be avoided and that everyone has a stake in and responsibility for the preservation of this order. The state is not liable. Neither are political actors or professionals on various levels. Responsibility is attributed to the individuals making up society, that is to all, and therefore to none?

THREE: *Diyanet Gazetesi*, 15 April 1975

Event: After a longer period of governmental crisis – five months of caretaker government under Professor Sadi Irmak – the first 'Nationalist front' government was set up on 31 March 1975 with Süleyman Demirel as prime minister (see above timeline).

### Togetherness and Separation

Preamble: O you who have believed, fear Allah as He should be feared and do not die except as Muslims [in submission to Him]. And hold firmly to the rope of Allah all together and do not become divided. And remember the favour of Allah upon you – when you were enemies and He brought your hearts together and you became, by His favour, brothers. And you were on the edge of a pit of the Fire, and He saved you from it. Thus does Allah make clear to you His verses that you may be guided (The Koran [SI], The Family of Imran 3: 102–3).

These noble verses declare very openly and succinctly how great the value unity [lit. oneness] and togetherness is for the life of the nation and also how separation and otherness and self-serving (egocentric) fights of individuals can lead nations to misery and disastrous cliffs, and it draws attention to this aspect.

In the first place, the verse commands piety/god-fearing (*takva*). Piety is to beware of Allah as is necessary and to protect oneself against disobeying of commands. The most appropriate description of piety is thus: to not abandon something that must be treated and to not treat something that must be abandoned, meaning to fear letting Allah's commands slip by and to act very rigorously in this respect. As is reported by many, the honourable Abdullah ibni Mesut[16] in his exegesis of this verse states:

> Piety is to be always in obedience to Allah and to never rebel, to recall Allah at all times and never forget, and to always be grateful and never fall into blasphemy and be ungrateful. Piety is the most honourable virtue in our religion. Truly becoming a wise servant is the greatest happiness. In order to reach this, these two points are given importance most particularly in this nobly stated verse:
>
> 1. To hold firmly to agreements made with Allah and to preserve devotedness to him.
> 2. The avoidance of discrimination, separation, nourishing otherness, defeatism, and the breaking up of the nation is the path to happiness in this world and the afterlife.

Our religion commands thus. Islam is a religion of unity. It is necessary for those who believe in Allah to live in oneness and togetherness. Islam seeks oneness of ranks and hearts. For society how great is the importance of oneness. The religion of Islam, which in the best way provides answers to the needs of society, gives importance in all respects to the necessity of oneness. Unity and oneness are amongst the exalted essential realities of Islam. These solid essentials in no way can be damaged. The value that is given in faith and worship to oneness is part of what everyone in Islam knows and appreciates. Often it is said that everyone should have their own way and act accordingly, yet in Islam this cannot be. The wolf seizes that which leaves the herd. The importance that is given to the community by not counting one who separates from it as among its members is enough to show the value of oneness. Mistakes disappear when community of Muslims are gathered together. The societal community of Muslims is amongst the noble proofs of Islam. Allah's mercy and help are with the community. On this topic many reliable *hadis* exist. Goodness is with the whole. The end of those who divide the nation is defeat.

The noble Koran, after inviting the believing society to oneness and togetherness and prohibiting falling into self-serving fights, separation and otherness, reminds of the blessings that Allah has for believers. It calls for taking a lesson from the past. With the help of religion and faith, individuals who are enemies of one another become brothers. Religion and faith are forces that bond people into oneness and create a peaceful environment for them. The most honourable and holy bonds bind people who are brothers in religion.

How could innocent people who believe in Allah and stand next to each other in worship in the mosque, that gathering place that we call Allah's house, be enemies? How could a person who has truly placed faith in his heart treat his religious brethren poorly? The noble Koran recalls that peoples who have been taken by passions and hatred and have fallen into divisions are near the edge of a cliff with fire at the bottom and can only be saved by brotherhood in faith, and this is a valuable point that should be considered carefully. What would happen to a people, Allah spare them, who are falling from a cliff into a fire? Even the mere thought of this is enough to frighten one who has the tiniest resemblance of love for his nation. Woe is the state of a nation in which son resents father, father remains angry at son, and brother holds grudge against brother! A nation fallen into this state cannot give rise to a strong community nor do they have a fighting chance in this world of struggles.

Thus, the Koran warns us by explaining in very succinct wording the harm of division. Communities that harbour separation and othering are pushed to the edge of the cliff into the fire. Thinking about their fall is very frightening. In order to be saved from this the nation must wake itself up, come to its senses and recall oneness and togetherness. As told by İbn-i Ishak,[17] the Aws and Khazraj tribes fought wars for a long period of about 120 years, and finally when they became Muslim, they became brothers and were saved from this separation and otherness, and they gathered underneath one flag. Thus, they were also protected from tumbling down this cliff into the fire. History is filled with examples like this. The noble Koran informs of the terrible ends of nations that are divided as a result of self-serving fights, by laying out this truth in the most vivacious fashion. Those who attempt actions of dividing and defeat of the nation by not paying heed to this advice are seeking to bring disaster upon the people. May the sins of these actions be upon them.

In the noble verse, oneness is recalled as one of the blessings from Allah. Let's know its value. Divisions are like cliffs with fire at the bottom; let's take a lesson from this. If we want to survive as a nation, we should heed this warning of the noble Koran. We should listen to God's words. Let's not separate from oneness and break our peace. Look what our national poet M. Akif Ersoy,[18] who talks about the benefits of oneness, has versified on the subject:

A people, to whom division hasn't entered, cannot be entered by the enemy. // So long as their hearts beat together, no pounding of cannonballs can intimidate them. (Author: Osman Keskioğlu)[19]

## Comment

The utmost virtue of Islam is god-fearing or piety. Piety requires obedience. The reason for this demand is the importance given to unity (oneness or togetherness) in Islam. Islam is the religion that best responds to the needs of society. Islam emphasises the necessity of oneness. Islam cannot allow a system where everyone goes his or her own way, an allegedly dominating trend in contemporary society. The proverb has it that the wolf seizes the one who leaves the herd. The most important proof of Islam's greatness is found in what it achieves in strengthening and consolidating the community of believers. God helps or supports the community of believers, rather than the believers as independent individuals. The precariousness of the single or lonely individual is thus expressed in blunt terms. To be divided is like standing by the edge of a cliff, under which lurks the fire of hell. Greatness and virtuousness go with the strong community. The strengths and benefits of a nation are measured in its power to guard unity and togetherness. Without such seamless unity, the nation will be at a loss. Individualism is seen as being at odds with unity, and therefore greatness.

Concerning the current political context, the sermon could be interpreted as an endorsement to the leader of Justice Party (Adalet Partisi, AP), Süleyman Demirel, who, after long negotiations, had been able to form a four-party coalition 'The first nationalist front', 'first', since there was also a second one formed by Demirel in July 1977. The 'front' was formed against the rival Bülent Ecevit and his democratic left Republican People's Party.

FOUR: *Diyanet Gazetesi*, 15 May 1977

Event: Mass meeting organised by leftist labour confederation DİSK (Devrimci İşçi Sendikaları Konfederasyonu) on Taksim Square on May Day 1977. The meeting ended in a tragic stampede with thirty-nine people dead (see above timeline).

*Fraternity in Islam*

Preamble: The believers are but brothers, so make settlement between your brothers. And fear Allah that you may receive mercy (The Koran [SI], The Rooms 49: 10).

Honourable community!

Believe Allah the exalted and his Messenger that all believers that gather under the flag of unity in Islam are like siblings born from one mother and father; this fraternity in Islam is not a temporary fraternity but rather ever-lasting (*Ebussuud Tefsiri*,[20] 5: 90). One of the duties of a Muslim to other Muslims is that in a quarrelling and fighting that arises between two Muslims, he should reconcile and make peace between the two Muslims. Thus, on this topic it is stated in one noble verse:

'The believers are but brothers, so make settlement between your brothers. And fear Allah that you may receive mercy' (The Koran, The Rooms [SI], 49: 10). Our beloved Prophet also states in a *hadis*: 'A believer is another believer's (religious) brother' (*Meşârık ul-Envâr*, İbn-i Melek: Vol. 2, 111).[21]

Honourable Muslims!

Our noble religion commands the fraternity of Muslims and living fraternally, and to live within unity and togetherness. For believers are to one another like the parts of one body. In another *hadis* our Prophet, Peace be upon Him, states, 'Believers love one another, have compassion for one another, and preserve one another like they are one body. If any part of the body becomes troubled, the other parts for this reason come down with sickness and insomnia' (*Câmi'uş-Şağîr, Azîziye Şerhi*: Vol. 3, 278).[22] Wherever he may be in the world, when one Muslim meets with a disaster, all Muslims feel sadness. Muslims are very compassionate towards one another. For compassion is the actual brother of love. Our religion informs that the life, property, honour and virtue of one Muslim are forbidden to another Muslim. When our Prophet, who is an example for us in all respects, gestured toward the Muslims who emigrated from Mecca to Medina and stated, 'Oh people of Medina! These immigrants are your brothers,' the noble companion Saad Bin Rebia (r.a.) took his immigrant brother to his house, showed him his property, and said, 'Look my brother, half of these possessions are yours.' Responding to this favour, his holiness Abdurrahman İbni Avf (r.a.)[23] was moved to the utmost and said, 'My brother, thank God for all of your possessions. You just show me the road that goes to the marketplace and leave the rest to me,' and he sold the bit of milk and cheese that he had bought from the marketplace and returned to his home in the evening (*Asrı Saadet*: Vol. 1, 307–9, old print).[24]

With this in mind, today for the temporary benefits of this world we see no harm in strangling and killing each other. As such we become weak against our enemies. One incidence of anarchy that was caused by a few people disturbs the nation as a whole.

Honourable Muslims!

In conclusion, let's avoid all types of activities that break the bonds of fraternity between Muslims. Let's know that the best people are those who do favours for others. Let's not forget that our language, our book, and our *qibla* are one (*El-Müfredât fî-Garîb-ül-Kur'an*, Rağıb-ı-Isfehânî: 13).[25] Let's know that consenting to evil is equal to doing evil and stay far from all types of actions that break peace.

Let us also not be helpers to those who seek to cause unrest. Let us never forget that we are each other's brothers. (Author: Kamil Şahin)[26]

## Comment

There is a striking contrast between the agitated and indignant feelings aroused by the day-by-day mounting political violence of which the May Day massacre became an alarming reminder, and the detached character of the above sermon. This is all the more remarkable as the labour conflicts touched sensitive strings in Turkish society. Seen in a European perspective Turkey's working class was relatively small, but the proportion of industrial labour in the total labour force had started to increase during the 1960s, raising problems and controversies concerning organisation.[27] Labour confederations on the national level had not been allowed until 1952, when Türk-İş (Türkiye İşçi Sendikaları Konfederasyonu), a politically moderate organisation engaged with the daily-life concerns of its members, rather than any long-term reforms set on empowering the working class. New dynamics were added to the labour movement after the socialist Labour Party of Turkey (Türkiye İşçi Partisi, TİP) was established in 1961, and especially after this political newcomer entered parliament with fifteen out of 450 representatives in the 1965 elections. DİSK, the leftist rival to Türk-İş, was formed in 1967, after which a fierce competition between the two labour confederations got underway. Worried by the challenges from the left, the sitting conservative Demirel government ventured new labour laws in the spring of 1970 in favour of the larger confederation, Türk-İş. Things came to a head when DİSK organised a strike encompassing 70,000 workers and a march from Izmit/Kocaeli to Istanbul gathering some 50,000 protesters (15–16 June 1970), leading to violent clashes and ending in the declaration of martial law in Izmit and Istanbul (Özdalga 1978: 92). These chaotic events were still fresh in the memory on May Day 1977.

Instead of inducing more substance into the *hutbe* by linking the sermon to the ongoing conflicts in the labour market, the text remains within the pale of conventional religious discourse. To engage in current labour issues does not necessarily mean that the sermoniser would have had to take sides. If the oratorical purpose was to convey a message of unity and solidarity, the effect of the text/talk could have been stronger had it connected to these ongoing, concrete controversies. In such a context the message could have been tuned to linking daily events to the religious tenets. But that is not the case. Instead, the exhortations are articulated in a general and abstract way, as when the audience is reminded that their language, book and *qibla* (the direction of Mecca – and praying) are 'one'. Thereby an opportunity to render the text more relevant to daily concerns is lost – a recurring characteristic of the *hutbe* texts as seen also in the following example.

FIVE: *Diyanet Gazetesi*, 15 January 1979

Event: Maraş massacre in December 1978, caused by communal (Sunni–Alevi) violence, lasting for several days and leaving more than 100 people dead and hundreds of shops demolished (see above timeline)

*Come, Let's Forget Resentments*
   Preamble: The believers are but brothers, so make settlement between your brothers. And fear Allah so that you may receive mercy (The Koran [SI], The Rooms 49: 10).
   Honourable Brothers,
   Allah the Almighty states in the noble Koran: 'The believers are but brothers, so make settlement between your brothers. And fear Allah so that you may receive mercy' [see preamble].
   This verse of the Koran puts forth that believers are brothers and should be found within the unity that is necessary for fraternity, and that they should abstain from all kinds of conflict and division. There is no doubt that the greatest strength to ensure our survival as a nation is unity and fraternity. For this reason, when Allah the Almighty stated in the noble Koran, 'And hold firmly to the rope of Allah all together and do not become divided,'[28] he commanded us to be in solidarity. This unity goes towards the advantage of the nation and the homeland in all areas and it will cause us to reach success. For communities that contain unity have the help and mercy of the Creator Almighty. A community that breaks unity also breaks peace. Communities whose members contend with one another lose their strengths. Thus, on this

matter verse forty-six of Sura al-Anfal should be recalled and announced, 'And obey Allah and his Messenger, and do not dispute and [thus] lose courage and [then] your strength would depart; and be patient. Indeed, Allah is with the patient' (The Koran [SI], The Spoils of War 8: 46). Our beloved Prophet also warns us on this topic by stating, 'Do not be enemies of one another, do not be jealous of one another, do not turn your backs and break with one another, Oh servants of Allah be brothers all of you.'[29]

My beloved brothers,

A Muslim knows another Muslim as his brother and approaches him affectionately. He could never wrong him. He abstains from words and actions that would sadden him. He meets the ideas of his brother that to him seem odd with tolerance. He is a helper to him in goodness and warns him of badness against him and protects him. He wishes the same things that he wishes for himself for his brother as well.

Causing division between brothers and separation by gossiping is a grave sin. The noble Koran has even informed that this is worse than murder. Our beloved Prophet advises that words and behaviours that break the oneness and peace of the community be avoided, and he gave great importance to the reconciliation between people not talking to each other and avoidance of separation. He strove with all of his strength for the unity between Muslims to not collapse. Once a discord between his friends arose. The moment he heard about it, the Prophet immediately went to the place of dispute and worked until the dispute was solved, and thus he was not able to go to the community at the time the mid-afternoon prayer was to be read and therefore his holiness Abu Bakr led prayer instead of him.

In that case my honourable brothers, come to fraternity, outstanding morals, and let's prevent the emergent resentments that in recent times have arisen among our noble nation who are renowned for truly loving one another. Let's avoid the utmost offensive behaviours against each other. Taking an example from the first Muslims and our ancestors, let's love one another like them. Let's show respect to our elders and love to our youth. If we do like this, we will have won the contentment of Allah the Almighty. (Author: Lütfi Şentürk, vice-director [of Diyanet])

## Comment

At the time this *hutbe* was written and recited in mosques around Turkey the Dersim massacres of 1937–8 were far away. The province Tunceli, where a large part of the population is Alevi,[30] many of whom also ethnic Kurds, had during the 1930s been subject to severe pressure from the Ankara government to conform to the new, republican centralist and laic order (Law of Settlement from 1934). The local tribes refused abandoning the semi-autonomous status they had enjoyed under Ottoman rule, but their armed resistance proved futile and was finally shattered with heavy military onslaughts claiming 13,000 deaths, indiscriminately aimed at men, women and children (Kieser 2011). The average Turk growing up in the post-war era would not know about these events. Even the name Dersim was erased from the map. However, those who were familiar with these areas would know, but they would not talk about it, at least not outside of their close circles. This was a non-issue at the time of the Maraş massacres in 1978–9, which did not mean that those involved were devoid of grim recollections of the Dersim mass killings.

That the author of the above *hutbe* should at all have hinted at these dark pages of earlier republican history, was out of the question. Nevertheless, what surfaced during the Maraş riots was by no means an unknown reality. The relationship between the two major Muslim communities in Turkey, the Sunni (around 80 per cent) and the Alevi (around 20 per cent), was not uncomplicated. But instead of linking the sermon to long-standing cultural and religious tensions, the discourse is drawn into the orbit of standard phrases of Sunni Islam, thereby leaving Alevi concerns unheeded.

As a matter of fact, the above *hutbe* portends what was to come over the next decades. With growing urbanisation, people from often poor Alevi villages in central and eastern Anatolia settled in big cities like Istanbul, Ankara or Izmir, or found work abroad, especially in Germany. Migration bolstered new ways of communication and organisation. Thus, Alevism as a cultural – and religious – movement, became increasingly visible during the 1980s. With growing numbers of associations and publications came demands related to official recognition of Alevi religious traditions, forms of gathering and rituals. In their – often deep – mistrust against Sunni, orthodox Islam, many Alevi have found a kind of refuge in Atatürk's secularism and have therefore mostly been loyal to the republican project.[31] Official Sunni circles have rarely looked with approval on the Alevi ethno-religious revival. However, rather than dissociating themselves from the Alevi veneration of the fourth caliph Ali, the Sunni response has been to embrace Muhammad's son-in-law, saying 'we are all Alevi', an attitude that has generally not gone down well in Alevi circles, where it has been interpreted as a way to deprive them of their distinctive tenet, a kind of 'hegemonic' inclusiveness. An especially critical issue over the coming decades has been the status of Alevi sacred abodes, *cemevi*s (see Olsson et al. 1998). Alevi communities are allowed to set up their own centres, but these complexes, in official parlance patronisingly referred to as 'cultural', not religious centres, have not been recognised as sacred abodes for ritual prayer. Thereby 'abode' can be added to the 'ones' enumerated above: 'one' language, 'one' book, 'one' *qibla*, and only 'one' type of religious abode, the Sunni mosque.

As to the question of how to overcome the rifts between the two communities, the audiences are reminded that they are all Muslims. In the light of that shared higher and ultimate ideal, all resentments should be forgotten and disregarded. The Prophet has shown the way. However, Sunnifying campaigns, such as inflicting mosques on Alevi villages, have not brought the two communities closer, as the development over the following decades shows.

### Official *Hutbe*s Related to External Threats – Armed and Cultural Jihad

SIX: *Diyanet Gazetesi*, 22 July 1974

Event: Turkish invasion of Cyprus 20 July 1974 (see above timeline)

*War*

Preamble: O you who have believed, shall I guide you to a transaction that will save you from a painful punishment? [It is that] you believe in Allah and His Messenger and strive in the cause of Allah with your wealth and your lives. That is best for you, if you should know (The Koran [SI], The Ranks 61: 10–11).

Honourable Muslims,

We are now living the most important days of our recent history. Our glorious military that has been written about in heroic epics for all of history has taken action to end the tyrannical behaviour against our religious brethren of Cyprus, which is a part of our nation. In this action we wish for the success of our armed forces by the power of Allah the Almighty.

War was born from within humanity. As long as humans continue to live, it too will continue. Our beloved Prophet expressed this truth with the words,

'War will continue until the end of the world.'[32] War is the battle of truth with falsehood, good with evil, just with unjust. For this reason, according to Islam, after believing in Allah the Almighty, the highest act of worship is war. When you say war, the first thing that comes to mind is defence of the nation. For every person and every nation, the foremost and most essential duty is this. Due to its duty of defending the nation, Islam counts military service amongst the most honourable duties. It is said that keeping guard one night for the military is better than 1,000 nights of prayer and days spent fasting for winning Allah's approval.

With this deduction and explication on the nature of war, our glorious military began an operation on behalf of the young nation of Cyprus. Cyprus, since the time of his holiness Osman, has been a place near to the select friends of our Prophet and filled with Turkish blood, inside which there are thousands of tombs of our martyrs and even martyrs from amongst the Companions. Those who live over there are our Muslim Turkish brothers. Greeks mounted an attack as they were about to annex the island to Greece by means of killing our Muslim brothers and trampling the tombs of our martyrs and the rising sound of the call to prayer from the mosque. In the face of this situation our government has decided to act against it and our military was deployed to the island.

Beloved Muslims,

This action is the first time in recent history that the opportunity for holy war (jihad) has been given to us. Take heed that I am saying 'opportunity for jihad' because by this means the continuous injustice and inhumane behaviours on the island will be put to an end, and the rights of our Muslim Turkish brothers will be protected. Those who die for this cause are martyrs and those who remain are warriors of the faith. Both of these are amongst the greatest of ranks. A man once asked our beloved Prophet: 'Which people are superior?' Our Prophet stated: 'No one is believed superior to one who wages war on behalf of Allah with his life and property.'[33]

One day our beloved Prophet sent Ebû Revaha's son Abdullah [Arabic: 'Abd Allah ibn Rawāhah] as the commander of a company of soldiers to fight the enemy. Commander Abdullah, at the break of dawn collected the troops and sent them to the battlefield and then went himself to the mosque to pray the Morning Prayer with our Prophet. They prayed. Our Prophet, as he greeted and turned his face to the community, saw Abdullah standing there. He asked him, 'You have been tasked with war – why did you leave your duty?' Abdullah responded, 'O, messenger of Allah, I fell behind from them in order to pray the Morning Prayer with you.' Our Prophet said, 'I swear to Almighty Allah, guardian of my soul, even if you never raised your head from prostration day and night in this mosque, you still would not reach the level of virtue of those military warriors. Make haste without stopping, and catch up with your friends.'[34] See how beautifully this event expresses the virtue of holy war.

My Muslim brothers,

Allah the Almighty has stated in the noble Koran: 'Oh you who have believed, shall I guide you to a path that will save you from a painful punishment? It is that you believe in Allah and his Messenger and strive in the cause of Allah with your wealth and your lives. That is best for you, if you should know.'[35] We should seize this opportunity for jihad placed before us by adopting this command of our exalted lord. We should hurry to help with both our material and spiritual resources. Only in such a case should we wage holy war with our earned possessions. We should support those fighting at the front line with our possessions and our lives. Our beloved Prophet told the good news that whoever equips the military going to war will receive a good deed as if they had gone to war personally. If paid attention to, it is commanded in both the Koran and *hadis* that we fight with our lives and our possessions for Allah. Fighting with our possessions is the result of righteousness and loyal faith. Those who believe show that they believe.

Our beloved Prophet called upon his noble Companions to help in preparation for the Battle of the Trench. Everyone put forth a piece of his possessions: some gave one-third, some a half, some a bit less, some a bit more. But amongst them only Ebû Bekir [Arabic: Abū Bakr] put forth everything. When our Prophet said to him: 'Oh, Ebû Bekir what did you leave for yourself and your family?' His holiness Ebû Bekir answered: 'I left their fate to Allah and his Messenger.'[36] Because he believed. And Allah gave everything that he gave back to him in a greater amount.

As such, we should all come together and support the heroes of our armed forces today fighting in Cyprus and those amongst our religious brethren who are living through very difficult days over there by taking up the example of the noble Companions and our ancestors. We should donate to our Air and Naval Forces Support Foundation and join the campaigns that work towards this goal with excitement.

If we do as such, Allah the Almighty will give us success in this righteous cause.

May your holy war be blessed, and may Allah bless us with his help and victory. (Author: Lütfi Şentürk, Mufti of Ankara)

## Comment

Two things set this sermon apart from the others presented in this chapter: first, the way it shows how easily the idea of holy war – jihad – presents itself in the official homiletic context, even in a secular country like Turkey; and second, the connection to a concrete event, in this case the Cyprus intervention.

Concerning jihad, the sermon maintains that when carried out in defence of truth against falsehood, good against evil, just against unjust, and national interests against foreign aggression, war is a sacred duty for every Muslim. Those who die for a higher cause are martyrs (*şehit*) and those who survive are rewarded with the honourable title of 'warriors of the faith' (*gazi*). War is seen as an act of worship. As a matter of fact, it is the highest form of worship. To keep guard during war, if only for one night, is better than a thousand nights of prayer or a thousand days of fasting. The sacred meaning of warfare is illustrated with an episode from the life of the Prophet. Abdullah, who was enjoined by the Prophet to lead an armed division was late to the war expedition, because he stayed for the morning prayer. For this he was reprimanded by the Prophet, since war held priority over everything else, even the community prayer. Implicitly, the sermon tells that Turkish Muslims are by no means unfamiliar with the notion of holy war. Jihad represents an idiom – a 'root-paradigm' (Mardin 1989: 3–5) – around which people unhesitatingly can be mobilised. Both preacher and audience seem to be on home ground with the notion of holy war.

In addition, the rhetoric of this sermon contributes some extra oratorical strength, since expositions on a concrete event, here the Cyprus conflict, takes the place of lofty and abstract reasonings. As a matter of fact, the jihadist discourse and the reality-related rhetoric support each other when it comes to strengthening the confidence in national unity. One assists in erasing internal, domestic conflicts; the other calls attention to an outstanding event, easy to grasp for everyone.

SEVEN: *Diyanet Gazetesi*, 1 August 1975

Event: Bringing American bases and other NATO establishments in Turkey under Turkish control (25 July 1975). Reclaiming sovereignty – and honour (see above timeline)

### Oneness and Togetherness in Islam

Preamble: O you who have believed, enter into Islam completely [and perfectly] and do not follow the footsteps of Satan. Indeed, he is to you a clear enemy (The Koran [SI], The Cow 2: 208).

As it is known, Islam seeks the improvement of the relationships between human beings from among its members and it has encouraged them towards this goal. Even when inviting another to belief in Allah, Islam advises calling through kind words, without injuring the heart of the addressee.

The noble Prophet, when spreading religion, planted the seeds of fraternity and oneness and while transfusing the people with the belief in Allah alone and the fundamentals of worship, he strongly recommended their brotherhood and the need for them to love one another.

In truth, Islam is a religion of peace and fellowship. A true believer could not do the actions that he does not want to be directed at him, nor could he direct the same actions he does not see as good for himself to others. The believer cannot disturb or perturb other people. All Muslims strive to follow the divine commands and the advice of the noble Prophet with the goal to reach perfect faith.

Considering that God says to be peaceful and fraternal, and to not attack your enemies even when your enemies break treaties with you and attack you, and considering that our noble Prophet (Peace be upon Him) has advised, 'Harming one Muslim, harms me, and whoever torments a *zimmi* [protected non-Muslim subject] is my enemy. Love one another and do not harm one another's honour, possessions or blood, and find mercy and compassion in your hearts for all living creatures,'[37] then surely a believer would not go after doing anything but these things.

A Muslim cannot be quarrelsome, angry or full of hate, nor be a slanderer or conspirator. He cannot murder his brothers of the same religion. With the help of faith, the believer does not come across any period of unrest or corruption. One who takes up such ugly actions cannot be said to have reached perfect faith let alone being counted as a true believer.

Those who divide or seek to divide the nation should carefully think of this *hadis* from the noble Prophet (Peace be upon Him), 'Those who make separations are not to be counted among us' (*Feth-ül Kebir* 3: 215),[38] and 'Those who hold weapons up to us, who create disorder and unrest among us are not to be counted among us' (*Feth-ül Kebir* 3: 187).

As such, there is no rioting, fighting, disorderliness, torture, crookedness, cheating, and anything that threatens people's rights to be spoken of in a believing community. In an Islamic community, there is never a space for such behaviours.

In an Islamic community, peaceful law and order comes about with faith and worship, trust and mutual love. Inside such a beautiful order every believer works with trust and joy to sustain and further the society of which he is a member. Because every Muslim that seeks perfect faith, that loves his Prophet from the bottom of his soul, cannot in any way forget the advice, 'In togetherness, there is mercy; in division, there is torment' (*Feth-ül Kebir* 2: 65) or 'A Muslim is another Muslim's brother, he cannot betray him, nor lie to him, nor shame or think small of him' (*Feth-ül Kebir* 2: 265) or 'help your religious brothers; save innocent people from oppression, the oppressor, or try to convince a tyrant to stop his oppression' (*Feth-ül Kebir* 1: 280).

Our religion that gives great importance to love, respect, fraternity, peace, goodness and beauty also accepts that to reach perfect or mature belief, one must accept these values as essential. No profit or ideology can remove and toss these values from a true believer's heart. No one can ever force him to abandon these characteristics. Because forgetting these essentials and antipathetically finding oneself in ugly and negative actions is yielding to temptation. Thus, God states: 'O you who have believed, enter into Islam completely [and perfectly] and do not follow the footsteps of Satan. Indeed, he is to you a clear enemy' (The Koran [IS], The Cow 2: 208). It follows that taking up the tactics of your enemy and destroying yourself are surely not the actions of an intelligent and logical person. The truth is that any individual possessing sound intelligence would not follow such a broken path.

A Muslim does not forget that even as an individual, he is part of a community. In a whole comprised of many parts, the negative behaviour of any part damages the whole and as the whole gets hurt then its parts also become rendered useless. In that case an intelligent Muslim keeps in mind that all actions he could take that would harm the community would also be harmful to himself. The health, survival and efficiency of the community are made possible by the mutual love, effort and togetherness between its members. Without this, God forbid, when the society is destroyed, would the individuals remain?

Our beloved Prophet (Peace be upon Him), says: 'Do not cultivate anger or hatred towards one another, do not cut your fraternal ties with one another, and do not turn your backs on one another. Oh, servants of God! Be brothers as Allah has commanded of you. For a Muslim it is not permissible to remain offended at his religious brother for more than three days' (*Feth-ül Kebir* 3: 313).

True Muslims are a community composed of people who to sum up become angelic and remain far from all types of ugly actions such as anger, offense, hostility, hatred, oppression, cruelty, and the bringing forth of all types of corruption and evil. It is not necessary to read all of history – those who doubt can look at the noble Prophet and his Companions. Those who are suspicious can look at our recent history; they can look at our Anatolia right before the War of Independence. These two viewpoints are enough to give an idea and from which to draw a lesson. Today we very much need the consciousness of the fraternity brought about by our fathers and grandfathers who built the spirit of the National Forces like a monument. Let's love one another in the way that Allah and the Prophet (Peace be upon Him) commanded; be brothers, and win the approval of God and the noble Prophet. (Author: Talat Karaçizmeli, Planning consultant [of Diyanet])[39]

## Comment

The character of this sermon is different from the previous one. The context is similar in that both are outlined against events related to Turkey's external politics. But whereas the previous sermon was meant to prepare the nation for war, this one is set on providing instructions about how to deal with other nations in time of peace. One carries the traces of an imagined speaker for the Ministry of Defence, the other those of an anticipated representative of the Ministry of Foreign Affairs. The *hutbe* can be read as a set of exhortations related to good diplomacy. Consequently, this sermon encourages constructive-minded forms of behaviour such as building beneficial relationships between human beings based on gentle, non-offensive statements. It speaks in favour of peace and reconciliation, be it aimed at friends or foes. Even if the main focus is on Muslims, non-Muslims are also embraced by Islam's benevolence and humanity. Islam is depicted here as a religion based on peace, fellowship and brotherhood, where there is no place for quarrel, anger, hatred, slander and conspiracy, since such behaviour has destructive effects on 'oneness and togetherness' (title of the sermon). For that reason, all kinds of rioting, fighting, disorderliness and other sorts of hostile behaviour (torture, crookedness, cheating, cutting fraternal ties, turning your back on others) are condemned. Unbefitting behaviour that harms the community of Muslims strikes back like a boomerang and harms each and every individual member of that community. So, the listener should know that vicious behaviour, whoever is targeted, is self-destructive. This is a far cry from the war heroism permeating the previous sermon. Still, on a higher level of discourse both sermons are assumed to be equally in tune with Islamic principles.[40]

EIGHT: *Diyanet Gazetesi*, 1 February 1977

Development: Western (Christian and/or Jewish) lifestyles and values brought in by modernisation, seen as a threat to authentic Muslim and Turkish traditions, and in the end a challenge to national unity

*Let's Protect Our National and Moral Values*

Preamble: And whatever the Messenger has given you – take; and what he has forbidden you – refrain from (The Koran [SI], The Gathering 59: 7).

There are two elements that allow a society to survive and cause its existence to continue. The first of these is material, and the second is spiritual.

If we compare the stones and bricks of a building to the materiality of a society, then the mortar that holds these parts together is like the spirituality of a society. Therefore, a building that is made without using mortar dryly interwoven and the non-solid walls within it are just like a society only held together with materiality and without spirituality. This building will decay, and it is bound to give way.

Our religion that is the source of our spiritual values has two foundations. The first of these is Allah's book the Koran, and the second is the tradition of our Prophet (Peace be upon Him) sent as the mercy and grace of the worlds. After these come the opinions of followers of our Prophet, and traditions of our ancestors with good customs and morals that are compatible with our holy book and tradition of the Prophet.

Allah the Almighty calls believers in the Koran to follow the book and the traditions and states with meaning, 'And whatever the Messenger has given you – take; and what he has forbidden you – refrain from.' (The Koran [SI], The Gathering 59: 7).

Again, Allah the Almighty shows the necessity and importance of following the Prophet in the Koran in the Sura The Combined Forces [Al-Ahzâb] and states, 'There has certainly been for you in the Messenger of Allah an excellent power for anyone whose hope is in Allah and the Last Day and who remembers Allah often' (The Koran [SI], The Combined Forces 33: 21).

Man and woman, every Muslim, should try to observe the faith, worship, morals and all practices in the Koran and the traditions of our master the Prophet (Peace be upon Him) and the good morals, customs and traditions of His valuable friends, and should keep alive the good customs of their ancestors. Those habits and customs that don't abide by religion, even if they are from our ancestors, should immediately be abandoned. Especially if these bad customs came from those who are not Muslims, then certainly in the shortest period of time they should be dropped. Unfortunately, in our time the bad habits and customs that came from Christian Europe are becoming more widespread amongst the members of our nation with each passing day.

We imitate Christian Europe in such a way that without separating the good from the bad, the useful from the useless, whatever we see, we take. This shrinks us. It causes us to lose our national character. We should take Europe's useful technology and positive science. Taking these is not objectionable to religion. Because our beloved Prophet (Peace be upon Him) stated: 'Knowledge and wisdom are like possessions that have been lost from the believer; wherever he finds them, he takes them.'[41] But the customs and habits and religious beliefs from those who are not Muslim that are not at all useful to us, that in fact harm us, we should not take. We have our own customs and habits that hold us together as a nation and cause us to love one another. Enemies that seek to demolish and collapse a nation from the inside will first remove that nation's religion, language, history, culture, habits and customs from the spirit of its people and then will try to put in its place their own religion, traditions, customs and culture.

In a *hadis* told by Ebu Said Hudri [Arabic: Saʿīd al-Khudrī], the noble Prophet (Peace be upon Him) states, 'Surely you all will meet and mix with the people who came before you and step by step go down their paths. Thus, perchance if they fall into a lizard hole then you too will be like them.' Companions asked, 'Oh Prophet! Are these peoples Jews and Christians?' The noble Prophet said, 'Who else but them could it be?'[42]

This reliable *hadis* warns the Islamic community not to follow or imitate the immoral actions and habits of Jews and Christians. The badness of imitating them is not exclusive to only Jews and Christians but rather it includes the bad customs and morals of all other nations that have passed in history.

Without doubt, every religion and social institution has its own specific culture and inherent characteristics separate from others, which is how nations preserve their unique character among other nations.

If a Muslim Turk abandons the customs and habits that tie him to other members of his nation and religion, and seeks to resemble those other than Muslims, the noble Muhammad (Peace be upon Him) gave this *hadis* accordingly; those seeking to resemble other than Muslims fall into the same class as those non-Muslims. The Prophet (Peace be upon Him) states that, 'Whoever a person resembles, from then on he is one of them' (Ebu Davud).[43]

Ibn Mesud, in another reliable *hadis*, says rather that it was stated, 'Whoever a person consents to their doings, he is one of them' (*Bulûğu'l-Merâm Tercümesi ve Şerhi: Selâmet Yolları* (vol. 4: 366).[44]

Without doubt whomever a person or class imitates the life, habits and customs of, he is an admirer of them and tied to them from the heart. May Allah save us Muslims from negligence. (Author: Arif Erkan)

Comment

The third sermon dealing with Turkey's relationship to foreign countries is different from the previous two in that its focus is not Turkey as a nation state, but as custodian of a civilisation, the guiding spirit of which is Islam. It is this spirituality, the 'mortar' that allegedly holds the 'material' blocks of society together, that is under threat. Turkey is confronted by a warlike situation. The influences from the West, predominantly represented by Christianity and Judaism, are getting increasingly extensive and powerful. Only moral rearmament based on Islam can turn the tide against these assaults on the 'nation's religion, language, history, culture, habits and customs'. Compared to the Islamist rhetoric of the National Salvation Party, this sermon may sound less chauvinistic, but is nevertheless dogmatic and polarising. It expresses deep suspicion against the 'Other'. The sermon further teaches that only science and technology should be imported from the

West, whereas cultural values at odds with Islamic principles are by definition despicable. However, what happens if such self-conceitedness strikes
a discordant note with Turkey's general efforts to be a leading actor in the
region and a trustworthy member of the global order? The willingness to
cooperate over national and cultural borders conveyed in the previous sermon is missing in this *hutbe*, indicating the broad spectrum of discourses –
at times contradictory – that find expression within an officially recognised
Islamic idiom.

To sum up, looking back over an economically and politically particularly unruly decade, it is but natural that 'unity and togetherness' (*birlik ve
beraberlik*) should be a recurrent theme – appearing almost as a mantra – in
the Friday *hutbe*s. The body, alternatively, the family or close kinship relationships are frequently used as imaginative symbols. Muslims should think
of themselves as 'siblings born from one mother and father'.[45] The ideal
relationship between Muslims is being like brothers – brotherhood being a
frequently repeated metaphor. The question, though, is how this brotherhood discourse has been conveyed. There are two options: it can either be
done by linking the sermon to what is happening in society at large, that is
adapting important events and developments into the *hutbe* address; or it
can be done by keeping current issues at safe distance by means of choosing
a generalising and elusive discourse. It should be obvious from the above
texts that the second alternative rules over the first. However, what are the
reasons behind such a preference? If the overarching aim is to forge a strong
community of Muslims and Turkish nationals, there is no obvious reason
why a discourse engaging in current events should be less effective than one
being overly generalising. Quite the contrary! In fact, there is more to say
on why a dry, restrained and abstracting style has dominated. It is not only
what is said, but also how it is said that is of importance. These rhetorical
aspects are addressed in the following section.

### Traditional Authority in a Secular State

The above reasoning has it that the detached character of the *hutbe*s is not
a matter of course. It requires an explanation. When looking for useful
perspectives, Patrick Gaffney's work about Islamic preaching in modern
Egypt (1994) is especially helpful. Gaffney introduces three Weberian types

of modern preachers: the affirmer of traditional authority; the advocate of religiously inspired modernity; and the apologist for the ideology of Islamic fundamentalism (Gaffney 1994: 194, 208, 238). The *hutbe*s displayed in this chapter come close to the first type. They can easily be described as following 'the classical standard', meaning a style that 'displays . . . zero-marking, that is, it is devoid of eccentric features and decidedly un-original in its stylistic externalities' (Gaffney 1994: 194). Alluding to traditional authority may be understood as if such oratory follows an old monotonous track merely by habit. However, being 'traditional' does not necessarily indicate yielding to routine. Instead, Gaffney argues, behind many often-repeated phrases and commonplace references to the holy sources lies a conscious intention of inducing solemnity and authority to the spoken word and the atmosphere surrounding the whole preaching event. This is accomplished by relying on reiterations of well-known phrases and Koranic quotations. In order to support his argument, Gaffney refers to Maurice Bloch's theory of 'formalisation' of speech. Together, these two contributions provide interesting keys to the sermons analysed in this book, and particularly the *hutbe*s reproduced in this chapter.

Bloch's theory builds on a distinction between 'everyday speech acts' and 'formalised speech acts' here schematically reproduced in the chart below. The first type of oratory is characterised by colourful and expressive language, where there is ample space for the speaker to use his own personality, experiences and initiatives in trying to catch the interest and attention of the audience. Imaginative narratives from history or daily life also belong to this kind of speech and the choice of vocabulary may vary extensively. Authority emanates from the imaginative power, eloquence and personality of the preacher, that is his charisma. The type of preacher described above by Gaffney as 'the advocate of religiously inspired modernity' often uses 'everyday speech acts', when, for example, he reproduces conversations from early Islam in contemporary, daily jargon (Gaffney 1994: 278–93). Formalised speech, on the other hand, is dry, solemn, repetitive, monotonous, meagre in narratives and/or anecdotes, and limited in vocabulary. The preacher keeps a low profile concerning his own experiences and does not share his opinions on contemporary issues. He does not act on his own account, only as a representative or mouthpiece of the religious tradition.

**Table 4.1** Everyday and formalised speech acts

| Everyday speech acts | Formalised speech acts |
| --- | --- |
| Choice (variations) of loudness | Fixed loudness patterns |
| Choice (variations) of intonation | Extremely limited choice of intonation |
| All syntactic forms available | Some syntactic forms excluded |
| Complete vocabulary | Partial vocabulary |
| Flexibility of sequencing of speech acts | Fixity of sequencing of speech acts |
| Few illustrations from a fixed body of accepted parallels | Illustrations only from certain limited sources, e.g., scriptures, proverbs |
| No stylistic rules consciously held to operate | Stylistic rules consciously applied at all levels |

Each category represented in the two columns leads to certain outcomes.[46] Regarding formalised speech acts, representing 'traditional authority', Bloch emphasises the following: first, they lead to impoverishment in choice of expression, meaning they leave the speaker little space for creativity, causing repetitiveness, that is recurrent use of certain standard expressions. Second, formalised language refers to general, rather than specific events, which means individuality and historicity are lost, that is '[s]pecific events are merged [with] events which are thought of as always pre-existing' (Bloch 1975: 15).[47] The third effect is related to the transfer of communication to a level where critical questioning becomes difficult. This outcome flows from the fact that general concepts take the form of widely accepted symbolic expressions, situated within an already given or established discursive universe. A shift towards formalised language therefore means a move in the direction of concord and unity and away from the kind of division or rupture that arises from critical or more unpredictable discourses. An audience entrusted with this kind of formal, thus unifying oratory, may experience that as an acknowledgement of its own inner strength or communal power. The fourth effect has to do with the ambiguity or equivocality – the double-talk quality – of formalised language, and the fifth its potential to hide or gloss over divisions and conflicts (Bloch 1975: 13–18). There is a tendency in formalised speech to evoke an either/or scenario, thereby leaving little space for intermediate alternatives. 'Communication becomes like a tunnel which once entered leaves no option for turning either to left or right' (Bloch 1975: 24).

Below are five factors of special relevance for the analysis of constraints encountered by the formalised style of above *hutbe*s:

- Repetitiveness and predictability
- Emphasis on the general and abstract, rather than the concrete aspects of events
- Language characterised by ambiguity and vagueness, amenable to many and conflicting interpretations
- Limited use of narratives and anecdotes
- Statements embedded in already accepted sacred archetypes, which cannot be critically questioned

Repetitiveness permeates all the eight sermons reproduced above, even if the first one – Islam is a Life-Sustaining Religion – stands out as the most striking example. From beginning to end, this *hutbe* summarises in well-known terminology the most basic tenets of Islam, as it has been taught in schools, Koran courses and other, freer forms of homiletics, such as *vaaz*. Other examples are provided by frequently reiterated Koranic verses, both those used as preambles and those quoted in the texts.

The use of generalised, non-specific, expositions is otherwise the most outstanding feature of the reproduced *hutbe*s. With the exception of the invasion of Cyprus (*hutbe* six) and the War of Independence (*hutbe* seven), there is no mention of any current concrete event, nor any specific person. In connection with the invasion of Cyprus, references are made to certain commanders, but these are historical or mythological figures from the time of the Prophet.

The sermonising language is also imbued with ambiguity and vagueness. For example, reference to those who 'lack [social] competence' (*hutbe* two) could be interpreted along a wide spectrum, stretching from governmental officials, professors, teachers, parents and relatives, to student activists. Such expressions as the 'needs of society', or 'taking a lesson from the past' (*hutbe* three), form associations with a great variety of contradictory demands.

The sermons are not utterly devoid of narratives or anecdotes, but such eloquence is scarce. When applied, like in the metaphor of the shepherd (*hutbe* two), the tale about the wolf, the edge of the deep cliff (*hutbe* three), stone bricks of a building, the lizard's hole (*hutbe* eight), they are condensed and taken from a narrow and too well-known, even worn-out repertoire. Stories and anecdotes, to the extent that they at all occur, mainly confirm already familiar accounts, while eye-opening narratives are almost non-existent.

Neither does the rhetoric leave much space, if any, for questioning and critical thought. The statements are obvious, closely pleaded into already endorsed, sacred archetypes. Who could, for example, question the idea of unity, togetherness, god-fearing (*takva*), entrustment, and law and order? The most telling example is again from the first *hutbe*, which is presented as a tightly knit, inviolable package.

The formalism exemplified here is often comprehended as a rhetoric that brings passivity and subjugation and that passes for being boring and unengaging, to the extent that audiences simply turn a deaf ear. As such, it does not lack critics, a topic dealt with in Chapter 6, where a scholar representing what Gaffney describes as 'religiously inspired modernity' (Gaffney 1994: 208ff.) explains his opinions about Turkish *hutbe* preaching. However, as suggested in the above discussion, it should not be overlooked that formal, authoritative speech also has strengthening effects on the sense of unity among the audience: first, an ever so often reiterated, therefore familiar discourse renders an atmosphere of ease and harmony among the audience; second, it conveys a sense of strength and stability, since it is experienced as belonging to a long, experienced and reliable practice, which, in its turn – and that is the third point – bestows honour and prestige to the congregation as a contributory upholder of this esteemed tradition. The significance of this kind of a Weberian type of traditional authority is persuasively argued by Gaffney, who illustrates how formalised speech-acts not only render authority to the sermon, but how this impression also extends to the congregation, the mosque, the surrounding community and even Islam as a civilisation (Gaffney 1994: 194–207). In contrast, freer, everyday speech and a more democratic, folksy or critically arguing approach do not self-evidently render the kind of prestige and authority the audiences seek. Thus, the formalised rhetoric speaks its own language – between the lines – in that it reinforces the notions of unity and togetherness so frequently repeated in the sermonised admonitions.

## Conclusions

The fact that the *hutbe*s discussed in this chapter were prewritten by functionaries within or close to Diyanet contributed to their formal character. However, the bent in favour of formalisation was not primarily due to the practice of preaching from a pre-written text – preachers representing various oratorical styles would ever so often use drafts – but that the text was prepared by someone different from the actual preacher. This distance between author and reader (reciter) added even greater restraints to an already formalised style, since it is rather unlikely that the preacher would feel comfortable to elaborate on or embellish an already completed, and officially approved text. However, this set-up, which obviously has enhanced formalism in Turkish Friday sermonising, is part of a special design for *hutbe* oratory pursued by the religious – and governmental – authorities. The explicit purpose for central control has been twofold: to obtain texts built on higher quality scholarship (education and judgement of local imams distrusted), and, to secure a discourse at safe distance from various manifestations of Islamic radicalism. The choice of formalism in oratory, on the other hand, was a less explicit, but nevertheless a seriously considered choice on part of the authorities, which should not mislead the observer into thinking that consensus exists in religious circles. Instead, voices have been raised in the direction of breaking the conservative trends and turn to everyday language and topics of greater day-to-day relevance (see Chapter 6). Yet, there has never been a real breakthrough in the direction of freer speech as far as the official *hutbe*s are concerned. It seems that for the secular state to rely on formal oratory, and thus a traditional form of authority (Gaffney 1994: 194), has been a way to contain religion. For religious groups, on the other hand, this has been a way to preserve the status and moral authority of religion. In this way, the unholy alliance between secular and religious interests, so characteristic of modern Turkey, found expression also in its official *hutbe* rhetoric.

## Notes

1. From 1,750 tractors in 1948 to almost 30,000 in 1952 (Zürcher 1994: 235).
2. Turkey State Institute of Statistics (1977); Özdalga (1978: 152–3).
3. The then existing electoral system gave the larger party an unproportionally large representation in parliament. Atatürk (d. 1938) was succeeded by İsmet İnönü, both as president and CHP leader.

4. The Democrat Party, the ruling party from 1950 to 1960, was closed, its leaders prosecuted in faked trials and banned from politics for many years, and the prime minister, Adnan Menderes, together with two ministers, sentenced to death and executed by hanging on 17 September 1961.

5. 5,042 people lost their lives in various incidents between 1976 and 1980 (Sayarı 2010: 201).

6. *New York Times*, 26 July 1975.

7. The Istanbul weekly *Nokta Dergisi*, 25 April 2007. Available at <https://m. bianet.org/bianet/siyaset/138133-1-mayis-1977-kanli-bayram> (last accessed 4 October 2020).

8. This event has been commemorated for decades. For one example, Yalçın Bayer in the Istanbul daily *Hürriyet*, 7 October 2008, see <https://www.hurriyet.com. tr/bahcelievler-katliami-nin-30-yili-10055243> (last accessed 4 October 2020).

9. The original Turkish texts are reproduced in Appendix III. In relation to that a note on references: the sources of quotations in the *hutbe* texts (mostly from the Koran and various *hadis* collections) are often given only by saying 'Allah says' (The Koran), or 'the Prophet or any of his close allies say' (*hadis*). In that case, the sources have been traced and added in endnotes. Sometimes, however, the sources are explicitly provided for, either in the running text or as endnotes of the *hutbe*, annotated as (1), (2), (3), etc. In that case, the source is given in parentheses within the text (not separated as endnotes). In addition, the English translations also contain annotated comments. In the Turkish originals (Appendix III) sources are given only as 'empty' numbers. All references and comments are found in this chapter.

10. The English translations of the Koran used in this work are from *The Qur'ān* (English Meanings), edited by Sahih International (SI) – a translation by three American women converts, Emily Assami, Amatullah Bantley and Mary Kennedy, published by the Dar Abul Qasim Publishing House, Saudi Arabia (1997). Available at <https://alrashidmosque.ca/wp-content/uploads/2019/05/ The-Quran-Saheeh-International.pdf> (last accessed 10 June 2021).

11. Authors of *hutbe*s, mostly identified with name and title, were persons active within, or otherwise attached to Diyanet. *Hutbe*s were also, but very rarely, signed with an anonymous 'Diyanet'.

12. This verse here serves as preamble for this *hutbe*.

13. This is a well-known *hadis*, found in among other things the *Sahih al-Bukhari* and *Sahih Muslim* collections, the two most often quoted *hadis* collections in Turkish *hutbe* oratory. The Bukhari version of the *hadis* reads as follows (in Dr M. Muhsin Khan's translation): 'Surely! Everyone of you is a guardian and is responsible for

his charges: The Imam (ruler) of the people is a guardian and is responsible for his subjects; a man is the guardian of his family (household) and is responsible for his subjects; a woman is the guardian of her husband's home and of his children and is responsible for them; and the slave of a man is a guardian of his master's property and is responsible for it. Surely, everyone of you is a guardian and responsible for his charges.' See *Sahih al-Bukhari*, number 7138 (book 93, hadith 2). In the *Sahih Muslim* collection the *hadis* carries number 1829 (book 33, hadith 24). Available at <https://sunnah.com/bukhari:7138> and <https://sunnah.com/muslim:1829a> (last accessed 2 March 2021).

14. For a reference in English, *Sahih al-Bukhari* number 59 (book 3, hadith 1), see <https://sunnah.com/bukhari:59> (last accessed 2 March 2021).

15. The Koran [SI], The Women 4: 58.

16. Abdullah ibni Mesut (Arabic: 'Abdullah ibn Mas'ūd), a contemporary of the Prophet, d. 652–3 in Medina, see İsmail Cerrahoğlu: 'Abdullāh b. Mes'ūd', (TDV *İslam Ansiklopedisi* 1988: Vol. 1, pp. 114–17).

17. İbn-i İshak (Arabic: Ibn Isḥāq) (704–68), Arab biographer of the Prophet Muhammad. See Ibn Hisham (1955).

18. See Chapter 6 for Mehmet Akif Ersoy – national poet, often cited in *hutbes*.

19. Osman Keskioğlu (1907–89), born in Bulgaria, migrated to Turkey in 1950; taught Arabic and religion at the Faculty of Theology, Ankara University; member of Diyanet High Committee for Religious Affairs 1966–76; prolific writer, also with recurring contributions in *Diyanet Gazetesi*. See Kamil Yaşaroğlu: 'Osman Keskioğlu,' TDV *İslam Ansiklopedisi*: Vol. 25, pp. 309–10.

20. Mehmed Ebussuud Efendi (also known as Hoca Çelebi, 1490–1574) (Arabic: Muḥammad Abū al-Su'ūd) was an Ottoman jurist of the Hanefi school and Koranic exegete, who, from 1545 until his death, was the Grand Mufti (sheikh ül-Islam) of Süleyman the Magnificent (entitled *kanuni*, 'the lawgiver') (1494–1566). Ebussuud's Koranic commentary (*tefsir*) covers twelve volumes (Schacht 1986: 152). For the specific reference used in this *hutbe*, see Ebüssuud Efendi (1928).

21. İbn-i Melek (Arabic: Ibn Malak) (d. after 1418), scholar of jurisprudence and *hadis* (Mustafa Baktır: 'İbn Melek' in TDV *İslam Ansiklopedisi*: Vol. 20, pp. 175–6). For the work cited here, see Ibn Malak (1886).

22. *Câmi'uş-Şağir* is a collection of *hadis* compiled by the renowned Egyptian scholar al-Suyuti (1445–1505). The work referred to here is a three-volume shortened edition of Jalal ad-Din al-Suyuti's vast collection (more than 10,000 *hadis*) by Ali bin Ahmet el-Bulaki Azizi (d. 1659) printed in Cairo 1887 (Haywood 1997: 913–16; TDV *İslam Ansiklopedisi*: Vol. 7, p. 112). See al-Bulaqi Azizi (1887).

23. Saad bin Rebia (Arabic: Saʿad ibn al-Rabī) and Abdurrahman bin Avf (Arabic: ʿAbd al-Raḥman ibn ʿAwf) were companions (*sahaba*) of the Prophet Muhammad. Therefore, their names are followed by 'May Allah be pleased with him' (R.A. or r.a.).

24. This is a well-known history of Islam by Muinüddin Ahmed Nevdi and Said Sahib Ansari. *Asrı Saadet* refers to the lifetime of the Prophet Muhammad, literally the 'Age of Happiness'. See Nevdi (1963).

25. Rağıb-ı-İsfehânî (d. 1108) (Arabic: al-Rāghib al-Iṣfahānī) was a scholar of religion, moral philosophy and Arabic literature, who is said to have had some influence on al-Ghazali (d. 1111). The work referred to is an alphabetical lexicon of Koranic vocabulary (Rowson 1995: 389–90; TDV *İslam Ansiklopedisi*: Vol. 34, pp. 398–401). See Raghib al-Isfahani (1961).

26. Kamil Şahin, Turkish theologian, prolific and awarded writer. Available at <http://kaynakca.hacettepe.edu.tr/kisi/95688/kamil-sahin> (last accessed 3 March 2021).

27. Workers constituted only 24.5 per cent of the total labour force in 1975, whereas in Sweden, for example, around 50 per cent of the total labour force were workers already at an early stage of the labour movement (end of the nineteenth century) (Özdalga 1978: 107).

28. The Koran [SI], The Family of Imran 3: 103.

29. For a reference in English, see *Sahih al-Bukhari* number 6064 (book 78, hadith 94). Available at <https://sunnah.com/bukhari:6064> (last accessed 4 March 2021).

30. The Alevi is an Alid-oriented ethno-religious community, mainly living in the central and eastern parts of Anatolia (especially Yozgat, Sivas, Tokat, Tunceli, Malatya, Adıyaman). Historically, they represent a mixture of settled, seminomadic and nomadic groups, who sympathised with Shiʿa-oriented Iranian rulers like Shah Ismail (1487–1524). For that reason, they were looked upon with suspicion by the Ottoman administration. They usually lived in smaller villages in distant areas, while Sunni Muslims dominated in Anatolian towns (See Olsson et al. 1998; Shankland 2003).

31. This loyalty to Atatürk may sound strange in the light of the afore-mentioned Dersim atrocities, but the Dersim Alevi were mostly of Kurdish origin. Their tribal ties were also stronger than in many other areas. Their resistance was therefore fiercer. At the same time such hostilities bore witness to the Alevi's thorny relationship with the larger Sunni society.

32. Müslim, İmare, 173.

33. *Sahih al-Bukhari*, number 2786 (book 56, hadith 5) Available at <https://sunnah.com/bukhari:2786> (last accessed 4 March 2021).

34. İbn Hanbel, V, 235 (unspecified/undated, shortened Turkish edition of Ibn Hanbal's vast collection of *hadis*).

35. The Holy Koran [SI], The Ranks 61: 10–11.

36. A *hadis* from Ebu Davud's (Arabic: Abū Dāwūd) (d. 889) collection. For a reference in English: *Sunan Abi Dawud*, number 1678 (book 9, hadith 123). Available at <https://sunnah.com/abudawud:1678> (last accessed 4 March 2021).

37. For a *hadis* reflecting the spirit of this quotation, see *Sunan Abi Dawud*, number 3052 (book 20, hadith 125). Available at <https://sunnah.com/abudawud:3052> (last accessed 4 March 2021).

38. *Feth-ül Kebir* is a collection of *hadis* based on the above-mentioned al-Suyuti's (d. 1505) vast collection, put together by the Palestinian scholar Yûsuf b. İsmâîl Nebhânî (1849–1932) (TDV *İslam Ansiklopedisi*: Vol. 32, pp. 471–2). See al-Nabahani (1932).

39. Talat Karaçizmeli (d. 2017) was a researcher and author. See, for example, *Gençlerle Sohbetler* (with Ahmet Okutan), Ankara: Diyanet Vakfı Yayınları (2010).

40. An initiated analysis of divergent interpretations of the same Koranic and *hadis* sources, see Jones (2020).

41. From medieval Uzbek *hadis* scholar Ebû Îsâ Muhammed bı saadet Îsâ Tirmizî (b. 824/d. 892) (TDV *İslam Ansiklopedisi*: Vol. 41, pp. 202–4).

42. Buhari, İ'tisam, 14 (unspecified/undated, shortened Turkish edition of Bukhari's often-cited collection of *hadis*).

43. From Ebu Dawud's *hadis* collection, see *Sunan Abi Dawud*, number 4031 (book 34, hadith 12). Available at <https://sunnah.com/abudawud:4031> (last accessed 4 March 2021).

44. The work referred to here, in English *Bulugh al-Meram Translation and Commentary: The Roads to Salvation*, is a Turkish translation and commentary by Al-Azhar educated scholar Ahmed Davudoğlu (1912–83) of the Shafii scholar İbn Hacer el-Askalânî's (d. 1449) *hadis* collection *Bulugh al-Meram*. See TDV *İslam Ansiklopedisi*: Vol. 9, pp. 52–3. Davudoğlu's translation was published in four volumes 1965–7, see Ibn Hacer el-Askalani (1967).

45. From *hutbe* number four in this chapter.

46. The two types of speech should not be conceptualised as a dichotomy, but a continuum bridging two extremes (Bloch 1975: 13).

47. In the context of a history of religion, these would correspond to sacred archetypes (Eliade 1974).

# 5

# DİYANET IN SEARCH OF AUTONOMY[1]

Turkey holds a unique place in the Muslim world when it comes to centrali-sation and state control of religious affairs. This is closely connected to its rigid implementation of secularism, or laicism, which since 1928 has been writ-ten into the Turkish constitution (Article 2). Less secular-oriented states, such as neighbouring Egypt and Jordan, have over the years entered a similar path, but at a more gradual and hesitant pace (Skovgaard-Petersen 1997; Antoun 1989).[2] In less centralised states of South East Asia, Indonesia and Malaysia, where the population is ethnically and confessionally more heterogeneous (still, Indonesia is home to the world's largest Muslim population) the Islamic upswing of the 1980s has been led by organised 'civil Islam', rather than by the state (Heffner 2000; Hoesterey 2016). The ambition of the official authorities in these coun-tries has been to control, but not to organise, religious life. Compared to other Muslim countries, Turkey offers a precursory example of the social and politi-cal dynamics – and predicaments – involved in having religion organised by a strictly secular and centralised state. The fact that the pro-Islamic Justice and Development Party (Adalet ve Kalkınma Partisi, AKP) assumed office in 2002 did not alter the state's centralistic and, as far as the constitution goes, secular character. This chapter offers an overview of Turkey's experience of official Islam by focusing on the Directorate of Religious Affairs, Diyanet.

Little mention has so far been made of this institution, the reason being its relatively minor importance during the first decades of the Republic. As a matter of fact, it was not until in 1965 that the Directorate was given a firmer legal structure and with that gained a more visible place on the map of official institutions. Thanks to tighter regulations, a more consistent production and effective distribution of *hutbe*s was also made possible – two processes that went hand in hand.

While the previous chapters concentrated on the ritual and discursive aspects of *hutbe* preaching, this chapter places emphasis on the organisational framework of these activities. The exposition starts with an overview of the development of the legal arrangements of Diyanet, with special emphasis on what happened after 1965. This year marks the start of a more sweeping reform, which also offered opportunities for institutional autonomy. The chapter deals with institutional developments that were in force until the turn of the millennium, when the political landscape changed and Diyanet, more blatantly than ever before, was drawn into the orbit of a particular political party, the increasingly authoritarian and Islamist AKP.

The consolidation and growth of Diyanet was no easy process. Becoming an integral part of the centralistic Turkish state apparatus brought different kinds of uncomfortable friction between prominent representatives of the secular state such as the military, the upper echelons of the civil bureaucracy, including the judiciary and the academia, on the one hand, and more liberal-minded business circles, media groups and political parties, on the other. A whole range of more or less high-pitched actors on both sides of the secularist–devout divide wanted to have a say. Against such interventionist attempts stood groups of religious professionals and their sympathisers, who acted on behalf of a more autonomous and politically neutral organisation. No doubt, Diyanet functioned as a mediator or filter between various hegemonic interest groups and popular sentiments. But it also acted on its own behalf, that is, in the name of those who filled its office rooms and corridors. With respect to these general observations, the following questions will be addressed in this chapter: What legal reforms were implemented? What kind of balance was reached between institutional autonomy and dependence? Which were the main powerbrokers in this tug-of-war, both in terms of leading individuals and organisations? In the name of which interests or worldviews did various actors engage themselves in these processes? The chapter aims to discuss the dilemmas involved in trying to maintain a relatively autonomous position, while having to accept being used as a medium for state and/or governmental interests.

### Diyanet

When Mustafa Kemal, as the prospective leader of the Turkish War of Independence, came to Ankara for the first time on 27 December 1919, the Ottoman mufti of that province, Mehmet Rıfat Börekçi (see Chapter 3), was already actively supporting the emerging nationalist resistance movement. When the first national parliament was summoned a few months later, on 23 April 1920, Börekçi was elected as member of parliament for the Muğla district, a position he left six months later (27 October 1920) in order to return to his position as mufti in Ankara. When the caliphate was abolished (1924) and Diyanet established, Börekçi became its first director, a position he held until his death in 1941.

The Ankara *müftülük* was housed in a small building just across the street from Hallaç Mahmut Mescit (or Kubbeli Mescit, close to Anafartalar Caddesi) in the Ulus district, the old centre of the city. When appointed director of Diyanet, Börekçi remained in the same humble place. The location amply reflected the modesty of the institution itself. In fourteen tiny articles (Law number 429), the guidelines for the new directorate were drawn up. For example, Article 1 stated that religion, in narrow secular terms defined as 'belief and worship' (*itikadat ve ibadat*), was henceforth to be administered by Diyanet, strictly subordinated to the parliament and, based on that, the government. Article 3 stipulated that the director was to be appointed by the president based on the prime minister's proposal; Article 4 that Diyanet should be linked to the prime minister's office; Article 5 that Diyanet was responsible for all religious appointments such as imam, *hatip*, *vaiz*, sheikh, muezzin, *kayyum* (caretaker); and Article 6 that regional muftis were bound to the directorate. This single-page document did not contain any provisions concerning the structure of the organisation, that is, the number of personnel, professional categories, systems of appointment, and so on. Such regulations were to a limited extent provided through an additional act issued in 1935. A more substantial reform was not enacted until in 1965.[3]

The precariousness or uncertainty characterising Diyanet's standing during the first decades is illustrated by the fact that it did not take long until the management of mosques (larger mosques, *cami*s, and smaller mosques, *mescit*s) and their personnel was transferred to another institution, the General Directorate of Charitable Foundations (Vakıflar Genel Müdürlüğü), also subordinated to the prime minister's office. This split of responsibilities related to religious affairs was realised through the budget act of 1931. Thereby, the command over religious abodes and personnel was retracted from Diyanet (see Article 5 above) and its authority reduced to dealing only with spiritual matters – 'belief and worship'. This division of labour was maintained until more liberal winds took over after the Second World War with greater sensitivity to religious sentiments and transition to a multi-party system. Thus, it was only on 29 April 1950, shortly before the first free elections, that the previous responsibility for mosques and their personnel was reverted to Diyanet, which, in force of its competence in theological and other religious matters, maintained a relatively greater autonomy vis-à-vis the government than the General Directorate of Charitable Foundations. The reform, which rendered Diyanet the basis of its present organisation, was realised in 1965. The new law (number 633) was implemented as part of a set of legal and administrative reforms carried out in the wake of the military coup of 1960 (Jäschke 1972: 64–8).[4]

Compared to Law number 429 (1924), which contained fourteen articles, Law number 633 contained forty-one, much more detailed, articles. The first article, for example, stating the aim of the organisation, was extended to include not only responsibility for 'belief and worship', but also the 'the bases of ethics' (*ahlak esasları*). Also added was the clause 'enlightening the people (society) on religious topics', which made the edifying purpose more explicit. However, it was especially concerning the structure of the organisation itself that the new law was more elaborated: four levels – directorate, central organisation, local organisation and organisation abroad – were specified (Article 2); the length of directorship limited to five years, with the possibility of extension for a second period (Article 3); a board consisting of sixteen members was drawn up, including details about qualifications, length of service, selection of board secretariat, rules for decision making, areas of responsibilities, including interpretation of religious queries (a fatwa-like function), research, following and reporting on religious groups outside of Diyanet, contacts with media, organisation of seminars and other larger consulting meetings (*din şurası*), and so on (Article 5); the

structure of sub-divisions, such as bureaus dealing with permission of opening a new mosque, service to prisons and other public care-taking institutions,
radio and television, women, youth and children, education, pilgrimage programmes, and so on (Article 7); educational qualifications and other terms of
employment of imams, *hatip*s, muftis and other Diyanet personnel (Article 9);
rules forbidding personnel within Diyanet to be politically organised, as well as
to speak for or against any political party (Article 25). It seems, however, that
this organisational upgrading to a large extent remained on paper. When future
director of Diyanet, Professor Tayyar Altıkulaç, took up the post as deputy
director in July 1971 he was shocked by the lack of order and discipline within
the organisation.[5] To a great extent, infusing fresh life into the new legal structure fell to him.

## New Prospects for Institutional Autonomy

By the 1960s, important changes had taken place in Turkish society. Urbanisation was increasing and the population was socially and politically mobilised in a new way. Religious education had been resumed and reorganised
during Adnan Menderes' time as prime minister (1950–60). The pressure on
the authorities to meet the religion-related demands of the common people
was growing; but so was the pressure of the political establishment to foster
its citizens. The progress achieved within public school education since the
early years of the Republic was modest, so that as late as in 1970 almost half
the population was still illiterate (Turkey State Institute of Statistics 1977).
Mosques therefore offered an essential alternative space for the authorities,
where these shortcomings could be compensated for, especially as regards
rearing faithful believers and loyal citizens.

During the interwar period, religion had been suppressed; now, there were
forces actively challenging the secularism of the interwar period. Thus, there
were two camps contesting each other on how to bolster loyalty to state and
nation: on the one hand, the hard-core guardians of the state, comprising
the military, the civil bureaucracy and the bulk of the academia; and, on the
other, the political-civil elite, who had come to power through free enterprise,
political parties and elections. The 'real' guardians represented the deeper or
secreted branches of the state, structures that bolstered mystified and reified
notions of the 'state' (Abrams 1988). The other elite represented the visible

part: parliament, government and government-related institutions. The rivalry between these elite factions – one secular, containing even fanatically secularist groups, the other relatively more religious-minded – determined an important part of the political conflicts and was also reflected in shifting attitudes and conduct vis-à-vis Diyanet and, by extension, the Friday sermons.

The interwar secularising reforms had deprived religious institutions of their authority. In Ottoman times, the sheikh ül-Islam – the highest figure in the religious hierarchy – had enjoyed the same status as the grand vizier. The legal system had largely rested on the *kadıs*, the specialised jurists within the ulema. In the new republican order, the religious organisation was reduced to a bureau under the prime minister's office, where local imams, positioned at the bottom of a formal bureaucracy, lost part of their autonomy. With the coming of a democratically elected government in 1950, however, new Imam-Hatip schools (preacher's seminaries) and faculties of theology were established, resulting in a certain improvement of the level of education among religious personnel. It was with these mixed cadres, representing both old (downgraded) and new (upgraded) forms of ambition – and frustration – that the state would henceforth have to engage in order to reach out to the congregations.

## Diyanet – Institutional Consolidation

Four months after the military intervention of 12 March 1971,[6] Tayyar Altıkulaç was appointed deputy director of Diyanet (15 July 1971). Before that – as a manifestation of the junta's concerns for a secular and West-oriented Turkey – the government had had the then deputy director of Diyanet, Yaşar Tunagür, dismissed. This purge was occasioned by Tunagür's alleged connections to the Nurcu movement, a Sufi-like network following in the tracks of the religious revivalist Bediüzzaman Said Nursi (1876–1960).[7] There was thus an urgent need to replace Tunagür with a supposedly more reliable staff member and it seems that the responsible minister, Mehmet Özgüneş, had found Altıkulaç a suitable person for that position.

In spite of his relatively young age, Altıkulaç was already known as a cleric especially proficient in reciting/chanting the Koran (*tilavet*), a special and relatively rare skill, which had occasioned him to take part in several recordings for radio broadcasting.[8] He was known as a dependable secular-minded nationalist, who did not associate with Islamist circles. On the contrary, he kept a clear distance from Islamist party politics. As related in his autobiography, Altıkulaç had been approached by leading figures from the 1969-formed pro-Islamic National Order Party (Milli Nizam Partisi, MNP). This happened when he was serving as imam in the eastern Tunceli province during his military service. The MNP people handed him a request to set up a district organisation on behalf of their party. They seemed to mean that as imam he would be especially suitable for such a mission. Altıkulaç rejected their appeal in straightforward terms, saying that to run a political party as if it were a religious community or movement could do nothing but harm to religion itself. He emphatically declared that by no means would he participate in that kind of undertakings (Altıkulaç 2011: 162–3).

The government also appointed a teacher with colonel's degree from the War College, Ahmet Okutan, as a second deputy director. The turnabouts in having the allegedly Nurcu-affiliated Tunagür exchanged for two more secular-minded deputy directors – one of them from the military ranks – is a good illustration of the kind of showdowns that arose and deals that were struck between state and government, on the one hand, and religious groups or communities, on the other. However, that Altıkulaç, on merit of his secular-mindedness, was chosen for this post does not mean that he was a man of the Establishment. Judging from the way in which administrative reforms were carried out under his leadership, he, in fact, managed to strike a balance, which bolstered the autonomy of Diyanet. This independence was realised through a momentum generated in the course of a number of reforms initiated under his management.

### Administrative Reforms

Altıkulaç had described Diyanet as being in a state of wreckage. Upon his arrival in 1971 he was stunned by the lack of administrative order and discipline. It was as if Diyanet was not a public institution, but an association lacking proper rules and regulations (Altıkulaç 2011: 183). First of all, the corridors were overcrowded. The reason for this agonising situation was that in order to have an appointment settled – as imam, muezzin or *hatip*, or any other position – people would have to busy themselves personally. Otherwise, their cases risked remaining undealt with for months. In addition, employees and their dependants would come from near and far to resolve personal problems which were outside the jurisdiction of Diyanet. People would bring up any issue related to health, education, family relationships and supply problems. The mere fact that Diyanet was an official institution situated in the capital drew people to go there for all kinds of problems. Parliamentarians would come and go at their own discretion in order to have their own and their supporters' dealings resolved. True, the problem with congested offices was not limited to Diyanet. The situation was similar all over the public sector, and just one example of the 'clientelism' (Heywood 2007: 386–9) permeating the Turkish governmental system. Still, it might have been that Diyanet was under heavier pressure because people expected a more sincere and generous reception there thanks to the religious glow and folksy character of this institution.[9]

The second problem pinpointed by Altıkulaç was the lack of proper archives. In order to find a requested dossier, the official in charge may have to search for days. In addition, personal security was inadequate. Dossiers containing confidential information were sometimes passed around without proper caution or protection. A third problem was what Altıkulaç identified as hidden unemployment. Women busy with knitting or crocheting during office hours has become a legendary synonym for low work output. This was also the expression used by Altıkulaç in his description of the lack of work discipline in Diyanet. He linked this laxity to the fact that office rooms were small, which made it difficult to implement control and supervision. A fourth, and even more serious problem, was the lack of discipline in the chain of order implementation. Decisions taken by the central authority were left to the discretion of the muftis at the provincial and/or district levels. 'Especially this situation made me very frustrated,' complains Altıkulaç (Altıkulaç 2011: 184).

Altıkulaç was eager to do something about these problems. In order to cope with the low production of work or services – 'hidden unemployment' – Altıkulaç ventured to intervene into the very architectural design of the office building. As an alternative to the small office spaces he introduced the idea of open-plan office. Walls were torn down and three larger halls were constructed based on an already existing division of labour between employment records (dossiers or files), rosters of permanent staff, and appointments (*sicil, kadro, tayin*). In this way two aims were met: a more well-arranged and rational organisation was reached; and a stricter supervision, thus work discipline, was achieved. However, as it turned out, it was not an altogether easy task to have this plan realised. Lütfü Doğan, the then director of Diyanet, was generally passive and unwilling to implement any kind of change and had repeatedly tried to postpone Altıkulaç's proposals until a later date. The opportunity to carry out the reconstructions came when Doğan went on a few days' trip to Istanbul. Altıkulaç tells in vivid colours how he made the preparations by begging for material support (financing and manpower) from a well-to-do friend from his own home district and how he, on the day of departure, escorted his superior to the airport and then rushed back in order to finish the construction within a few days. On his return, the director did not say anything encouraging, but neither did he oppose against the new open-plan arrangements (Altıkulaç 2011: 187).

With respect to archives, there were around 50,000 personnel files in pressing need of systematisation. With the purpose of finding a useful and effective model, Altıkulaç applied to the General Staff (High Military Command), the Ministry of Justice and the Ministry of Education; he found that the General Staff provided the best model, and the Ministry of Education the poorest, wherefore the first one was chosen. What colleagues in Diyanet estimated would amount to several years' work was finished in a couple of months. But this was not reached without tough measures concerning working pace and discipline (Altıkulaç 2011: 188–9).

Concerning the need to clear the offices from crowds, Altıkulaç decreed a prohibition against outside visitors. However, outside visitors could not just be dismissed and were instead advised to see the heads of divisions or the deputy directors. The aim was to provide peace and quiet to the personnel at the lower levels. In addition, Altıkulaç made an effort to teach the staff how to write official letters in order to raise the general quality of services (Altıkulaç 2011: 189–91).

A reform that deserves special mention concerned the way in which appointments of imams, *hatip*s and muezzins around the country were carried out. To begin with, there was the basic problem related to the scarcity of personnel, that is, the available personnel were not sufficient to cover the needs of all the mosques in the country. Besides, the available personnel were unevenly distributed. From a survey arranged by Altıkulaç, it became apparent that imams, muftis and other religious personnel too often got their appointments based on the power of certain politically influential parties or personalities. For example, in Isparta, which was the home province of Süleyman Demirel, a long-standing leader in Turkish politics, cadres were filled to 100 per cent. In some humbler provinces, on the other hand, the coverage went down to 20 per cent. In order to avoid this kind of injustice, Altıkulaç introduced a regulation (*tüzük*) in seven articles, stating which criteria to follow when distributing available cadres. He points out that preparations were made in silence, without shouting them out from the rooftops. Thanks to these procedures, powerful political groups were kept at a distance, which meant that Diyanet was able to maintain a certain amount of independence and autonomy. When confronted with visitors, even if those were parliamentarians or other influential people, the personnel at Diyanet were now able to decline their requests by referring to existing regulations. In 1979, the government of the day tried to change these regulations, which had been accepted only four years earlier, but Altıkulaç did not succumb to the pressures. He asserted his own position in a formal report. What lent substance to that report was that it was signed not only by himself, but also by the members of the High Committee for Religious Affairs (Din İşleri Yüksek Kurulu, DİYK), a situation that requires special explanation and clarification (Altıkulaç 2011: 194–8).

It was by force of the High Committee that the director was able to withstand the pressures imposed by various political circles in and around the central government and local administrative bodies. The committee thus constituted an important instrument for any frontrunner or leading group within Diyanet, who strived to maintain and strengthen the independence or autonomy of the directorate. The strategic significance of the committee was also linked to the far-reaching authorities assigned to the director, especially concerning appointments of the personnel. In this sense Diyanet had – or was able to claim – a more autonomous status than many other official institutions (Altıkulaç 2011: 692). These regulations were based in Law number 633 from 1965, which also defined the legal framework of the High Committee.

Law number 633 thus offered the underpinnings of a relatively strong clerical independence. The regulations stipulated that out of twenty-seven candidates appointed by local organisations throughout the country, nine were to be chosen by the director. It was thus in his power to choose those he found best qualified. However, until Altıkulaç was appointed director of Diyanet in February 1978, this committee had not yet succeeded in constituting itself – the reasons being a lack of candidates with the required qualifications and interference in the appointment process by political groups, especially the pro-Islamic National Salvation Party (Milli Selamet Partisi, MSP), who picked candidates according to their own political leanings, rather than professional qualifications.[10] It seems that Altıkulaç's predecessors were not as keen, neither concerning the significance of the committee for the maintenance of institutional autonomy, nor the kind of manipulations they might be exposed to. For Altıkulaç, however, it became a number one priority, to see to it that the High Committee was formed and activated. It was thus thanks both to his personal resolve and insight into the importance of the High Committee that he was able to maintain relative integrity and independence for Diyanet. In what comes out of his autobiography, this had not been an easy task, but the formation of the High Committee represented an important take-off for his own mission as director (Altıkulaç 2011: 343–6). After having obtained a certain degree of control over Diyanet, Altıkulaç could concentrate on particular critical issues, such as strengthening Diyanet's representations abroad, especially in Germany; improving the organisation of pilgrimage (*hac*); raising the level of education for imams and other religious personnel; strengthening the control of various 'free' religious communities and increasingly obtrusive Islamist party interests; finding the correct time to start fasting during Ramadan; and reinforcing Friday sermonising (Altıkulaç 2011: 336).

### New Regulations concerning the Friday Sermons

*Hutbe* oratory was definitely in need of reform, according to Altıkulaç. The weekly homiletic addresses were especially important, since it was by means of the Friday sermons that the people could be reached in larger numbers for religious education and enlightenment. Therefore, it was particularly regretful for a leading theologian like Altıkulaç to notice that the level of education of those delivering the homilies was so poor. At the beginning of the 1970s, the great majority of practising imams and *hatip*s had but a primary school diploma. Those with higher education were not more numerous than they 'could be counted on one's fingers' (Altıkulaç 2011: 413). This must be seen in the context of the overall poor level of education in Turkey.

When describing how Friday sermonising was carried out in Turkey, Altıkulaç separated between four different styles: (1) *hutbe*s selected from various collections available in the book market or in libraries; (2) *hutbe*s chosen from texts produced and delivered by Diyanet in Ankara, especially through the fortnightly (or monthly) published *Diyanet Gazetesi* (see Chapter 3); (3) *hutbe*s written by the imam or *hatip* himself; and (4) *hutbe*s delivered extempore (Altıkulaç 2011: 413). Altıkulaç was especially concerned about *hutbe*s delivered extempore, since they allegedly allowed for more emotional and politically seasoned addresses and therefore were regarded by him as particularly problematic. Such alleged 'misuses' of the *minber* was from time to time reported by members of the congregations to the local mufti, who in his turn could – but by no means always did – forward such complaints to Diyanet in Ankara.[11] It even happened that imams were applauded as a result of an expressive sermon. Altıkulaç saw these kinds of departures as signs of insufficient education. Poor quality in the art of sermonising was for him first and foremost a problem of inadequate education. Here was, in his evaluation, a field in need of reform, regulation and discipline.

The issue was delegated to the High Committee for Religious Affairs. However, since several members of the committee were absent during the initial round, Altıkulaç, displeased with the performance, returned the first proposal. The seriousness of the issue required that every member was present during the deliberations. When finalised, the new regulations were distributed to all muftis on district as well as provincial levels. The document comprised the following principles: (1) *hutbe*s should be read from a previously prepared text (not extempore); (2) certain exceptions were allowed for persons specially appointed by the central Diyanet organisation, muftis serving on district and/or provincial levels, and/or imams with special permission from officially appointed muftis; (3) priority should be given to *hutbe*s that had either been published, or carefully examined and approved by Diyanet. Special permission from the district or provincial mufti was required for imams, who preferred to make use of existing *hutbe* collections, or who wanted to write their own *hutbe*s; and (4) each provincial *müftülük* was required to set up a programme for the Friday sermons that aimed at conveying religious knowledge to the audiences. The aim was to sermonise on the same topic in all mosques in the same province (Altıkulaç 2011: 414–15).[12]

However, the problem concerning how to improve the Friday sermons did not end there. In addition to poor training, there was also a lack of commitment. Altıkulaç complains about imams who did not even bother to read through an already prepared text before reading it to the congregation. 'The number of imams, who do not even bother to read through the *hutbe* before they read it to the congregation are really not wanting!' (Altıkulaç 2011: 428). So, in order to raise the level of active involvement, Altıkulaç issued a ruling making it obligatory for each employee working within the organisation to subscribe to *Diyanet Gazetesi*. As expounded in Chapter 4, this fortnightly magazine contained one, sometimes two *hutbe*s, ready to be used by the local imams and *hatip*s during the Friday noon service. This obligatory subscription, particularly imposed by Altıkulaç, had already started in March 1980, and was therefore not related to the dictates of the military regime of September 1980, even if voices critical of Altıkulaç' demanding style wanted to describe the forced subscription that way (Altıkulaç 2011: 428–30). For several decades *Diyanet Gazetesi* (in 1991 changed to *Diyanet Aylık Dergi*) served as the main forum for authorised *hutbe*s.

**Distribution of Official *Hutbe*s through *Diyanet Gazetesi***

Due to scarce resources Diyanet did not publish any periodicals of its own during the first decades of the Republic. Short of the means to reach the common people through such media, the religious institution issued other types of publications, mainly books, addressing its own personnel. Among twenty-three editions published during the years 1924–50 were translations of *hadis* and commentary on the Koran (*tefsir*), books explaining the principles of Islam (*ilmihal*) and the two *hutbe* collections examined in Chapter 3 (Akseki 2005 [1928]; Akseki 1936–7; Bulut 2015: 13–14).

The first periodical issued by Diyanet appeared in 1956. It was planned as a sixty-four-page annual publication, but it took another five years for the next issue to appear and then in the format of a yearbook (1960–1) (Büyüker 2015: 22–3). A more regular periodical publication did not get on its way until November 1968. However, to start with, this sixteen-page fortnightly 'newspaper' (*Diyanet Gazetesi*), appeared more sporadically with a longer one and a half year break between April 1969 and October 1970. After this staggering beginning the publication continued to appear on a regular basis until 1991, when it was reshaped into *Diyanet Aylık Dergi*, a monthly, more professionally laid-out and comprehensive 'magazine'. In the wake of the breakdown of the Soviet Union and, as a result of that the social and political changes in the region, government representatives as well as leaders within Diyanet felt a need to strengthen the profile of the country's religious institution, not only inwards but also towards the outside world. That initiative was also meant to bolster the image of Turkey in the newly opened-up Central Asian, Turkic republics.[13]

The model sermons of the previous, officially authorised *hutbe* collections (1927–8 and 1936–7) offered imams and *hatip*s around the country a publication from which they could pick and choose – and expound – according to their own discretion. Official control was exerted more in the negative than the positive, meaning that rather than demanding or commanding a certain given text, warnings, or in the worst case, dismissals, would occur where the preacher challenged the borders set by the secular laws or regulations. However, with the regularly issued publications the character of the official voice changed. It did so in two respects. First, the centre drew closer to the periphery, which implied a stronger sense of supervision from above. To this was added the compulsory character of *Diyanet Gazetesi*, that is, the imposed obligation on every imam and *hatip* to subscribe to the publication. Second, even if the published *hutbe*s, for several years entitled 'Address from the pulpit' (*Minberden sesleniş*) or simply '*Hutbe*', did not have to be followed to the letter, they provided the guiding principle for exhortations delivered by individual imams and *hatip*s all over the country. This inevitably led to the strengthening of a nationwide sermonising discourse. Through this process, the hitherto provincially limited public spheres in and around the local mosques gave way to the emergence of a religiously tinted public sphere on the national level.

The issuing of Friday sermons through *Diyanet Gazetesi* both increased central control over local congregations and strengthened the sense of unity on the national level. The consequence, however, was that it put a damper on the preaching act itself, concerning both its contents and its potential to spur emotional excitement. The first was related to the inconvenience involved in conveying the same message to people coming from very different geographical areas, and cultural, ethnic and educational backgrounds. This problem – closely linked to the magnitude and heterogeneity of the country – was, as a matter of fact, widely recognised by official circles as well as the wider mosque audiences.

Concerning emotional involvement, it goes without saying that a text, written by officially employed clerics and academics, or Islamic-oriented intellectuals at safe distance from the daily realities of local congregations, would hardly capture and respond to the sentiments of actual mosque-goers. Not only with respect to the content, but also on the emotional level, it was a question of finding the lowest common denominator, a register that suited all and that did not offend anyone. The immensity and heterogeneity of the audiences set limits for what could be said and how. Diyanet was obviously facing a dilemma: the stronger and more all-encompassing it became as an institution, the weaker and more undistinguished the power of its official homiletics.

## Conclusions

By the end of the 1970s, Diyanet had reached a new level in its development as a governmental authority with a certain amount of autonomy. This was, as a matter of fact, the result of its leadership's efforts to keep both official secularism, most markedly held in control by the military, and political actors with an Islamist agenda at arm's length. A balance was struck between an overall secular political order and a religious institution fending for itself as long as it remained within certain restrained borders. For a couple of decades, a more broad-minded and enlightened (less fanatically *laic*) atmosphere thrived – a situation favouring a softening of state-religion relationships, which in its turn allowed for more public space to religious-mindedness. AKP entered the political stage and consolidated its power under these more easy-going conditions. However, as the party's grip on power became stronger and more authoritarian, especially after its third straight election victory in 2011, Diyanet bowed to the pressures. Under the AKP, the religious institution was considerably strengthened, both in terms of economic allocations and an increase in the number of personnel, but at the same time it was transformed into a weak-willed tool. The Islamisation that was a result of this new rapprochement between an empowered Diyanet and an increasingly authoritarian government under the AKP did not necessarily impede secularism. As Jakob Skovgaard-Petersen has argued concerning the development of state–religion relationships in post-war Egypt: 'While it may be conceded that Islamization must be the antonym of secularization, its advance may nevertheless result in another form of secularization.' As long as the market economy holds sway, 'it may be asked whether simply labelling an institution or a business "Islamic" is enough to make it truly Islamic' (Skovgaard-Petersen 1997: 222–3). On the contrary, Islamist-imputed control may have an undermining effect on religious identities, since any managerial failure – or misuse of power – will recoil on religion itself. That is also what has happened in Turkey: rather than befriending the religious concerns of the wider society, Diyanet's merger with the ruling Islamist party has had damaging effects.

## Notes

1. For an already published, slightly different version of this chapter, see Özdalga (2020).
2. In Egypt, the sharia courts were not abolished until 1955, three years after Gamal Abdel Nasser's (1918–70) *coup d'état* in 1952 against King Farouk I (r. 1936–65). In spite of this change to secular laws, serious pressure was brought to bear in favour of sharia during the 1970s and 1980s, which meant that the secular reforms were seriously contested (Skovgaard-Petersen 1997: 166, 183, 200–2).
3. The law is available at <https://www.tbmm.gov.tr/tutanaklar/KANUNLAR_KARARLAR/kanuntbmmc002/kanuntbmmc002/kanuntbmmc00200429.pdf> (last accessed 29 January 2021).
4. Available at <https://www.mevzuat.gov.tr/MevzuatMetin/1.5.633.pdf> (last accessed 29 January 2021).
5. Tayyar Altıkulaç served as vice director between July 1971 and September 1976 and as director between February 1978 and November 1986.
6. For developments relating to the military ultimatum of 12 March 1971, see Zürcher 1994: 271–6.
7. Bediüzzaman Said Nursi, of Kurdish origin, was arrested and tried several times between 1935 and 1953, accused of using religion for political purposes (Mardin 1989; Zürcher 1994: 201). For Yaşar Tunagür, see Lord 2018: 111.

8. The following discussions are based on Professor Tayyar Altıkulaç's testimony about his years as deputy director (1971–6) and director (1978–86) of Diyanet (Altıkulaç 2011), supplemented with a longer interview I conducted with him on 19 May 2014. Instead of waving Professor Altıkulaç's own account aside as an expression of pure subjectivity, I have wanted to give prominence to the fact that as the key character in this process he has offered a rare inside account of this important period in Diyanet's and Turkey's modern history. As author, Altıkulaç maintains a critical distance to events and personalities, including himself, but at the same time he manages to convey a strong sense of what it takes to press for reforms, including sacrifice and compromise. The book was well received in different political and academic circles, including being recommended as reading for students of religion and religious personnel.

9. The folksy character of Diyanet was also reflected in the living conditions of its director, Lütfü Doğan (1968–72), who resided in a *gecekondu* area (squatter-town), and had meals, according to old traditions, sitting on the floor (Altıkulaç 2011: 183).

10. MSP representatives insisted that appointments should be based on how many votes any particular imam or mufti could expect to acquire for their own religious party, the MSP. They were also of the opinion that the lion's share of any sermon should be reserved for the promulgation of the MSP's mission (*dava*) (Altıkulaç 2011: 483–4).

11. The sensitivity of this question increased after Necmettin Erbakan had formed the MSP. If the imam said, 'Let's stay with *justice*' (*adaletten* ayrılmıyalım), that meant support for Süleyman Demirel, leader of the Justice Party (Adalet Partisi); if he said, 'May Allah render *salvation*' (Allah *selamet* versin), then this would be interpreted as alluding to Necmettin Erbakan and the National Salvation Party (Milli Selamet Partisi) (Altıkulaç 2011: 413–14).

12. These principles were confirmed by the DİYK and signed by Altıkulaç, 1 December 1981 (Altıkulaç 2011: 415).

13. Diyanet started to issue a magazine for children in 1979 – *Diyanet Çocuk Dergisi*. In 2013 a supplement featuring family questions was added to the *Diyanet Aylık Dergi* (Görgülü 2015: 26; Arslan 2015: 38–9).

# 6

## WRITING AND LISTENING: VOICES FROM INSIDE

The main subject matter of this volume's previous chapters has been official Friday sermons as texts. The chief purpose has been to describe basic themes and styles, but also to interpret the homiletic discourses in the light of existing social, political, institutional and historical contexts. In this chapter, focus is moved to persons engaged in and around *hutbe* performances. What are, in their eyes, the merits and shortcomings of Friday sermons, especially the *hutbe*s delivered by Diyanet? What difficulties are encountered in writing a Friday sermon, as well as listening to it? How important is the selection of mosque? What is the significance of the congregation, with whom the believer shares the service? How much does the sermon affect an individual's beliefs and general mood? Does the address occasion reflection and discussion with other congregational members afterwards? What other activities take place around the Friday noon service? In a smaller survey carried out in Istanbul and Ankara in 2014, I directed these questions to preachers and sermon writers, as well as auditors. Six of these interviews are reproduced below: one with a person with longer experience of and insights into the production of *hutbe*s, and five with persons regularly attending the Friday noon prayer. Most of the interviewed listeners were students.[1]

Before giving an account of the interviewees' evaluations of *hutbe* preaching, a short summary of developments in Turkey after 1980 is delineated. This reminder of the country's turbulent and problem-ridden recent history brings the apolitical character of the Friday sermons into sharper light. To this is added a presentation of *hutbe* topics from this period meant to serve as a backdrop to the testimonies emerging from the interviews. The chapter is wound up by a thematical evaluation of the interviews in light of that wider context.

## Neo-liberalism and Beyond: Turkey after 1980

Once the military had seized power on 12 September 1980, the mounting political violence of the previous decade quickly came to an end. Ordinary people could breathe a sigh of relief in more than one respect. Not only was it again possible to sojourn in the streets without fear, the prospects that the economy would recover looked promising. Turgut Özal, finance minister of Süleyman Demirel's last coalition government (1979–80), was appointed deputy prime minister in the junta-installed cabinet, with responsibility for the economy, together with the implementation of the IMF stabilisation programme of 24 January 1980.

Turgut Özal pursued an economic policy based on export-oriented, free market principles. He applied to Turkish conditions the neo-liberal theories of the Nobel Prize winner Milton Friedman and UK Conservative Party leader Margaret Thatcher. After the 1983 elections, when Özal's newly formed Motherland Party (Anavtan Partisi, ANAP) gained almost a two-thirds majority in parliament, he served as the country's prime minister until he was elected president in 1989. Under his leadership the economy grew and diversified: foreign capital was drawn into the country for investments in industry and tourism; infrastructure, such as big dam projects were initiated (the Euphrates and Tigris), and road networks were improved, including a new bridge over the Bosporus; telecommunications were modernised; and consumer goods, previously hard or impossible to find in the Turkish market, became available. For someone living in Turkey during these years the changes were remarkable. Speaking for myself and my close middle-class environment, the 1980s was the decade when we were able to install a telephone; buy an automatic washing machine and a dish washer – supported by an instalment plan; freely – and openly – purchase foreign currency, when going abroad. Health services also improved and hospitals offering services on par with other European countries were established. Turgut Özal's sudden death in 1993 meant a setback, not only for the economy, but for the general political atmosphere as well. Özal had not only brought governmental stability; he had also contributed to a more relaxed mood in the public sphere, especially concerning two politically sensitive issues: the Kurdish problem and the role of religion in Turkish society.

The social and political tranquillity secured by the military in 1980 had come at a heavy price. The repression that followed targeted all kinds of leftist, rightist or extreme nationalist, and Islamist opposition groups. But the most severe prosecutions hit the Kurdish resistance movement. 'After the military takeover of 1980, Diyarbakır Prison No. 5 became a place in which to crush the Kurdish activists with the use of unspeakable torture' (Başaran 2017: 29). The draconian measures also included prohibition against the Kurdish language (1983). So, for example, cities and towns were forced to adopt Turkish names. Martial law was imposed, followed in 1987 by a state of emergency that was not lifted until 2002. The Kurdish armed resistance organised in the PKK (The Kurdistan Workers' Party) struck back in August 1984 by attacking Turkish security forces in the Kurdish towns of Eruh and Şemdinli. This marked the beginning of an armed struggle between the PKK and the Turkish state that has still not reached a resolution. During this drawn-out conflict, between 30,000 and 40,000 people have been killed, including civilians, PKK guerrillas and security personnel; around 4,000 villages have been evacuated and 4.5 million people displaced (Başaran 2017: 31).

Turgut Özal did not take sides with the military leadership on the Kurdish issue. He shared their concerns in fighting the PKK, but at the same time he argued for a less repressive, more liberal solution, which included an acknowledgement of Kurdish cultural and political demands, including the idea of forming a federation. His liberal stance was also evident in his approach to the role of religion in the public sphere. This concerned the veiling issue especially, which aroused strong feelings in the aftermath of the 1980 military coup; on this issue the military had also pursued a policy of repression. The Council for Higher Education (Yükseköğretim Kurulu, YÖK), established on the initiative of the military command in November 1981, implemented a set of regulations, according to which the Islamic headscarf was banned from university classrooms. Over the following years this led to bitter confrontations between students and staff, sometimes with the intervention of the police and gendarmerie; expulsions from educational programmes; and drawn-out court cases (Özdalga 1998). Having a religious family background, also with Sufi leanings (the Nakshibendi order), Özal did not approve of the ban on the Islamic headscarf (*tesettür*) but made efforts to try to find legal arrangements against such prohibitions. So, with Özal gone an important voice in favour of more open-mindedness was lost. Instead, social and political antagonisms increased, but in new ways.

After the military takeover of 1980, the street violence between leftist and nationalist/rightist groups of the previous decade had been replaced by conflicts related to ethnic minority and Islamic issues. The political landscape changed, but the unity of the country was now challenged on even more serious and insecure grounds. That the solutions to these sensitive and complicated problems lay in consolidating democracy, not circumscribing it, did not penetrate the leading security cadres, or prominent sections of the intelligentsia. It is true that efforts were made to draw Turkey closer to Europe, with the hope of strengthening its democratic institutions, but they were not enough. Neither were they granted sufficient international support. For example, in January 1987 Turkey ratified the rights of individuals to apply to the European Court of Human Rights, and in April the same year Özal applied for membership of the EU. However, to the great disappointment of himself and the democratically minded public, the latter was turned down.

That the unruliness of the 1970s cooled down did not mean that social and political developments became less worrisome. The relative optimism after the military had handed over political leadership to a democratically elected government in 1983 did not last very long and, as already mentioned, the scene took a turn for the worse after Özal's death. Examples of especially dramatic events include the Sivas massacre in July 1993, when thirty-seven authors and intellectuals of mainly Alevi origin, who had gathered for a conference at the Hotel Madımak, were burnt to death by a mob consisting of thousands of Sunni locals pouring out from the Friday prayer in a nearby mosque. The car-bomb assassination of Uğur Mumcu, a leading journalist at the Istanbul daily *Cumhuriyet*, in January 1993, a murder which caused deep indignation in wide circles, was also part of the rising wave of violence. March 1995 marks the date of several days of riots in the Alevi-dominated, working-class neighbourhood of Gaziosmanpaşa in Istanbul. During these events, known as the 'Gazi Quarter riots', twenty-three people were killed and 1,400 wounded, including rioters, police and civilians. To this should be added that, especially after 1993, forced evacuations and burnings of Kurdish villages took place, as well as extrajudicial killings of Kurdish businessmen and activists and the disappearance of hundreds of Kurdish people (Başaran 2017: 31).

Also, when it came to institutional politics, dramatic developments took place. Pro-Islamic Recep Tayyip Erdoğan, an outspoken member of the Welfare Party (Refah Partisi, RP) was sensationally elected mayor of Istanbul in the local elections of March 1994. The following year, the same party took the lead in the general elections, scoring 21.4 per cent of the vote. This may seem a modest figure, but as the biggest representation in parliament (158 out of 550 seats), this granted the formerly demeaned party power to join the government. These were spectacular events that caused outrage among secularists and enthusiasm among Islamists. This polarisation of sentiments and reactions culminated in a military intervention in February 1997, the 'post-modern coup', which led to the dissolution of the Erbakan-led coalition government, closure of the Welfare Party, and a banning from political participation of its chairman and other leading party cadres. Again, the political turmoil came in combination with a deepening economic crisis. The renowned World Bank economist Kemal Dervish was called back to Turkey to shoulder the position as minister of economic affairs. As such he was expected to guarantee that the severe conditions stipulated by new IMF loans were properly applied.

The above-mentioned accounts are but examples of agonising events that in the post-1980 coup period engaged newspapers, TV programmes and a growing number of conferences and workshops organised by the flourishing civil society organisations. However, almost nothing concerning all of this was visible in the official *hutbe*s of the time.

### *Hutbe* Topics

The reluctance to engage in macro-level issues is demonstrated in the titles of authorised *hutbe*s enumerated below. I have classified the topics of 1,283 *hutbe*s published between 1968 and 2006, first in *Diyanet Gazetesi* and after 1999 in *Diyanet Aylık Dergi*, in five categories: religious beliefs/worship; morals/ethics; religious memorial days or seasons; worldly concerns pertaining to daily life, work and health; and political issues, pertaining to the larger society, the nation and the state. Examples of topics in each group are as follows:

Religious beliefs/worship:

'The importance of the congregation (community) in Islam' (30.10.1971), 'There is no place for superstition in religion' (15.11.1971), 'On the subtleties of the [Prophet's] Farewell sermon' (15.01.1973), 'The meaning of the Koran' (01.05.1978), 'The exemplary life of the Prophet' (15.07.1981), 'The first command enjoined by Islam was "read"' (01.12.1986), 'Islam is a religion based on oneness' (04.04.2003).

Morals/ethics:

'The responsibility of parents towards their children' (15.05.1971), 'Business ethics in Muslimhood' (25.12.1971), 'Trouble-making' (01.08.1972), 'Duty and responsibility' (01.08.1973), 'Bread wastage' (15.01.1975), 'Our religion forbids all kinds of smuggling' (01.02.1976), 'Summer vacation and how to bring up (educate) children' (15.07.1978), 'Islam and shopping' (01.05.1979), 'Let's help the blind and the disabled' (15.01.1980), 'Economics and the benefits of saving' (01.07.1981), 'Drinking (of alcohol) is the mother of all evil' (01.03.1982), 'On neighbouring rights in Islam' (01.11.1982), 'Workers' rights and duties' (01.02.1984), 'Visiting someone who is ill' (01.10.1985), 'On supporting foundations and charity organisations' (01.12.1986), 'Respect and tolerance in Islam' (01.08.1988), 'Avoid gossip, slander and the telling of lies' (01.11.1989), 'Telling lies is the mother of all evils' (01.05.1990), 'Security of life and property in Islam' (01.07.1996), 'To control your anger' (01.01.1998), 'On the harm of gambling' (01.08.1998), 'Respect for the elderly' (19.01.2001), 'On the importance of greeting in Islam' (31.08.2001), 'On the harm/damage of smoking' (02.08.2002), 'On the role of religion in society' (13.06.2003), 'On the role of women in Islam' (01.08.2003), 'On good intentions and sincerity in work and deeds' (14.01.2005), 'Communication between generations' (12.08.2005), 'A Muslim desires well-being for others' (13.01.2006), and 'Hospitality' (28.04.2006).

Religious memorial days or seasons:

'Ramadan and fasting' (22.11.1968), 'Sacrifice [*kurban*]' (30.01.1971), 'What the miracle of ascension brings forth' (15.08.1973), 'The [Ramadan] feast and preparation for the feast' (15.01.1973), 'The Night of Pardon [*Berat gecesi*]' (02.08.1972), 'The birth of our Prophet' (15.02.1978), 'Pilgrimage [*hac*] worship' (01.10.1978), 'Emigration [to Medina, *hicret*]' (01.12.1979), 'The night celebrating the birth of the Prophet [*Mevlid kandili*]' (01.01.1982), 'Alms and the due required to be given at the end of Ramadan [*zekat ve fitre*] (01.05.1988), 'The Night of Power [*Kadir gecesi*] and the virtue of the Koran' (01.04.1989), 'On the role and significance of sacrifice [*kurban*] in our religion' (01.07.1989), 'On the meaning and importance of fasting' (01.12.1998), 'The month of Muharrem' (18.02.2005), and 'Let's preserve/protect what we have achieved during Ramadan' (04.11.2005).

Worldly concerns pertaining to daily life, work and health:

'Cholera' (01.11.1970), 'On the importance of cleanliness' (15.12.1970), 'The importance of science' (30.12.1970), 'Cancer' (30.03.1971), 'Primary education' (30.09.1971), 'Islam and art' (15.11.1972), 'Our religion and trees' (15.13.1973), 'Agricultural efforts' (15.05.1974), 'Travelling' (01.09.1974), 'Seamanship/navigation' (15.07.1973), 'Let's protects our forests' (01.09.1977), 'How to protect ourselves from malaria' (15.01.1978), 'New Year's Eve' (15.12.1977), 'The protection of animals' (01.04.1978), 'Remedies against drought' (01.08.1978), 'On the health of children in Islam' (15.06.1979), '"World food day" and the importance in Islam to live a modest life' (01.10.1981), 'Remedies against tuberculosis' (01.01.1983), 'Islam and tourism' (01.05.1983), 'Islam and sport activities' (01.05.1984), 'On the protection of our environment' (01.11.1984), 'On the health of body and psych in Islam' (01.09.1985), 'Traffic accidents' (01.06.1987), 'On the harm of smoking' (01.04.1988), 'On the importance of books and libraries' (01.06.1988), 'The relationship between workers and employers in Islam' (01.11.1988), and 'Ecological balances in Islam' (01.10.2001).

Political issues pertaining to the larger society, the nation and the state:

'Water sleeps, but not the enemy' (15.07.1971), 'To defend your country is like a huge worship' (30.08.1971), 'The importance of military service in Islam and the victory of [30] August' (15.08.1972), 'Let's strengthen our navy' (15.09.1972), 'With respect to the National Day' (15.10.1972),

'Patriotism and defence of the country' (01.05.1973), 'To stay away from imitation/copying [foreign powers/cultures]' (15.12.1973), 'Moral crisis' (15.11.1975), 'On the conquest of Istanbul' (15.05.1976), 'On the conquest of Anatolia by Muslim Turks' (15.08.1977), 'Jihad in our religion' (01.12.1979), 'The drama of the Afghan people' (15.01.1980), 'The reasons for political violence [*anarşi*] and the remedies in knocking it down' (15.02.1980), 'Allah commands justice' (01.02.1981), 'Unity and fraternity' (15.04.1981), 'The importance of the celebration of the victory of [30] August [end of War of National independence] (01.08.1981), 'Our fidelity to our national and religious traditions' (01.12.1981), 'The Çanakkale victory [1915]' (01.03.1982), 'The victory of Malazgirt [1071]' (01.08.1973), 'The Republic' (01.10.1983), 'Patriotism' (01.02.1985), 'Human rights' (01.12.1985), 'The virtue of tolerance' (01.01.1986), 'The role of Islam in our national life' (01.09.1986), 'Martyrdom and war heroism' (01.03.1989), 'On the importance of unity and togetherness in Islam' (01.08.1996), 'Women's rights in Islam' (01.03.1997), 'Justice in Islam' (01.09.1997), 'Let's protect our national and moral values' (01.10.1997), 'The foundation of our Republic' (01.10.1998), 'Our nation is under threat' (01.10.1998), 'The 700th anniversary of the Ottoman Empire' (01.02.1999), 'On the relation between religion and state' (01.08.1999), 'Hypocrisy is a sin that pollutes our society' (27.12.2002), 'Native country/motherland, nation and state for ever' (29.08.2003), 'It is a common duty to contribute to the development of the country' (18.06.2004), 'The Republic represents the social will' (29.10.2004), and 'Respect for human rights' (02.12.2005).

The result of the examination was that the categories related to 'religious beliefs/worship', 'morals/ethics', and 'religious memorial days or seasons', scored around 25 per cent each, while 'worldly concerns relevant to daily life, work and health' and 'political issues, pertaining to the larger society, the nation and the state' scored around 13 per cent each. It goes without saying that these shares are only approximate, since topics are not always easily separated as belonging to one or the other category. Still, even as a rough estimate, it sets the issues related to the wider society, the nation and the state into perspective. However, when looking closer into the topics here classified as 'political', that is, those linked to societal or political macro-issues, they, almost unexceptionally, deal with fixed or canonised national memorial days or other topics of similar abstract or general nature.

They contain but standard nationalist expressions, far removed from current events or developments. The only sermon touching on topicality is 'The drama of the Afghan people', issued on 15 January 1980, the month after the Soviet army had invaded Afghanistan. Another example is the sermon 'The events in Azerbaijan and our brotherhood duty', issued on 1 February 1990, related to a recent crackdown by the Soviet army on independence-minded civilians in Baku.[2] Another sermon alluding to a current topic is 'The Turkish Lira and our national reputation' from 31 August 2001, occasioned by the then ongoing deep crisis of the Turkish economy. To underline even further the magnitude of the silence, it should also be added that during the Arab Spring of 2011, almost a decade into the AKP's holding on to governmental power, not a single *hutbe* touched upon these, for a politically concerned Muslim, crucial events. The deposition of the Tunisian president Zine El Abidine Ben Ali on 14 January 2011, and of President Mubarak on 11 February 2011, the murder of Muammar al-Gaddafi in October 2011, and the political violence leading to civil war in Syria – all these stirring events went unnoticed in the Turkish Friday *hutbes*. The only event of any wider social or political interest that was at all hinted to, was the attack by the PKK in Çukurca in the province of Hakkari on 19 October 2011, with twenty-four soldiers killed, eighteen wounded and an even larger number of PKK fighters killed.[3]

Official Friday sermons rarely touch upon public issues of current interest. When it does happen, it is typically related to events outside the country's borders, and issues that appeal to Turkish nationalist or Muslim *umma* sentiments (such as Azerbaijan and Afghanistan above). It is against that background that I now turn to the minor field investigation of listeners and sermon producers and what they have had to say on the Friday *hutbe* and other related questions. To be sure, the interviews are reproduced in such a way that each interviewee speaks for himself. Interpretative comments are provided only after the presentation of the empirical material.

### Scholar and *Hutbe*-writer (Interview I)

*A critical voice*

Bünyamin Erul (BE) is a professor at the Faculty of Theology, Ankara University. He has specialised in *hadis* literature and has published extensively in this area of research. Professor Erul has close connections to Diyanet, for example as a member of the High Committee for Religious Affairs (Din İşleri Yüksek Kurulu, DİYK) from 2008 to 2020. He has also acted as imam, *hatip* and muezzin and has travelled to various countries in the Muslim world and the West.

BE starts by calling attention to the fact that the word *cuma*, both for Friday and for the Friday noon prayer, is related to gathering, coming together. This corroborates what has been emphasised several times throughout this book that the *cuma* stands out in its capacity as a societal or shared event. It is not religiously valid if performed in solitude. It has to be in a place where the congregation is gathered. Therefore, it is particularly important that the messages given during the Friday sermon are meaningful and edifying. According to BE, however, Turkish official *hutbe*s leave a great deal to be desired in that respect. The focus of BE's critique is especially on repetitiveness, irrelevancy, governmentally pre-ordered sermons, ethnic nationalism, and the lack of engagement and passion in preaching. However, BE underlines that any assessment has to be seen against the background of what Friday *hutbe*s were like in Ottoman times, when, as he claims, the whole ceremony was exclusively in Arabic. Thus, delivering the Friday sermon in Turkish started with the Republic, and is therefore relatively new (see also Chapters 1 and 3).[4]

*Repetitiveness*

Lack of variation, meaning repetition of the same themes, even whole sermons, and cited sacred texts is an important problem, according to BE.

**BE**: Lately, things have improved, that's true. However, during the earlier periods of the Republic there were only a couple of books published by Diyanet[5] and they were read in all the mosques over and over again. Just imagine! Here is a book containing fifty-two *hutbe*s and an imam who has served in the same village for maybe twenty years. So, the congregation has got used to these messages. People already know too well what the imam is going to say, because they have listened to the same admonitions many, many times. And the *hodja* himself does not really know how to write a sermon, because he has not got sufficient education to do so.

In addition, the same narrow selection of Koranic verses is repeated over and over again. Then, there are also certain topics that are constantly reiterated like care for your mother and father, god-fearing (piety), cleanliness, and so on. These are all routinised and stereotyped topics far away from real social problems, from difficulties or frictions in state–government relationships, and from what is happening in the world outside the country's borders.

*Irrelevancy*

The above criticism is closely related to another troubling issue, namely the lack of relevance to daily events and developments, both in local, and larger national and international contexts.

**BE**: Until some six or seven years ago all *hutbe*s were written by Diyanet. The same sermon was read out in all provinces and in all mosques . . . Just think about it! Let's say there is this *hutbe* about traffic. That means traffic rules are brought up as a topic also in villages in the south-east, where there are neither proper roads, nor vehicles! That's absurd . . . However, these kinds of allegedly 'off-side' *hutbe*s have been abandoned.[6] So now, at least, the relevance of the topics may have improved. The problem now, however, is that the texts are poor. Let's say that a couple of district muftis, preachers and religious officials come together in their provincial centre. What they accomplish in terms of language, style and content may not be that bright and edifying.

*Sermons made to order*

Another problematic aspect brought up by BE is state patronage, which manifests itself in ministries and other official administrative units wishing to use *hutbe*s for their own information campaigns.

**BE**: There were times when the state or this or that ministry ordered *hutbe*s to be written on special topics. So, for example, I remember having listened to sermons warning against stomach-flu[7] or other infectious deceases [ordered by the Ministry of Health] . . . There was also a *hutbe* about the dollar, yes, against exchanging dollars in the black market. The thing is that politicians and ministers used to think that a comfortable way to reach out to the people with important information was through the *hutbe*s. And, yes, that's logical, because you reach out to some twenty million people [men] during the Friday noon service. But, if the demands from politicians, ministers, ministries or the government do not conform to the spirit of Islam, and instead verge on absurdness, then it is up to Diyanet to stand up against that.

That is also what has happened, according to BE, because during his time as board member of Diyanet, under directors Ali Bardakoğlu [2003–10] and Mehmet Görmez [2010–17], he has not come across this kind of demand.

*Ethnic nationalism*

Nationalism is a delicate problem. Turkey has a Kurdish minority of around 20 per cent of its population, approximately half of which is living in the eastern regions of the country, and the rest in big cities in the western parts, especially in Istanbul. During the spring of 2013, official initiatives had been undertaken to improve relations – the so called 'peace process' – so at the time of the interview in June 2014, the general atmosphere in Turkey was rather optimistic concerning the odds to reach a lasting solution to a more than thirty year-long conflict. It is against the background of these relatively promising developments that BE expresses his criticism against exaggerated emphasis on Turkish national interests. Ethnic enmities, which had grown increasingly serious for several decades, were generally played down at this time.

**BE**: The *hutbe*s express a nationalistic discourse . . . Well, of course, during the republican era there was unavoidably a stress on Turkishness, the Turkish nation, Turkish society, the Turkish republic, an so on. At that time this was perhaps not an expression of racism, but nowadays it is different. You know, the Kurdish problem, the eastern problem; these are burning issues. If a preacher talked about 'the Turkish nation' during the forties and fifties, this was not understood as a discourse that separated Kurds from Turks. These were rather uttered within the framework of a common nation state. However, later on, during the last thirty to forty years, non-Turkish groups have started to feel uncomfortable about this.

Yes, such [ethnic] expressions are now being criticised. For example, I experienced a similar thing, when I was travelling in the Arab world. They would talk about the 'Arab nation', but here am I, and I am not an Arab. When they make separations like that, I inevitably show a reaction, asking 'So, who am I here?' However, they [preachers] should rather use umbrella concepts such as 'the Islamic community' or 'the community of Muslims', which would include all Muslims, without making any difference between race, colour, and language . . . Because what we have learned from the Koran and the Prophet is that we should not use a dissociative, but a unifying language . . . The language of preaching (*hitap*) should not be a language that divides, but that unifies.

There is all this talk about fostering good citizens. Now, this may be evaluated in two ways. A state would always want to be spared troublemakers. This holds true for any political system, any religion. In the end, why do we have religion? In order to secure peace in society and among its people. This is so for Christianity, Buddhism and other religions. So, to raise good [nation-minded] citizens is not in itself a negative thing.

However, what we want is not to foster good citizens only. For us, that is, us Muslims, the real fatherland (*vatan*) is the Muslim/Islamic abode (*İslam coğrafyası*). The concept we really should consider is *umma* [Turkish: *ümmet*], meaning any community sharing the same religion. Christianity is an *umma*, Jewishness is an *umma*, and Islam is an *umma*. Wherever there are Muslims living within the Islamic geography, they are brothers. The Prophet used the beautiful image of 'being like one body'. If any part of the body is ill, that person encounters problems, like insomnia, getting high temperature. In a similar way, no Muslim can stay inconsiderate to any problem existing in the Islamic abode. People starving to death, terrorism, earthquakes . . . Muslims reach out to such problem-stricken areas and come to their rescue. They pray for an end to fighting and chaos. Muslims should think about such support as a whole. Not only limited to us, living here in Turkey. A brother living in Malaysia should think about problems in Turkey as part of his own problem. So, when we say fatherland (*vatan*) we should not only think about the present national borders. Yes, it is true that this is our fatherland, [the country] in which we are living, but a Macedonia, a Bosnia, an Azerbaijan, a Turkmenistan is also our fatherland. Because the people living there are also our brothers. We think in broader terms, and therefore the language we use in our *hutbe*s has to be far from such ethnic elements and embrace Muslims in the broadest possible sense. So, we should not only promote good citizens. Our aim should be to foster good Muslims.

**EÖ**: So, what is then meant by being a good Muslim?

**BE**: Our [religious professionals] ideal is to convey an image of the good Muslim, which is based on the principles of the Koran, and all available knowledge related to the Prophet as a role model. When trying to reach out to the believers through our *hutbe*s, our aim is to show Islam as a friendly, coherent/logical religion.

Unfortunately, however, today, as well as in the past, there are people who have misused the *hutbe*s, who have tried to use them for their own political aims, their vile personal ambitions, prejudices, animosity.

### Engagement and passion

Eloquence is also something that is missing in Turkish *hutbe* oratory, according to BE. Homiletic traditions are much more powerful in the Arab world than in Turkey. There, the proficiency of the preachers is also on a more distinguished level.

**BE**: The person performing the *hutbe* [in Arab countries] may be a university teacher or a famous religious scholar, ulema . . . As a listener, you don't even have to know Arabic in order to understand how powerful their speech is. Without using any notes or documents whatsoever, they hold their addresses extemporaneously. They speak out directly and in a very convincing and energetic way. Yes, they really deliver their *hutbe*s so powerfully.

**EÖ**: And how about Turkey?

**BE**: Unfortunately, we have not reached that level. We are still suffering from shortcomings, flaws. For one, concerning language and style we have not reached the right maturity. We have not found that affectionate pitch, the kind of discourse, language and style that draws the interest of the audiences. If only a few out of a hundred people coming out of the mosque remember what the *hutbe* was about, that means the topic was uninspired, that the address was not stirring enough . . . Our *hutbe*s are dead, if I may use such an expression.

### People expect better hutbes

**EÖ**: So, what are the remedies? How does one come to terms with these inadequacies?

**BE**: Yes, that's what people say: 'We expect more powerful *hutbe*s from Diyanet.' They find the Friday sermons poor. Maybe it is all right for someone only having a primary school education, but for someone with a university degree, a general director, a bureaucrat, a university lecturer, such people expect something more satisfactory, more qualified.

People would say: 'When I go there and when I listen to the *hutbe* for five or ten minutes, then I also expect to learn something.' When the same messages are repeated, it is like serving hash to the congregation. Or, let's say the *hatip* starts his sermon saying: 'Dear congregation, Today's topic is, honour your father and your mother.' Well, then people just stop listening! Oh, the same old stuff again! No, what we suggest is that the preacher should start the sermon in such a way that it triggers the curiosity of the audience. To hold a long speech is easy. But to prepare a sententious text is more difficult.

Voice is also important. Reading a text without compassion or proper diction is also worthless. Once I prepared a *hutbe* for Diyanet on 'time consciousness'. Well, this time I had to listen to my own *hutbe*, read by another *hatip*. Oh, my dear, I said to myself. I should have asked the permission to read this myself. That beautiful text fell on deaf ears, because it was read without proper empathy and diction.

I have suggested – but without success – that, in Ankara, for example, instead of having the same *hutbe* for all mosques we should select some four or five of the biggest and most popular mosques, those having several thousands of auditors, and then announce in advance both the topic of the *hutbe* and the name of the preacher for each of those mosques. In that way people could decide for themselves which mosque to attend, which *hatip*, which topic to listen to. As things now are, people routinely go to the mosque closest by or the one most comfortable to reach.

*Civil disobedience*

How has BE in his practice as imam and *hatip* handled the described shortcomings? Sometimes, this means having to force given rules and regulations.

**BE**: Here at the Faculty [of Theology] we hold our own *hutbe*s. We have not asked Diyanet to have one of their imams appointed to our *mescit*.[8] Instead, we rotate among each other. So, sometimes, I also lead the Friday *hutbe*. Now, of course, the people coming here – some 2,000 attenders – are people from various universities in and around our neighbourhood, so here we have the opportunity to act according to our preferences. What we do is, we print 300 copies of the *hutbe*, which we place at the entrance door. If the audience like the sermon, they take a copy on their way out. So, if we run out of copies, it means they approved of it. If we don't, we understand they found it boring.

Young people, such as our assistants, tell us: 'Please, prepare more sophisticated [lecture-like] *hutbe*s.' However, a *hutbe* should not be like a scholarly presentation. The *hutbe* is not a place for academic lecturing. On the other hand, however, the texts should be above the level of Diyanet's *hutbe*s.

Before I started my university studies, I stayed as imam for about a year at the central courthouse in Ankara. There is also a small *mescit* and the congregation is made up of judges, prosecutors and lawyers. The State Security Court was also located there. There was a press centre as well. So, that was the context, in which I held my *hutbe*s.

This was at a time [middle of the 1980s], when we were obliged to read the *hutbe*s published by Diyanet's monthly magazine. But I did not pay regard to that. What I did was wrong [against the regulations]. If anyone had complained, I could have been subjected to an investigation. I could have lost my job.

Well, the alternative would have been to write the *hutbe* and send it to the *müftülük*. The *müftülük* would then have passed it on to Diyanet in order to await approval. A long procedure! Maybe I was too rebellious. But here I was among people who all had a university degree, they were all jurists . . . So, I had to offer them different things. I did not know then how long I would stay there, but as long as I remained in that position, I would have to offer some proper instruction . . . During the first three months I told them about the basics of belief . . . the belief in Allah, how to conceptualise the Prophet, the understanding of predestination, afterlife. After that I passed to the forms of worship and kept talking about that for a couple of months . . . I, for my part, studied concepts from their field such as justice, rights, jurisprudence, persecution, testimony, and so on . . . They showed great interest. After the Friday prayer, on my way to another part of the building to have tea with a friend, I was stopped by one of our lawyers, who was fervently talking to two women, friends of ours. He turned to me and said: '*Hodjam, hodjam* [my *hodja*], please come! I was just telling about your *hutbe*.' So, if my sermon had become a topic related to these friends after the *hutbe* . . . [that was an important acknowledgement].

Similar thing, when I served as imam in an industrial part of the city, artisans and craftsmen made up my audience. There, I chose topics more related to loans, marketing, business transactions, rights and laws . . . I chose these kinds of [for them relevant] topics and I held very fervent, exciting and striking sermons. The mosque overflowed and people continued to gather outside.

## Vaaz *and* hutbe

Two principal shortcomings with respect to Turkish *hutbe* preaching are raised in the interview with BE: the inadequate address of current social and political issues, and the poverty concerning oratorical eloquence. As a matter of fact, both questions are closely interconnected. What BE draws attention to is the relationship between the liturgical and the preaching (*vaaz*) part of the *hutbe*. In the example taken from his experience of *hutbe* performances in Arab countries, the sermonising part, where the imam addresses problems of more current public interest, is much more pronounced there than in his own country. In Turkey, the *vaaz* section has more or less atrophied or withered. This pattern is even more pronounced in the Central Asian Turkic republics. BE describes the situation there in the following way:

**BE**: A while ago I was in Kazakhstan and stayed there for two weeks . . . In Kazakhstan the *hatip* only symbolically mounts the *minber*. He reads a verse from the Koran and a *hadis*, and then he descends. He does not deliver any message at all. What is the reason for that? Well, maybe because of the state. If [the *hatip*] ventured to give an address, he may get himself into trouble. In the end, it suits the interests of the state authorities to keep such problems off. Do people perform their *namaz*? Yes, they do! Do they say their prayers? Yes, they do! Then, that's enough.

## *Summing-up*

In spite of the striking similarities, the Turkish version of the Friday sermon is not as simplified or shortened as the Kazakh. Still, in Turkey, the spoken part is far from being as distinct and significant – often eloquent – as in Arab countries, such as Egypt and Jordan. However, even if BE looks with some envious admiration towards Arab practices, he is also aware of the fact that eloquence and freer oratory comes at a price. In Egypt and Jordan, for example, *hutbe*s have been used for promotion of personal ambitions and mobilisation of the masses for a political cause (see Gaffney 1994 and Antoun 1989). This constitutes a problem for their governments, who have increased central control of *hutbe* preaching, that is, entered upon a Turkish course.

What has been said above does not mean that there is no place for freer preaching in Turkish religious life. *Vaaz* is a common way of addressing audiences inside the mosques as well as in other places and at different times of the week. But, as BE points out, in Turkey the *vaaz* has partly been separated from the *hutbe*, while in the Arab world the *hutbe* also includes a longer *vaaz* exposition. In Turkey, it has become customary to have a *vaaz*, which can be very long, before the Friday noon service. However, the fact that a longer *vaaz* is separated from the *hutbe* also means that it loses some of its official authority.

Looking at the Turkish *cuma* as a ceremony, where the sermonising (*vaaz*) part is of minor importance, further strengthens the notion of the *hutbe* as a primarily liturgical event. When the space allowed for free oratory and eloquence is limited, ritual elements get the upper hand, an observation that supports the overall conclusions of this book.

## Audiences (Interview II)

SA was born in the middle of the 1960s. He has a village farmer-family background and got his secondary education in an Imam-Hatip Lisesi. For his higher education, he studied law and has worked as prosecutor, and, at the time of the interview, as judge in Ankara.

*Religion – the most important source of national unity*

According to SA, religion, with its various forms of worship and holy abodes, is one of the most important institutions when it comes to providing national unity in Turkey.

**SA:** Since the last one or two years we are facing different kinds of problems in this country, aren't we? [PKK; Gezi events in Istanbul, May–June 2013, spreading over the whole country; corruption scandals, December 2013]. Look at other countries! Look at Ukraine, for example. In that country we can witness similar antagonisms, but there, people flew at each other's throats. They even went to war. In our country developments did not go that far.

**EÖ**: Is there a reason for that?

**SA**: Well, the basic reason is this: here, we have this unity and togetherness amongst people. Even those at the utmost right and the utmost left have certain things in common. They participate in funerals together. They go to the Friday prayer together. Such common activities reduce enmity among people.

According to SA, mosques contribute to the safeguarding of national unity, but that is not enough to obtain nation-wide unanimity.

**SA**: No, it is certainly not enough, but this unity in religion constitutes a very important common point in our relations. Yes, we have a unified country, Turks and Kurds . . . If they have been able to live together for years, one of the most important factors is related to our beliefs . . . The most important common point in our country is religion.

This also means that the topics raised during the *hutbe* have to deal with common issues. Common issues mean issues related to religious questions. Political issues are generally avoided in *hutbe*s, because the congregation consists of people coming from very different environments – both concerning political parties and general outlook. Entering into thoses kinds of [controversial] issues means the common ground is at risk . . . Therefore, I think that Diyanet is doing the right thing. It is successful in the sense that it avoids focusing on topics that may cause trouble.

However, when it comes to the performance of the imams, SA is not so sure about their qualifications and judgements.

**SA**: Imams, that's a different thing!

*Sincerity and piety in worship*

The mosque is a symbol for unity and togetherness, according to SA. So, what determines which mosque to choose for the Friday noon prayer?

**SA**: What is the purpose of religious worship? We talk about god-fearing [*takva*]. Sincerity [*samimiyet*] in worship is also very important in our belief . . . So, what the listener considers are things like the style of recitation.

For example, who reads the Koran most beautifully? . . . However, most of the time you don't have much of a choice. If you are at work and you have a lunchbreak between twelve o'clock and one o'clock, then you would generally choose the mosque nearest by. But, if you have some free time, then you can choose a mosque that offers the Koran-recitations you like better, that is, where the Koran is recited more beautifully, more sincerely. But the physical appearance of the mosque is also important. Then, for example, you can choose to go to 'Diyanet's mosque' [pompous mosque adjacent to the Directorate's main building in Ankara, built 2009–13], or the Kocatepe mosque [impressive mosque in central Ankara, built 1967–87] . . . It is not much different from how you evaluate the place you live in. If your home is beautiful, you feel more peaceful, don't you? Yes, it adds something, when the place is more spacious.

**EÖ**: How about the congregation? How important is it that you know the people gathering for the Friday *hutbe*?

**SA**: True, the congregation is also important. Just like in the university. There is a difference between listening to a lecture together with people you like, and listening to the same lecture together with ordinary people you don't know. However, generally, the congregation is not something you choose. People are not coming there for any other purpose than to take part in the prayer.

However, according to SA, there was a time, when the congregation (*cemaat*) made a great difference.

**SA**: It was something quite different, when we were students. There was this mosque close to our faculty. So, we would generally go there many students together. The *hodja* was young. We were about twenty years old at that time. He was in his thirties. Then, he really took up touching subjects. And he would speak extemporaneously, very facilely. For example, I will never forget his sermon about Mehmet Akif [see Interview V, below] and the circumstances related to his writing of the national anthem . . . This sermon was held in relation to a kind of anniversary, and it impressed me so much. This was sometime between 1986 and 1990. We went there every week. He spoke livelier, more fluidly. We would skip our lunch in order to go there. So, we sacrificed our lunch . . . Maybe our excitement was due to our youthfulness, or maybe it was because this *hodja* really was able to convey different impressions and feelings.

## Audiences (Interview III)

BC is a fourth-year political science student, who is making plans for advanced studies. He comes from one of Turkey's eastern provinces and has Arabic as his first language. His relatives originate from Syria, which, at the time of their migration, was still part of the Ottoman Empire. The five-time prayer is routine in his family. As for himself he adopted this practice in high school.

*Islam is more than just worship*

BC is critical when it comes to the topics addressed in the Friday *hutbe*s.

**BC**: Yes, we [me and my friends] often discuss the *hutbe* topics among ourselves [after the noon service]. Generally, we discuss more if the *hutbe* has been on a topic related to daily events. Last week the *hutbe* was on praying. How is praying performed, and things like that. To be honest, we did not mention about that very much . . . But, if the *hutbe* concerns a current event, it is different. For example, three or four weeks ago it was related to Somalia. Then, when we got out, we discussed that question among ourselves. For example, what was the reason such a topic was chosen? How could that be explained? When the *hutbe* is related to daily events, we discuss it more.

Look at all the problems around! In spite of this, *hutbe*s are prepared as if these problems did not exist . . . Instead, the Friday *hutbe* should be recognised for what it is, namely a weekly gathering for Muslims. It is like a weekly conference for believers. In that situation, it is not appropriate to just talk about topics such as the origin of our *kandil*s [blessed nights], when and how they have been practised, our obligations in relation to these festivities, and so on. It is as if they think that Muslims are detached and unaware of what is going on in the real world around them.

On second thoughts, however, BC notes the problems and complexity involved in finding the right pitch when composing a Friday sermon.

**BC**: Everyone interprets the *hutbe* according to his own background and understanding. Some people are more traditional and approve of the emphasis on *hadis* and traditions. Others are supporters of reform, that is, they prefer an understanding of religion that is more in tune with the contemporary world. They [the latter] are generally more critical. After all, everyone makes an evaluation according to his own thoughts and values.

And, BC adds, in the middle of these differing strands, Diyanet pursues its own principles.

**BC**: Those who share [Diyanet's] position do not generally have a problem [with the *hutbe*s]. Their emphasis is on worship . . . But, as I see it, one cannot separate worship from daily life. Worship and daily life are integrated into each other. Both are of equal importance. That's why I object to the course taken by Diyanet. It puts too much emphasis on worship.

Because Islam is not only a religion for worship. Islam is a religion that bestows a way of life that encompasses everything. Therefore, it is not enough to speak about worship only; for example, how to celebrate the *kandil*s, how to read this, how to do that . . . That is not enough for me. True, there has to be a place for these sacred commemorations as well, but it is not enough.

**EÖ**: So, should there be more emphasis on political questions?

**BC**: The thing is not to bring up politics every here and there, but to give more emphasis to societal issues of relevance for the audiences.

*The importance of good imams*

Diyanet is criticised by BC for not bringing up relevant public issues, but would it be better if each imam/*hatip* prepared his own *hutbe*?

**BC**: Actually, I don't think so. Because, unfortunately, imams are neither particularly refined intellectually, nor enough qualified when it comes to religious knowledge. On some topics they are really deficient. Therefore, it would be wrong to take such a risk. So, to let every imam write his own *hutbe* may not be the best thing to do. And, I don't say this out of elitism . . . Think about a university: all faculty members don't hold the same standard. Similarly, all imams are not equally good.

**EÖ**: An example?

**BC**: Think about an imam who talks about an event from the life of the Prophet. However, his knowledge is not very good, so he starts enlarging on the topic, telling stories according to his own mind. And, even if he is not telling outright lies, he claims that these stories are true. I don't approve of such storytelling at all. So, rather than having imams steering in the wrong direction, the present situation is better . . . People in the higher ranks of Diyanet have better theological and academic qualifications. Therefore, it is, in spite of it all, more appropriate that they prepare the *hutbe*s. It is just that I would like the topics to be more focused on societal [*toplumsal*] issues.

*Hutbe*s dealing with contemporary social and political events are rare, according to BC, but they are also the ones that stand out as especially memorable.

**BC**: For example, a couple of years ago I listened to a *hutbe* related to the Middle East and Syria. It was about brotherhood. It was not a new *hutbe*. But at that time there was a great need for that kind of sermon, because the Syrians [as refugees] were really alienated and in a bad condition. They were discriminated even by Muslims. This was a topic that touched upon both social and religious issues. So, in both respects this was a strong *hutbe*.

*Being part of a large congregation*

As much as the imam, the mosque also plays an important role for the general atmosphere of the performance.

**BC**: I usually go to the mosque nearest by for the Friday *hutbe*; around 90 per cent [of the time] I do that. But I have also made it a habit to visit well-known mosques when I go to a different city. I am, so to speak, 'touring' different mosques.

**EÖ**: What is so special about a bigger mosque?

**BC**: If you perform your prayer in a *mescit*, the whole ceremony is trivialised. For example, the *mescit* on our campus is like that. It is mediocre. You don't experience much of the spirituality in that atmosphere. But if you go to a mosque like Kocatepe [see above], there would be maybe 10,000 people gathered for prayer. That's extraordinary . . . The preacher is very good, the imam is very good, and the sound system is terrific . . . That really affects you. So, to pray in mosques like that is much more exalting, I think.

There is a big difference between praying together with five people and doing so together with 5,000 people. There you are, as one of this big crowd. That really gives you the sense of belonging to a society. That's a great experience.

## Audiences (Interview IV)

CD is about to finish his university studies in history in one of the high-ranking universities in Turkey. His parents, who are both government employees, came originally from a middle-sized town in central Anatolia and are both practising Muslims. As a small child CD would attend the Friday *hutbe* together with his family, but at the end of primary school, he started to go on his own initiative, especially if his father was away from home. That there is a deeper dimension to the question of why a person attends the Friday sermon, is brought up by this person, who stands out in his religious mindfulness.

### Whose free will?

**CD**: To say that I went to the mosque based on my own free will [*irade*] is not quite correct. It is not that my family would force me to do so, that's not what I mean. However, such an act is ultimately based on the mercy of God [*Allah'ın bir lütfüdür*]. Yes, with that reservation, I could maintain that I went there of my own, yet insignificant [*cüz-i*], free will.

Concerning the five daily prayers, I try to do that, but I have not been doing so ever since I was a child. It was only after I had started at the university that I tried to make that a practice. It would, however, have been better, had I started earlier. No, it was at the university that I started to do so.

### Listening to the hutbe requires training and awareness

Before evaluating the messages conveyed through the *hutbe*s, CD emphasises the general character and significance of this performance.

**CD**: There are certain rules or guidelines which give the *cuma* its special character. First, it has to be performed in a mosque or *mescit* together with a congregation. Second, it contains a *hutbe*, and third, it includes a *namaz* made up of two prostrations [*rekat*] . . . These three acts together constitute a religious obligation [*farz*]. To listen to the *hutbe* is as much obligatory as it is to perform the obligatory prayer.

Before I was really aware of the importance ascribed to the *hutbe*, I can't say I listened very carefully all the time. Through the years I sometimes have; sometimes I have not been able to pay that much attention. However, there are also other things that may affect the atmosphere. A few years ago, I used to live in a place close to the prime minister's house [Recep Tayyip Erdoğan]. When he came to the mosque things would turn to disarray. Such things surely may disturb the concentration . . . However, since becoming aware of the importance attributed to the *hutbe*, I listen with pure attention.

That does not mean that CD would look up the *hutbe* on Diyanet's homepage in order to be better prepared for the sermon.

**CD**: No, I would not look up the *hutbe* on the Internet beforehand, even though I know it is displayed there. If I did, I could easily read it in a minute, but that would distract my listening during the *hutbe*. Which does not mean that I sometimes, on the way to the Friday prayer, try to imagine what it is going to be about.

*Common concerns*

During the Friday sermon Muslims are brought together to share common concerns. CD believes that this is fundamental for the safeguarding of the religious community.

**CD**: One shouldn't fail to acknowledge that the meaning of the Friday noon prayer is for Muslims to come together in order to contemplate shared daily concerns . . . The aim is to raise the level of consciousness and awareness among the believers. It is when people come together to help each other to become better Muslims that they really consolidate themselves as a community [*cemaat*]. That's one of the most important characteristics of the *hutbe*. That's how I see it.

**EÖ**: How about the mosque?

**CD**: When it comes to mosques there are a couple of alternatives around here, but I usually go to the smaller *mescit* on campus. The people gathering there are mostly students my age and I feel I belong more to that congregation. We have our studies and our approach to Islam in common.

*To invite someone for lunch after the* hutbe

The Friday sermon doesn't end with the noon service, according to CD. It is also the starting point for wider socialising under the spell of the preaching ceremony.

**CD**: Of course, we often discuss the *hutbe* when the ceremony is over. Even if we don't exactly touch upon the topics addressed during that particular sermon, our conversations and discussions take place under the impact of what has been said. That's also one of the deeper meanings of the *hutbe* . . . It encourages us to take up discussions related to the word of God and the deeds of the Prophet. Thereby, it is ensured that important common Islamic concerns are voiced and reflected upon, which is another important thing [about the *hutbe*].

One should not overlook that there also are *hadis* related to what to do after the *hutbe*. According to some Prophetic traditions, the believer is urged to offer a meal. Other *hadis* encourage people to continue busying themselves with daily chores for the sake of their daily bread. Or continue their business in the market as usual.

As for us, we take up socialising, while we also carry on with our conversations about the *hutbe*. Maybe you see a friend on the way out from the mosque, and you take him to a cafeteria, or you invite him home for lunch, or you go to some other place. And, like that, our company and discussions continue, related or unrelated to that day's sermon.

*Difficulties in writing a good* hutbe

**CD**: Generally, a *hutbe* starts with a Koranic verse or a *hadis*, or both. Then follows a commentary and an exposition on its meaning. After that follows an interpretation of these holy texts based on quotations or extracts by leading scholars.

**EÖ**: So, how difficult is it to write a *hutbe*?

**CD**: In technical terms it is not so difficult, I guess. Someone with a degree in theology could easily compose a well-designed *hutbe*. However, to choose appropriate and relevant topics, which are related to current, daily events, means you need to know Turkey very well – both how Islam is understood and lived in this country, and what the social and political problems facing Turkey are like. That's what makes it so difficult. For that reason, it is also essential that [*hutbe*s are prepared] by a recognised authority.

**EÖ**: So, to have the imams prepare their own sermons is not a solution?

**CD**: Let's say the imams were enjoined to write their own *hutbe*s. God forbid! This could even trigger disputes about the *hutbe*. It is true that in other parts of the Islamic world imams prepare their own *hutbe*s. There, one imam may, from his mosque, criticise what another imam has said from his location. That's not possible in Turkey. Here, such practices would be conceived as a big threat.

*Diyanet – a necessary and expanding authority*

Even if the interviewee is critical of many things done and delivered by Diyanet, there is a need for an acknowledged authority.

**CD**: To maintain religious authority is very important. A religious authority is important in order to prevent factionalism [*fitne*], discord [*tefrika*] and political party divisions. In this respect Diyanet fulfils an important function.

Still, to be honest, Diyanet has its limits. According to my understanding, the religious authority should not be subordinated to the political. Politics is only one section of a larger whole, and that is religion. But the dominant understanding today is the reverse. It is a system in which religion is treated as if it were an institution below the political. Diyanet is, as is well known, subordinated to the prime minister's office. So, in a system based on modern/secular laws there is a limit to Diyanet's area of influence. But this is changing now.

CD is of the opinion that, lately, Diyanet has expanded its areas of influence.

**CD**: Diyanet is on the rise. It is penetrating deeper into society. We notice this in the way Diyanet grows and is branching out. Then, there are also other religious foundations working in close cooperation with Diyanet. You can also notice this trend in the diversification of publications issued by Diyanet. In addition, it has also come in as an actor in foreign relations, something that can be observed in many different ways. Our directors [Diyanet] travel to Africa, where they meet with religious leaders on various levels. They gather information about their problems and report them back to Turkey.

### Audiences (Interview V)

DE is a third-grade engineering student who grew up in Istanbul. His mother is a member of well-known Sufi network and it was she who taught DE how to pray. He also attended Koran courses, which are usually organised during the summer holidays.

*May your* cuma *be blessed!*

**DE**: I come from a generally conservative and religious family . . . In the high school I went to, there was no *mescit*. Neither would the principal give us permission to go to the nearby mosque for the Friday *hutbe*, because it overlapped with course hours. But, once – I think it was on one occasion – it was towards the end of the last semester, we were allowed to go, and that was really very nice.

Now, at the university where I am studying, there is a *mescit*. And I usually go there for the Friday *hutbe*. I usually go there on my own, but since it is on campus, I usually come across friends there, or someone I know. But what I like most about going to this *mescit* is that when we come out from the Friday prayer we embrace and congratulate each other, saying 'Tekabbel Allah', which is Arabic, meaning 'Allah kabul etsin' [May God accept it]. We usually use the Arabic phrase. But we also say: 'Cuman mübarek olsun' [May your *cuma* be blessed], while we greet each other by taking the other person's hand between our own two hands, which is an expression for *salavat* [blessings on the Prophet and his descendants].

These greeting habits add sincerity, a sense of solidarity and intimacy to the Friday gatherings, according to DE. Otherwise, the *hutbe* itself does not generally become a topic of deliberation.

**DE**: We really don't discuss the topic of the *hutbe*. Actually, and I am sorry to say this, we usually forget the subject. Sometimes we think that the same topics are repeated over and over again. There should be more talk on concrete and current daily events. In that respect the Prophet himself constitutes a good example. It would be great if we could live up to that. But it seems we can't. We are stuck with unspecific and abstract topics. We [me and my friends] are not so happy with that all the time. That the *hutbe* is read from an already prepared text also has a dampening effect. Maybe it would be better if the imams prepared their own *hutbe*s as they used to do in former times, instead of having them written by people at Diyanet.

However, DE adds, the *hutbe*s are not that disappointing all the time.

**DE**: Sometimes [the *hutbe*] may also leave deeper imprints. For example, there is one particular *hutbe* I remember very well; it's a *hutbe* I will never forget, because it impressed me a lot. This happened recently. It was a *hutbe* on the *hadis* 'The person is with his beloved one'. Well, the message was that if you lose someone you love, or if someone leaves for a faraway place and you know that you will never meet again, you should not grieve too much, because you will meet in the next world . . . So, therefore you should not go against that. Now, that sermon was also supported with verses from the Koran. I liked this talk very much, because at that time I was having troubles, was kind of depressed . . . so therefore I will never forget this sermon . . . Of course, it so happens that we talk about the *hutbe* afterwards, but normally it is not a subject for discussion.

So, according to DE, an interesting *hutbe* may beat distress and inattention.

**DE**: When I feel distressed, for example, if the coursework is too heavy or my friends do things that upset me, I cannot concentrate on what is being said. But, as I just said, if the topic of the *hutbe* is interesting, or if there is a verse from the Koran or a *hadis* that catches my attention, then I am all ears. And, I forget my other problems.

### A crowded congregation

A large congregation outweighs a beautiful mosque or an eloquent *hutbe*.

**DE**: Of course, aesthetics play a role. It is great to be able to go to the newly restored Ortaköy Mosque [by the Bosporus], for example, or Sultan Ahmet [Blue Mosque] or Süleymaniye [all in Istanbul] with their classical Ottoman architecture. I wouldn't say that the Friday prayer therefore is more meaningful or valuable. You can't say that there are more powerful and less powerful *cuma*s. It is rather that they are different. They provide a different experience. Sometimes I perform the prayer in a melancholic mood; sometimes I feel more spirited. For example, when I go to the Süleymaniye Mosque I perform my prayers with greater zeal.

**EÖ**: So, what is the reason for that?

**DE**: Well, I think, it is because this mosque was founded by Süleyman the Magnificent [Kanuni, 1494–1568] and built by Mimar Sinan [famous Ottoman architect, 1489–1588]. Here, you really feel the atmosphere and it renders a deeper feeling of mystique, yes, it is different.

But, the extent of the gathering is very important. It doesn't matter how beautiful the mosque, or how eloquent the *hutbe*, or how compelling the atmosphere, if there is just a small congregation it doesn't work. Then, I really can't enjoy it.

### National unity for the sake of Islam

Mehmet Akif Ersoy (1873–1936),[9] author of the national anthem, is the by far most often quoted poet in the *hutbe*s. On the question of whether there is a special reason for that DE answered:

**DE**: Mehmet Akif is a symbolic name. There is something special about him. On the one hand, he is the author of the national anthem; on the other, he suffered a lot from the Kemalist ideology. Those were difficult times for him.

He was courageous. He was prepared to carry the Islamic mission to the very end. So, when his poems are cited in the *hutbe*s it makes a difference. You are reminded about your duties. Like, you are a Muslim, be careful! Watch your step! As said in the Independence March, 'you are son of a martyr, don't offend your forefathers'. You owe something to your own history. This is what I understand from his poems.

Mehmet Akif did certainly not write poems for artistic reasons. His mission was different. It concerned all the losses suffered by Muslims! He could not accept that state of affairs. He especially could not stand the defeats suffered by the Ottomans against the West. He wanted Islam to reclaim its supremacy. His mission was that Islam once again should prevail on earth. Not in a political sense, though. 'Establish an Islamic state, and let's live there!' No, it was not that kind of thing. He wanted to arouse awareness among Muslims; a willingness to show their superiority to the rest of the world; superiority in being the most prominent, the most outstanding human beings. Yes, his aim was to wake them up.

He often made references to history. We know that he was giving examples from Turks, Ottomans, Seljuks. His frame of reference was for the period after, not before Islam. Ethnic roots, ethnicity, was not a priority for him. However, what he wanted to say was that the Ottomans, together with the Seljuks, were the carriers of Islam for about nine to ten centuries. Maybe this was the most powerful Islamic statehood in history. Therefore, I think he thought that we [the people of Turkey, heirs to the Ottoman and Seljuk sultanates] must maintain our special entitlement [to Islam]. This is what I sense from his poems.

The relationship between Islam and national unity is complex. Islam plays an important role in securing national solidarity, but, says DE, national unity also constitutes a support for Islam.

**DE**: National unity is of course very important. But the ethnic aspect should not be exaggerated . . . The problem today is not so much with Turkey as with Muslims living in other parts of the world. For example, Egypt is having big problems, Palestine is another issue and Afghanistan is yet a different case. Looking around, maybe Turkey is the most suitable place to be a Muslim.

Therefore, we should protect our national unity, so that again we will be able to say: 'We are the protectors of Islam, we protect Islam.' We should act in such a way that we deserve to say so.

It is sad to learn about all this disintegration and splits among Muslims. Muslims are suffering in Palestine, in China, that is, Xinjiang – from China to Africa, lots of suffering. However, Turkey can act as a guardian here. Turkey can prevent these break-ups. That's also what [the government's] foreign policy is aiming at. That's how I see things.

### Audiences (Interview VI)

EF is a fourth-year economics student. He has no intentions of taking up higher studies. Instead, he is trying to get out into the job market and is looking forward to earning his own money. He comes from a middle-sized town in south-west Anatolia. His father is a retired imam, and he is the youngest of five siblings. Thanks to his father's profession EF has a degree of inside information when it comes to sermonising; so what does he think about Diyanet's Friday *hutbes*?

**EF**: *Hutbe*s are useful. Not because they particularly often become a topic of discussion, but because they serve as important reminders in a society marked by haste and rush, where we tend to forget our religious values.

*Hutbe*s are also important because they provide a kind of measure with which to evaluate what you go through or experience over the period of a week. There must be some recognised standards, both concerning religious and daily current issues.

But Diyanet would reach out to their audiences more powerfully if they prepared more captivating *hutbe*s. There is, for example, a lack of diversity. There should also be other professional groups like economists, sociologists and psychologists in the *hutbe* commissions, not only people from within Diyanet itself. But maybe they already recieve help from such specialists. That's more than I know.

*An imam intent on writing his own* hutbes

**EF**: My father was an imam, so that means I started to go the mosque very early. Even though I didn't know the rituals I was taking part in the daily prayers, pretending I knew how to do it. The congregation was generally made up of elderly people. I was having a very good time with them.

My father spent a lot of time in the mosque, since at that time imams were responsible for almost everything related to the mosque – even the cleaning.

My father enjoyed preparing his own *hutbe*s. There was an episode that he often told us about. It happened when he was serving as imam in a village and a couple of inspectors came there to listen to him . . . At that time, as far as I know, imams prepared their own *hutbe*s, either the whole or part of it . . . My father had a considerable library at home. He used to say that he prepared very good *hutbe*s, based on what he had collected from his books. Well, after that, he was appointed to a larger city in that region. I don't know for sure, but it seems that the inspectors noticed his performance and used that as a reference in his favour.

My father used to think that Diyanet's *hutbe*s caused laziness among imams. He used to say: 'Imams are constantly reading the same sura, whereas in our time we read all of them. At an early age we would know the whole of the Koran. Nowadays they become imams only by knowing a few suras.'

## Diyanet

Diyanet has on and off been criticised for exaggerated centralisation and control. Some voices, especially in conservative religious circles, have also been raised against what they see as undue influence of the military in religious affairs, for example during the military intervention of 1980, a period that EF's father has told him about.

**EF**: One should not exaggerate the effects of the military regime [1980–3]. It had an impact, of course, but there were also other reasons for Diyanet to control the Friday *hutbe*. One of them was related to the deficient level of education among imams. They had not yet reached the level of competence necessary to prepare their own *hutbe*s.

## The Koran

**EF**: My father reads the Koran very often, and also in Turkish. At home, we have a lot of books on *ilmihal* [catechism] and, as well as that, we also have numerous interpretations [*meal*] of the Koran. And, yes, he knows the Koran by heart, but not the Turkish adaptation.

It is not easy to memorise the Koran. It is very difficult and requires very serious discipline. So, they especially let small children become *hafız*, because it is easier to learn by rote when you are very young.

*Mehmet Akif – author of the national anthem*

Concerning the special significance of national poet Mehmet Akif Ersoy, EF adds:

**EF**: Even though he is an imam, my father keeps the works of Mehmet Akif in his library. Also, around Anatolia, people having only some three or four books would, every so often, have a book by Mehmet Akif. Because Mehmet Akif is regarded as a poet who shows a way back to moral values in a time characterised by a break with Islamic ideals.

**Interpretative Perspectives**

When the believer, after mandatory ablution (*abdest*), takes off his shoes and enters the mosque for the Friday sermon he does so for several reasons. Joining the '*cuma*' is a religious obligation (*farz*), but that does not mean that participation takes place out of simple routine. Participation is also associated with certain deliberations related to the outcome of the ceremony. Based on the interviews, the responses have been structured around four aspects: the gathering itself, that is, the formation of the congregation (*cemaat*); the inner experience of peace and sincerity; admonitions delivered during the sermon; and the wider relevance of the discursive address, in what constitutes the preaching (*vaaz*) part of the *hutbe*. In the following section, the interviewees' reflections are reviewed along these lines.

*Gathering as a congregation*

There are two principal facets to the act of gathering during the Friday *hutbe*: the ritual and the social. The first is related to the manifestation of the congregation as a vital part of the religious ritual. When the history student (Interview IV) talks about Muslims consolidating themselves as a community (*cemaat*), maintaining that this occurs when they help each other to become better believers, he touches upon the ritual aspect of gathering. The gathering community is perceived as a key ritual element in the larger sacred ceremony.

Comments related to the density or crowdedness of the praying community, such as 'there is a big difference between praying together with five people and to do so together with 5,000 people' (political science student, Interview III) or '[i]t doesn't matter how beautiful the mosque, or how eloquent the *hutbe*, or how compelling the atmosphere, if there is just a small congregation it doesn't work' (engineering student, Interview V), are more emotionally loaded, subjective expressions of what it means to be partaking in such a ritual community.

There is also a social aspect of the ritual gathering. Youthful memories of skipping lunch, hasting away to the Friday prayer together with other co-students (judge, Interview II) illustrate the social networking active around, or brought about by, the *hutbe* gathering itself. Likewise, inviting friends for lunch or in other ways continuing to socialise after the *hutbe* offers another example (history student, Interview IV). However, such *hutbe*-related social activities may also contain symbolic greetings like *salavat*, through which the sacred character of the *hutbe* gathering is carried out to the courtyard surrounding the mosque (engineering student, Interview V), thereby creating a kind of transition zone between the sacred performance and closely linked social activities.

However, the repercussions of the sacred gatherings go further. They are believed to extend to the whole nation. To participate in a Friday prayer or a funeral reduces enmity among people and contributes to the strengthening of the Turkish nation (judge, Interview II). Religion is therefore the most important institution in securing national unity. In that perspective, the *hutbe* congregation serves as a metaphor for the nation. Since these gatherings take place within a mosque, it follows that the sacred abode stands out as a symbol not only of Islam, but of the nation – the *unified* nation – as well. The towering minaret is an unmistakable part of this symbolism.

*Sincerity and honesty in worship*

'Sincerity (*samimiyet*) in worship is very important in our belief,' says SA (judge, Interview II). This is also a recurring theme in Diyanet's *hutbe*s. 'Sincerity' expresses concentration, the ability to close off the world around and focus on worship itself. Such composure is best accomplished in the mosque, even if prayer can be carried out wherever the person happens to be – at home, at work, even in the field or the street. Regarding the Friday *hutbe*, however, the prayer must take place within a mosque, or a *mescit*. Therefore, the choice of mosque is important for the understanding of what audiences cherish in relation to the *hutbe* ceremony.

What most interviewees say is that due to time limits – Friday is a normal weekday in Turkey – they choose the mosque or *mescit* closest by. So, that choice is made out of convenience. They really do not have much of a choice. However, if there is more time, they choose a bigger mosque with space for a larger congregation. Or, if possible, they consider an abode that is architecturally more impressive, historically renowned, and generally more magnificent; or, where the imams recite the Koran more proficiently and the voices of the muezzins are more powerful – aspects that are often coinciding. By performing his *cuma* in a smaller *mescit*, the believer fulfils his religious obligations all right, but, says the political science student (Interview III), 'the whole ceremony is trivialised . . . You don't experience much of the spirituality in that atmosphere'.

With one exception, none of the interviewees mention the sermon itself or the preacher (*hatip*) in their choice of mosque. The exception is the judge (Interview II), who remembers going to the same mosque week after week together with his student friends, because the imam 'took up touching subjects' and 'spoke livelier, more fluidly'. The rule, however, was that neither the sermon, nor the preacher seemed to raise any particular expectations, therefore being of slight importance in the selection of mosque to attend. So, what were the alleged reasons for this lack of attention to the sermonising part of the *hutbe*? That's the topic of the next section.

### Admonitions

The most common emphasis of the *vaaz* is on advice and admonitions, that is, do this, avoid doing that. That's also what goes into the concept of preaching in the first place. However, it seems that the admonitions outlined in the official *hutbe*s too often suffer from routine and reiteration. When preacher and *hutbe*-writer BE warns of *hutbe*s starting with the phrase: 'Dear congregation, Today's topic is honour your father and your mother', adding that such a salutation rather bars than encourages people from listening, he critically suggests that the topics are both too repetitive and trivial. Other examples are cleanliness, god-fearing (piety), how to be a good citizen. The problem is not with the essentiality of the topics, but with their repetitiveness and the stereotyped ways in which they are brought up. His own experience, on the other hand, advises that to bring up admonitions related to the audience's real concerns – either in an industrial or a legal professional context – promotes interest and enthusiasm (Interview I).

In the Faculty of Theology where BE is professor, assistants require 'more sophisticated *hutbes*' (Interview I), an appeal that touches upon another dimension of the sermonising exposition than that dealing with advices and admonitions, namely contemporary social and political concerns. Similarly, when the political science student says that 'Islam is not only a religion for worship. Islam is a religion that bestows a way of life that encompasses everything' (Interview III), he implies that *hutbe*s should also bespeak topics related to society outside of the mosque and the religious service. This leads to what apparently is the more problematic and hard-to-define aspects of the homiletic address.

### Relevance and Eloquence in Preaching

All the interviewees seem to agree that the official *hutbe*s in their present form leave a great deal to be desired. According to *hutbe*-writer BE, people expect more powerful *hutbe*s from Diyanet. When it comes to *what* they expect, the answers vary. Political science student (Interview III) believes that there should be more emphasis on issues related to developments in other Muslim countries, especially in the unruly Middle East and particularly in Syria. Due to the large number of refugees since the Syrian civil war started in 2011, what is happening in that country is of utmost importance. Somalia is another example. Even though it does not share a border with Turkey, the turmoil there is of great concern to Turkish believers and should therefore be reflected in the official *hutbe*s.

Engineering student DE (Interview V) also thinks that there should be more emphasis on concrete and current issues. However, when recalling an especially memorable *hutbe*, he mentions one related to an existential, more personal kind of problem – 'The person is with his beloved one'. The economics student (Interview VI) remembers a *hutbe* related to the importance of fostering good conversational habits or dialogue in close relationships.

Rhetorically, that address was also well structured, he emphasises, with suitable verses from the Koran and *hadis*. The problem, according to him, is that the cadres preparing the texts are too narrowly recruited. In order to reach out to the audiences, Diyanet needs to add other professional groups, like economists, sociologists and psychologists to their *hutbe* commissions.

To sum up, none of the interviewees seem to be very appreciative of the Friday sermons. They all agree that the topics mostly fail to catch issues relevant to their own time and living conditions. Parallel to that, the *hutbe* addresses are also poor in oratory. Memories of imams speaking extemporaneously, lively and/or fluidly (Interview II) are rare. Still, eloquence is the less challenging part. To explain what goes into the notion of relevance is harder, both because it greatly varies between different groups, and because to form a synthesis out of such diversity requires knowledge and empathy. The history student (Interview IV) brought this up, saying that 'to choose appropriate and relevant topics, which are related to current, daily events, means you need to know Turkey very well – both how Islam is understood and lived in this country, and what the social and political problems facing Turkey are like'. As an experienced *hutbe*-writer and preacher BE describes how he has tried to get as close as possible to his audiences. But that means that he, in the capacity of *hatip*, writes his own *hutbes* in tune with the social and professional context – and mood – of the particular congregation he addresses. However, in Turkey the authorities do not look with approval on such initiatives, for which reason he had to take a risk when challenging existing regulations.

The mosque-goers participating in this study largely agreed that delegating the responsibility for the *hutbes* to the imams or *hatips* was not a solution. This means that neither Diyanet nor the audiences really have confidence in the proficiency or judgement of the preachers. Lack of sufficiently authoritative *hutbe*-preaching therefore seems to boil down to a problem of the qualification of the imams themselves. It is true that Imam-Hatip education after years of neglect, followed by disruptive politicisation, is a challenging problem in itself. However, it is not all about education. The experience so far shows that official authorities – be they secularists or Islamists – have been unwilling to allow more preaching independence. The stakes of governmental control obviously run higher than that. However, mistrust in the country's imams and *hatip*s is but one instance of a wide-ranging lack of social trust in Turkish society.[10] Looked upon from the point of view of *hutbe* preaching, the situation signifies a catch reminding of the maxim 'practise what you preach!' How can *hutbe* oratory, meant to bolster trust and solidarity, promote its own cause if preachers are not entrusted to speak their minds?

## Conclusions

Judging from the above interviews, the Friday sermon is for the most part a disappointing affair. People participate in the *cuma* for the obligatory (*farz*) character of the event itself and what it offers in terms of joining the congregation. The sermonising part (*vaaz*), however, seems to be of minor, almost insignificant importance. On the one hand, Turkey has a growing and globalising economy, a society based on increasingly complex relationships and a political structure easily generating hard-to-solve impasses; on the other hand, there is a sermonising discourse more or less disconnected from these developments and devoid of power to connect people to their daily life and experiences – their destiny as a society and a nation. On the one hand, it is a vibrant and conflict-ridden society; on the other, there is a distribution of what Richard Antoun, in his Jordanian study, aptly referred to as 'canned sermons',[11] ready-made addresses that end up 'offside' (Interview I), that is, fail in providing stimulating and healing visions.

Judging from this somewhat discouraging analysis, has Diyanet been assigned an impossible task? Under prevailing circumstances, it seems so. However, if coping with this problem includes allowing freer preaching, this cannot be achieved without the state loosening its hold both over Diyanet as an official institution, and over civil society at large. Such liberalising efforts were made towards the end of the 1980s under Turgut Özal's prime ministry and presidency with effects also on Diyanet's organisation. The directors succeeding Tayyar Altıkulaç represented a reform-oriented group among Turkish theologians, with support from leading and modernist-oriented faculties of theology. The greater tolerance towards religion that followed in the wake of this trend also opened the way for the Justice and Development Party, which was founded in 2001 and came to power with an overwhelming majority in the general elections the following year. However, with the Islamists in power Diyanet was steered into different waters. This did not occur overnight, but after two more election victories, which also brought more authoritarian leanings to the AKP leadership. Thereby, Diyanet lost the relative autonomy it had achieved under Tayyar Altıkulaç and his successors. Instead of continuing with attempts to improve the quality of its personnel through decentralisation and better training, Diyanet allocated its resources to propagandistic mass media campaigns. The effect of these initiatives on *hutbe* preaching is the topic of the next chapter.

**Notes**

1. Among the interviewees only one is a preacher and *hutbe* writer. Since Professor Erul is a public figure, he appears with name and title and has given his consent to publication. The other interviewees are anonymised.
2. This interference was triggered by a massacre by Azerbaijanian nationalistic groups on Armenians living in Baku in January 1990.
3. This was the deadliest PKK attack on Turkish security forces since the 1993 ambush, which killed thirty-three soldiers. Diyanet's *hutbe*, delivered two days after the event (21 October 2011), was addressed 'To Our Beloved Martyrs . . .' (*Aziz Şehitlerimize . . .*).
4. As much as this is a common understanding, commentators do not wholly agree, since there seems to have been exceptions. More research is needed for a stronger assessment of *hutbe* preaching during Ottoman times.
5. Professor Erul is alluding to Akseki's well-known *hutbe* collections, discussed in Chapter 2 of this volume.
6. Professor Erul hints here at the changes that took place in 2006, when each province was enjoined to set up a *hutbe* commission and produce sermons specially adjusted to agendas of their own province. On what happened to this reform, see Chapter 7.
7. The mention of 'diarrhoea' in a *hutbe* context is a not infrequently heard criticism. For example, in his memoirs, former director of Diyanet Mustafa Said Yazıcıoğlu (1987–92) lodges a similar complaint (Yazıcıoğlu 2013: 267), a topic obviously conceived as a low-water mark concerning triviality in *hutbe* preaching.
8. In December 2020 BE called attention to a change: 'for a couple of years, the Faculty has a Diyanet-appointed *hatip*, and only *hutbe*s authorised by Diyanet are delivered.' The interview was held in 2014.
9. Mehmet Akif [Ersoy] (1873–1936) was born in Istanbul. His father was of Albanian origin; his mother had Uzbek-Tajik roots. He supported the War of National Independence (1919–22), during which he held patriotic sermons

rallying the people against the occupying 'imperialist' powers. After the establishment of the Republic and the abolition of the caliphate, he fell out with the Kemalists, left the country for Egypt and did not return until a few months before his death in 1936.

10. The percentage of the population answering 'Most people can be trusted' was 12 per cent in Turkey in 2014. The corresponding figure for Sweden was 63.8, Germany 42 and USA 38.2 per cent. Available at <https://ourworldindata.org/trust> (last accessed 23 January 2021).

11. The somewhat provocative expression 'canned sermons' (Antoun 1989: 136) has been used for various collections of sermons either distributed for free by governmental agencies, or otherwise cheaply available in the book market. 'Provocative', because the usage of these kinds of ready-made texts have been seen as a sign of weakness or low status on part of the preachers themselves, either because of insufficient training and education, or because of subordination – and humiliation – to excessive state control. 'Canned' associates well with the above-reported interviewees' experiences of Friday sermons as dry and tasteless.

# 7

## PULPIT UNDER ISLAMIST BANNER

The new millennium started out in an atmosphere of promising optimism for Turkey. When the AKP came to power in 2002, it was against the sinister background of a 'lost decade'. The 1990s had been marked by unstable governments and mismanagement, not only in the economic field, but in other vital areas, such as civil–military relationships and the Kurdish question. The shortcomings culminated in a deep economic and financial crisis in 2000, entailing an IMF-sponsored stabilisation programme under the supervision of the specially commissioned former World Bank expert Kemal Derviş. After the change of government in 2002, it fell on the new pro-Islamic government to follow up on the implementations of this restrictive economic programme, in actual fact winning the AKP leadership widely recognised respect, domestically as well as internationally. Inflation decreased from 50 per cent in 2000 to less than 10 per cent in 2012, and GNP per capita increased from around US$3,700 in 2002 to almost US$11,800 in 2012 (see Appendix IV, Table IV.1). Economic stability and general goodwill towards Turkey among EU countries and the USA led to a significant increase in foreign investments and favourable credit on the international market – developments with considerable impact on governmental spending, allowing for several reforms related to infrastructure, education and health care. As a result, this development also had positive effects on lower income groups, so that the percentage of the population below the poverty line decreased from

13 per cent to 2 per cent between 2006 and 2012. To this reassuring picture should also be added improvements concerning human rights and the rule of law. In addition, the European Council had, at its meeting in Helsinki in 1999,[1] recognised Turkey as a candidate country for the EU, an initiative that was followed up by membership negotiations in 2005.

## Growth of Diyanet

Diyanet could hardly remain unaffected by these developments. As shown in Appendix IV, Tables IV.2 and IV.3, the organisation grew both in terms of personnel and budget. While the number of employees was around 80,000 in 2006, it increased to more than 105,000 in 2012 and reached well over 120,000 in 2013. Similarly, the annual budget increased from around US$1 billion in 2006 to more than US$2 billion in 2011 and US$2.8 billion in 2013. These increases were realised in response to complaints brought forward in Diyanet's annual activity reports, concerning difficulties in meeting the needs of personnel in the country's continuously growing number of mosques, itself an effect of the steady rise in population. Needless to say, however, there were also political and ideological factors involved in the enhanced investments, since the ruling Islamist-oriented party considered Diyanet part of its own special domain. This possessive attitude became especially apparent after 2011, when the AKP firmly consolidated its power.

When evaluating the demands circulating within and around Diyanet during the first decade of the new century, the following sources stand out: firstly, two sets of annual reports, namely *DİB* [Diyanet İşleri Başkanlığı] *Faaliyet Raporları* (Diyanet Activity Reports) and *DİB Din Hizmetleri Raporları* (Diyanet Religious Services Reports); and secondly, an extensive survey of Diyanet and various groups surrounding the Directorate, from ordinary mosque-goers to representatives of civil society organisations and academics (Çakır and Bozan 2005). The presentation starts with the survey, from which three aspects of special relevance for *hutbe* oratory are selected: preaching, especially Friday sermonising; supply of religious staff; and educational qualifications of existing personnel.

The findings of Çakır and Bozan correspond well with the opinions conveyed in the interviews reported in Chapter 6. Most striking was the scepticism voiced against the standardisation of *hutbe* preaching, since it meant that the sermons failed to meet the expectations of widely differing mosque congregations. 'Ready-made' sermons also prompted indolence among the clerics, with damaging effects on their prestige and authority.[2] The criticisms raised in Chapter 6 also confirm what was spelled out by Çakır and Bozan concerning the lack of sufficient proficiency and education among Diyanet's personnel. Their survey also showed that there was general agreement in circles close to Diyanet that the Directorate should make greater efforts to raise the level of knowledge among its personnel and to do so in a systematic way, without delay. Diyanet should also offer guidance for long-neglected reforms of secondary, and higher, academic religious education (Imam-Hatip schools and faculties of theology respectively) (Çakır and Bozan 2005: 337). Also emphasised in the survey was the general shortage of personnel, a claim supported by figures showing that 23,542 out of a total of 76,445 mosques were deprived of a religious functionary. Asked on a TV programme (2004) whether such figures meant that vacant mosques had to stay closed, the then director of Diyanet, Ali Bardakoğlu (2003–10), responded:

> Even if we [Diyanet] are not able to assign a functionary, people do not lock up the mosque. They open the mosque and make arrangements with someone in or around the neighbourhood who they think looks like a *hodja*, and they place him in front of the prayer niche (*mihrap*) and say to him, '*Hocam* [my *hodja*], teach us about religion', and those people expound on religion. Then, what those *hodja*s teach will only be known to Allah and the congregation itself. When you visit that place after some four or five years, you encounter an atmosphere marked by a very different religious formation and understanding. And, there you are, with problems to grapple with. (Çakır and Bozan 2005: 71)

### *Hutbe*s under Examination

The criticisms brought up in Çakır and Bozan's study did not come as a surprise in Diyanet circles, where similar complaints had circulated for a long time. For example, in his memoirs from 2013 the former director of Diyanet, Mehmet Said Yazıcıoğlu (1987–92), recalls his concerns both about badly chosen, distasteful topics (see Chapter 6) and the fact that some imams from time to time felt the need to distance themselves from the obligatory Friday sermons by saying: 'I am hereby reading the *hutbe* delivered by Diyanet' (Yazıcıoğlu 2013: 267–8). The heavy centralisation of *hutbe*s obviously caused alienation among religious officials, since it was almost impossible to find topics that could attract the interest of all in such a heterogenous population. The sermons would have to be produced in closer dialogue with the audiences and the realities of their daily lives, but that would require better trained and educated imams and *hatip*s (Yazıcıoğlu 2013: 268–70). The fact that the religious profession had not reached that level presented itself as a dilemma and had eventually also found its way into the Directorate's annual reports.

An indication that the critical assessments related to the Friday *hutbe*s were taken seriously was the decentralisation of *hutbe* production in 2006. Instead of bestowing one and the same sermon upon the whole country, each of the eighty-one provinces should produce its own weekly *hutbe*, better anchored in and therefore supposedly more sensitive to the special atmosphere and concerns of each province. That was seen as a remedy to the regretfully missing preaching zeal. Consequently, in the 2006 activity report it stated:

> Until the end of June, the Hutbe Commission continued preparing the exemplary *hutbe*s, published in *Diyanet Aylık Dergi* [monthly magazine] or on the Internet. Starting from June this task was transferred to the provincial mufti administration, where the Provincial Hutbe Commission advised on appropriate *hutbe*s to be delivered.[3]

However, it should also be added that the *hutbe*s produced by each provincial *müftülük* had to be submitted to Diyanet in Ankara at least one month before being read to their respective audiences, an arrangement that seemed counter-productive, to say the least. So, even if the intentions were set on easing – and reforming – the existing centralised system, Diyanet was not prepared to venture more than very cautious steps on the way to oratorical freedom.

This lack of confidence in what could be achieved by the cadres on duty in the provinces was also reflected in the way chosen *hutbe* topics were followed up in the annual reports. However, this was done in a dry, entirely quantitative and formalised mode, where the yearly 4,455 *hutbe*s[4] were divided into a variety of categories and sub-categories, represented in a large number of colourful diagrams. The division of topics could vary over the years. Thus, for example, in 2008 and 2009 the *hutbe*s were divided into the following categories: social, belief, moral, worship and 'other' (2008, 2009). In 2010 three categories were added, namely family, health and woman. The distribution between the categories was as follows in 2010 and 2011 respectively (percentages in parentheses): social (20/19), belief (13/13), moral (9/10), worship (14/15), family (6/7), health (4/3), woman (1/1) and other (33/32).[5] In the 2013 report the 'other' category had been removed and instead the number of categories had been increased to twelve, resulting in the following categories (with percentages in parentheses): moral (13), family (5), worship (17), doctrine (7), woman (2), society and social life (16), virtues and sins (3), religious and national days (18), work and economic life (4), the human being (7), health and cleanliness (2), science/wisdom and education (6).[6]

Since neither the choice of thematic categories nor their relative distributions were commented upon, they do not contribute much to the understanding of possible purposes underlying the particular design of Diyanet's overall *hutbe* programme. Rather, they seem to indicate that Diyanet was following a tradition that was carved out at an early phase of the Republic, itself modelled on a longer Ottoman and wider Islamic tradition. That themes related to society, the economy, family and woman are spelled out (2013) instead of being bunched together under an unknown 'other' (2008–11) may be taken as a sign that the aim of the Directorate was to increase the visibility of more society-oriented issues. In particular, the fact that 'woman' stands for itself and is not subsumed under 'family' may be interpreted as an effort to meet the demands from women's rights organisations. This was also in line with a greater openness towards women, both within Diyanet's own cadres, and its activities inside as well as outside of the mosques.

However, illuminating as these reports on thematical categories and their distributions may be, the immediately following evaluation of the quality of Friday preaching is more revealing. These were collected under the heading: 'Shortcomings of the *hutbe* texts prepared by the provincial mufti administrations (*müftülük*)'. Even if not fully disapproved of, their performances were subject to a number of serious criticisms (in free translation):

> instead of being authentic, they rely on sentences copied from various other texts; instead of addressing the hearts of the audiences, they are written in a dry and indifferent language; one has not followed the instructions given by Diyanet, advising on the importance of thematic consistency and the use

of the proper Koranic and *hadis* quotations and references; inappropriate and ill-chosen expressions have been used . . . [examples provided, especially related to unfaithfulness in marriage]; the topics chosen have been far from the daily concerns of the audiences; and some provincial commissions do not even bother to write their own *hutbe*, but make use the one written by Diyanet in Ankara or any other provincial commission.[7]

Based on this critique and in an alleged effort to minimise the listed deficiencies the report further suggests (in free translation):

that the provincial *müftülük*s see to it that their *hutbe* commission takes its task more seriously, by paying closer attention to the given instructions; that topics are chosen more carefully; that dubious expressions, open to misinterpretation are avoided; that competitions are organised or that *hutbe*s are assigned to selected persons, inside or outside of the local *hutbe* commissions; that successful *hutbe*-writers are rewarded; that the number of *hutbe*-writers is increased; that one takes advantage of people experienced in *hutbe*-writing and organise meetings, conferences and panels for that purpose; that the provincial mufti reads and gives the final shape to the *hutbe*s before they are submitted to Diyanet in Ankara; that enough time is allowed for examination, since the text must be submitted to Diyanet's Religious Services Information Management System (Din Hizmetleri Bilgi Yönetim Sistemi) in Ankara one month before the actual address; that the traditional *hutbe* prayers are allowed, in addition to the prayers designated by Diyanet; that due attention is provided to the way the *hutbe* is delivered and that the religious personnel is offered proper education in diction; and that the audiences are asked for feedback related to the *hutbe*s.[8]

Even if these self-critical reports were signs of good intentions, they do not seem to have led to much progress. The above paragraphs were taken from the 2011 service report. In the 2012 report, these paragraphs were reiterated verbatim. The only sentences left out were the examples offered of ill-chosen expressions related to unfaithfulness in marriage. However, with the 2012 report a new initiative was added, namely the setting up of a guiding or preaching commission in Ankara (Merkez İrşat Komisyonu) consisting of twenty-two experienced sermon writers, with the purpose to 'minimise the observed deficiencies' in *hutbe* preaching. This was part of a larger plan encompassing a number of symposia gathering preachers and muftis on higher levels in Diyanet's hierarchy. These meetings resulted in a list of rec-ommendations, which largely overlapped with those already stated in the report (see above). Worth noticing, however, is that in addition to these reiterated recommendations were also the supplement of a new electronic resource, consisting of a selection of 500 *hutbe*s drawn from sermons written and delivered by Diyanet during the period 1999–2012. This was meant to serve as a pool of *hutbe*s to be used by preachers around the country. To this was also added, as a common resource, ten *hutbe*s, provided by the Director-ate, delivered throughout the country.[9]

Moving another year ahead, the 2013 report looked quite different. The critique and the recommendations listed in the 2011 and 2012 reports were gone and what had been done in order to improve the quality of the *hut-be*s was now limited to the enumeration of a couple of symposia gathering sermon-writers, preachers and academics from in and around Diyanet. An electronic database consisting of 250 previously written and delivered Friday sermons was provided, along with twenty-seven *hutbe*s produced by Diyanet and delivered around the country.[10] One cannot help asking what happened to the previous plan of having the *hutbe*s produced on the provincial level, if half of the Friday sermons were produced at Diyanet's headquarters in Ankara.

Coming to the 2014 report the *hutbe* database is provided with 500 old (between 1999 and 2012) and forty-two (out of fifty-five) newly written *hut-be*s.[11] In 2015, the database contains 250 old *hutbe*s and fifty-three new *hut-be*s, delivered around the country,[12] and in 2016, Diyanet produced fifty-five new *hutbe*s, enough to fill a whole year's programme.[13] In the 2017 report, an alleged reason is added, saying:

> 2017 was a year when a number of important events took place in our coun-try [among other things, military operations in northern Syria]. Therefore, the *hutbe*s prepared every week at the centre of the Directorate have been delivered in all mosques around the country. The title of all the *hutbe*s deliv-ered throughout the year are listed at the end of this section.[14]

A similar, even bolder formulation is found in the 2018 report:

> Keeping in mind the important developments in our own country, the region and the world at large, the *hutbe*s prepared during 2018 by our General Directorate were delivered in all mosques throughout the country.[15]

These statements, both in the 2017 and 2018 reports, were followed by a list of the topics of that year's centrally produced *hutbe*s, and a diagram illustrating the thematic distribution of topics based on the twelvefold classification initiated in the 2013 report.[16]

The efforts to decentralise the production of Friday sermons initiated at the beginning of the 2000s, thus making them more relevant to local and provincial audiences, obviously failed or were simply abandoned. Concerning its commitments to offer the country's citizens cum believers meaningful Friday sermons, Diyanet was now back at point zero. No real progress had been achieved over the past decade and a half. However, during the same period the Directorate had expanded as it had never done before, both regarding financial resources and personnel. This indicates that instead of venturing into raising the level of *hutbe*-preaching, Diyanet was steered into spending its boosted revenues in other areas or projects.

### Diyanet under Authoritarian Islamist Rule

After the AKP's third straight election victory in 2011 the political landscape changed – not so much in terms of leading actors as in mode of governance. The authoritarian eclipse started to make itself felt with a step-by-step increase in governmental control of the judiciary and the public media. However, what was really at stake became more apparent during the Gezi Park events in and around Taksim Square in Istanbul in May–June 2013. Invitations to settle the conflict with peaceful means was categorically rejected by the government, despite the president and former AKP-member Abdullah Gül's and many other leading voices' insistent efforts in that direction. The governing party had clearly switched to a higher gear in its efforts to forcefully suppress the protesters, and not only mobilise the security forces, but the whole state apparatus for its own purposes. In this process, Diyanet represented an easily conquered institution, endowed with valuable symbolic power. The commandeering of Diyanet occurred along three lines: control, expansion and instrumentalisation, that is, adjustment to the AKP's political agenda.

The first was related to the relationship between Diyanet and the government. The closer the religious institution was drawn to the executive power, the more powerful the government's impact. In 2012, Diyanet was raised in the official order of precedence from number fifty-one to number ten. Thereby, an important obstacle was removed concerning the director's use of his official garb – a long embroidered white gown and turban. As long as Diyanet was positioned lower down the hierarchy, directors had refrained from using this outfit, partly because it unnecessarily signalled Diyanet's deficient status – something that could have prompted negative reactions among religious-minded groups.[17] After the enhancement in the order of precedence, however, the director could, and was in fact encouraged to use his official dress as often and as widely as possible. Now the way was paved for more visibility and symbolic power.

Another step in the process of drawing Diyanet closer to the centre was the decision in 2014 to link Diyanet directly to the prime minister, instead of, as had been the practice before, to one of the deputy prime ministers. From now on, Diyanet's director Mehmet Görmez (2010–17) would more often be seen in the company of Prime Minister Erdoğan on various domestic and foreign events and missions, turbaned and dressed in his official white garb.

### Beyond the Mosque and Diyanet's Entrenched Borders

Tighter relations with the government went hand in hand with Diyanet's expansion, both concerning its annual budget and number of personnel (see Appendix IV, Tables IV.2 and IV.3). However, the enlargement also manifested itself in its widened and diversified areas of activity outside of the mosque and Diyanet's entrenched institutional borders. Diyanet had already in 2009 obtained its own TV channel, first as 'TRT Anadolu' and after 2012 as 'TRT Diyanet'; an outlet that almost trebled its number of programmes from 1,148 in 2011 to 3,157 in 2014.[18] This was part of the Directorate's wider effort to extend its services 'outside of the mosques' and 'bring it directly to the people', often by visiting ordinary people's homes. One example was the broadening of 'conversation activities' (*sohbet faaliyetleri*), informal meetings offering religious guidance (faith, belief, ethics and worship). Such *sohbet* activities were organised in mosques and *mescit*s, but most often they took place in people's homes. Once such home gatherings had been added to the annual reports (2013), the number of *sohbet* meetings increased from 42,081 in 2013 to 113,350 in 2014.[19] Since women were especially targeted in these *sohbet* campaigns, it was also women that were especially mobilised for these operations.[20] 'Home visiting' was strikingly similar to the door-to-door campaigning methods that for decades had paved the way to the AKP's election victories. Venturing to reach the believers outside of the mosques had also included active promotion of Koran-reading and other forms of religious instruction such as courses, seminars, conferences, exhibitions, and social activities like bazaars and picnics.

Diyanet's extended outreach also included deeper cooperation with the Ministries of Health and Education. Family counselling and other forms of social and psychological support in coordination with other public institutions also increased, targeting children (childcare centres), students (housing), women, disabled and elderly people, martyrs' families, seasonal workers, drug and alcohol addicted, prisoners, and, since the civil war started in 2011 in neighbouring Syria, refugees. For this purpose, special Family and Religious Counselling Offices (Aile ve Dini Rehberlik Büroları) were set up in all eighty-one provinces (*il*) and 264 districts (*ilçe*), providing assistance to the *müftülük*s around the country. The aim was to offer people guidance on religious and family issues and, if need be, advise them on where to apply for further assistance on health and various social problems.[21] To this should also be added the change in the marriage law in 2017, through which imams and muftis were allowed to perform civil marriages.

As well as being expressed in figures, Diyanet's expansion into new areas is also evidenced in the mission statements, pronounced in the annual activity reports.[22] The change in scope of activities is apparent, when comparing the 2009 and the 2018 annual Activity Reports (*Faaliyet Raporları*).[23] In the 2009 report, merely religious issues – belief, worship and ethics – are clearly focused. Such concerns are more closely related to praying, preaching and Koran-reading, practices which traditionally are carried out in the mosque or *mescit*. In the 2018 report, however, focus on 'enlightenment and guidance on religious topics' spills over into other scholarly platforms like panels, conferences, seminars, symposia, or into other social spaces inhabited by somewhat more targeted social categories, such as women, families, the youth, the disabled and 'the other sections of society' (2018). In addition, reading rooms, electronic and mass media (radio and TV) outlets are emphasised as important fields for religious instruction.[24] Underneath this stress on using and developing other settings for religious instruction is the notion that the mosque constitutes a limitation, both when it comes to engaging well-educated groups and reaching out to the broader masses, especially youths and women (groups also targeted by the AKP).

Concerning the range of activity, the 2009 mission statement is more focused on Diyanet's own organisation. For example, when mentioning training programmes for further education, the reference is to Diyanet's own personnel, not, as in the 2018 report, to institutions or administrative units, outside of its own boundaries. As a matter of fact, the 2018 Activity Report expresses an aim to extend Diyanet's activities into wider administrative areas, and to do so on the basis of organised collaboration. It is not only, as in the 2009 Activity Report, a question of offering instruction on religious issues to 'society', meaning the citizens of Turkey in general, but to penetrate other institutions. Specially mentioned are prisons, childcare centres, homes for elderly people, hospitals and other health institutions. Diyanet also undertakes to 'monitor' and 'evaluate' Islam-related activities, including various forms of scholarly and propaganda publications. Similarly, it also pledges to analyse and deliver an opinion on printed, oral or visual productions submitted to the Directorate for evaluation. Worth noticing is that the screening and assessment of various Islam-oriented publications is not limited to Turkey alone, but also includes such production outside the country's borders.[25] This brings us to another important change in Diyanet's mission statement – its approach to international undertakings.

## Diyanet beyond the Nation's Borders

In the 2009 Activity Report, Diyanet's outreach beyond Turkey's national borders is limited to the country's own citizens or kinfolks. This is either in its provisions of religious services to Turks working or living abroad, especially in immigrant-dense countries in Europe, and travel and accommodation support to Turkish pilgrims when visiting the holy sites in Saudi Arabia. In the 2018 Activity Report, however, commitments targeting countries outside of Turkey are expressed in a new way. The aim is now, on the one hand, to collect information about other religious networks and, on the other, to distribute to Muslim communities around the world Turkish religious publications, translated into their own languages. The term 'outside the country' (*yurt dışında*) is used six times in the mission statement of the 2018 report, against only once in the 2009 report.[26] This phrase, as well as the mission statement in its entirety, may not be so significant. Still, it hints at a shift in focus of attention from the domestic to the transnational. What this interest amounts to in practice is implied from a series of additional special reports: *Dini İstismar ve Tedhiş Hareketi DEAŞ* (2016), translated to English as *Exploitation of Religion and Terrorist Organization DAESH* (2017); a report on FETÖ, the officially used acronym for Fethullah Gülen Terör Örgütü (organisation), the alleged power behind the 15 July 2016 coup attempt, entitled *Kendi Dilinden FETÖ – Örgütlü Bir Din İstismarı* (2017) (FETÖ in His Own Words – Organised Exploitation of Religion); and, *Suriye Fırat Kalkanı ve Zeytin Dalı Faaliyet Raporu* (2018) (Report on the Operations Euphrates Shield and Olive Branch).[27]

The 'DAESH report' is the result of an appeal launched in eight different languages in June 2014, followed by an international conference gathering some 150 scholars from the Islamic world held in Istanbul in July the same year. As a substantiation of these efforts, a report was published in 2015, followed the year after by the above-mentioned, further extended edition. The purpose of these efforts was to refute the radicalism of DAESH or ISIS (the Islamic State of Iraq and Syria), showing that this ideology represented a distortion of 'true' Islam. The report also includes explanations for the rapid advance of this kind of violent activism by especially referring to the detrimental 'economic, political, social and cultural conditions' prevailing in immigrant communities in Europe. The report especially targets the youth, that is, Muslims who have grown up in non-Muslim, often Islamophobic contexts and, for that reason, are especially vulnerable to extremist ideologies. But attention is also directed at the despair spreading in the Muslim world as a result of the foreign occupations of Afghanistan and Iraq, the deadlock on the Palestine question, and the indifference in the world at large to the suppression of the democratic demands put forward during the Arab Spring.[28] The FETÖ report, written on the special directive of President Erdogan,[29] is a critical assessment of Fethullah Gülen (b. 1938), his thinking, personality and leadership, stretching over a period of more than fifty years, encompassing his comprehensive, domestic as well as global, organisational networks. Gülen went into voluntary exile in the USA in 1999, where he still resides.

The Operations Euphrates Shield and Olive Branch Report is different in character. While the 'DAESH' and 'FETÖ' reports are more theoretical and arguing, the 'Operations Report' offers a detailed account of Diyanet's activities in northern Syria following the two military operations carried out in August 2016–March 2017 and January–March 2018. Diyanet appears here as an agency not only engaged in setting up its own religious institutions and networks, but in coordinating wider humanitarian aid programmes focusing on health, education and housing. Taken together, all reports bear witness to the fact that Diyanet was drawn closer than before into the orbit of the government and the ruling party. Since the effects of this rapprochement on the organisational practices of Diyanet is most obvious in the report on the efforts spent in northern Syria, that is the focus of the following discussion.

## Diyanet in Northern Syria

Turkey became especially involved in Middle Eastern affairs through the 'Arab Spring'. In the wake of Hafez al-Assad's death in 2000 the relations between Turkey and Syria had started to improve, but this rapprochement did not survive the tensions of the Syrian civil war, which started after the brutal suppression of protests in Deir ez-Zor and other cities around the country on 15 March 2011 – 'The Day of Rage'. As the situation in Syria deteriorated, Turkish–Syrian governmental and diplomatic relations broke down, whereby Turkey joined the USA-led coalition's support of the Syrian opposition. As the civil war has dragged on, Ankara's commitment to a policy of regime change in Syria has caused further complications in Turkey's regional relationships, including a course of four military operations into Syrian territories. Diyanet has in different ways been used as a tool in these risky and uncertain endeavours.

As already mentioned, this is not the first time that Diyanet has acted outside of the country's borders, but this time the purpose is radically different and more hazardous. Already in the 1970s (see Chapter 5) officials were sent on missions to migrant-dense countries in Europe (Germany, the Netherlands, Belgium and Sweden) in order to provide religious services to their fellow nationals. Diyanet was also engaged in projects promoting Turkey's economic and cultural agendas in the Central Asian republics, initiated during the 1990s, after the fall of the Soviet Union. Turkey's interference into Syria and northern Iraq, however, is set on controlling territories outside of the country's recognised border and is therefore more offensive and challenging. Drawing the religious institution into such ventures means that Diyanet has become an instrument in the ruling party's foreign policy efforts.

A little more than a month after the failed coup attempt on 15 July 2016, Turkey started its Operation Euphrates Shield (Fırat Kalkanı Harekatı). This was a cross-border campaign into Syrian territory, conducted by the Turkish Armed Forces and Turkey-aligned Syrian opposition groups (Turkmens and Sunni Arabs). The campaign did not develop as smoothly as the Turkish leadership had anticipated, but by March 2017 the area between the Euphrates to the east and the rebel-held area of Azaz to the west was under Turkish control. No sooner was this occupation accomplished than Diyanet extended its networks into the area. In the above-mentioned report on the Operation Euphrates Shield and Operation Olive Branch, Diyanet's activities are summarised both with respect to this and the Afrin area, the north-westernmost part of Syria, occupied during the subsequent Operation Olive Branch (Zeytin Dalı Harekatı, 20 January–24 March 2018). As such, this report offers insights into Diyanet's contributions to a wider drive set on a de facto integration into Turkey of these areas, including education, health services, police and postal services, renaming of streets and parks after prominent Turks, and transfers of Turkish lira (TL).[30]

Diyanet started its mission with an inventory of people suitable to carry out the religious functions in the area, upon which 1,019 local imams, *hatip*s, muezzin, *kayyum* (mosque guardian) and teachers in Koran-reading were enrolled, coordinated by five officials from Diyanet and paid by Türkiye Diyanet Vakfı, TDV, a foundation close to Diyanet.[31] The number of personnel rose to 1,472 in June 2018 (407 in Azaz; 101 in Jarablus; 325 in al-Bab; and 639 in al-Rai). Between May 2017 and June 2018, Türkiye Diyanet Vakfı paid 5,465,050 TL in salaries to these new cadres.[32] Diyanet's 'Syrian personnel' were also offered education, both locally in Syria and in Turkey. A one-week educational programme (7–12 April 2018) held in a hotel in Antalya, for example, included lectures on topics related to basic developments in the contemporary Islamic world; the crisis in Syria; the negative effects of the war and what religion can do to reduce them; the importance of promoting brotherhood between the Turkish and Syrian peoples, and what Turkey is contributing to that end; and the threats against the Islamic world caused by seemingly Islamic, separatist structures such as DAESH/ISIS, al-Qaida, Hezbollah, and FETÖ. The course also contained lectures on the services accomplished by Diyanet at home and abroad, and more belief-oriented topics based on Turkish official interpretations of Islamic doctrines and practices. And, not to forget, the course also offered instructions in the use of computers and the Internet, and ended in visits to religious sites in Istanbul, Konya and Urfa.[33] When similar instruction was offered inside Syria, it followed a more extended time schedule.[34]

Except for expanding its own organisation, including training programmes, into the occupied areas in northern Syria, Diyanet engaged in the restoration of war-damaged mosques.[35] The Directorate also provided humanitarian aid, such as accommodation, food, clothing and medical care. Distribution of Arabic translations of Diyanet's publications, especially those targeting school children, was also part of the mission. Special programmes were added during Ramadan and the Feast of Sacrifice, when people in Turkey could pay for animals to be slaughtered and distributed among those in need in the occupied areas.[36]

## Concluding Words

The purpose of the above deliberations is not to offer an analysis of Turkey's expansionist efforts across its southern borders. Neither is it meant to give a full picture of the AKP's increasingly close and domineering relations to Diyanet, even if it should be obvious from what has been pointed out so far, that the AKP had found in Diyanet a willing ally – a platform from which it more easily could carry out its policies. The purpose is instead to give examples of what Diyanet was busy doing, when *hutbe* sermonising stopped being a priority on its agenda. After 2011, when the AKP firmly consolidated its power, the emphasis on centralised instead of provincially produced Friday sermons rolled back, and by 2016 Friday sermons were again exclusively produced by Diyanet in Ankara. This relapse into strict centralisation was accompanied by uncompromising exhortations as to the prohibition of any deviation whatsoever from the original text. For example, 'it is strictly forbidden to add or extract anything from the *hutbe*s sent from central office of the directorate' and 'preaching is by no means allowed to be carried out by anyone lacking permission or sufficient competence'. Concerning nationalist duties, the following refrains are voiced: 'emphasis should be given to topics strengthening national unity and togetherness' and 'while calling attention to the malice of all kinds of separatism, the benevolence of social solidarity, mutual support and everything that contributes to national integration and unity should be emphasised'.[37] There is no mistaking in the tone of command, which was nothing short of that of former secularist hardliners in Turkey's National Security Council.

## Notes

1. This was under Bülent Ecevit's prime ministership (1999–2002).
2. In July 2016, Egypt's Ministry of Religious Endowments launched a campaign for a 'unified written Friday sermon', similar to already long-standing Turkish practices. The arguments raised against such a programme by leading Egyptian clerics were almost the same as the criticisms quoted above from the Turkish context. For example, critical voices warned that the text of the ministry's sermon would create a barrier between preacher and audience, to the detriment of the given message. It would be hard to find a common denominator for groups of greatly different educational and social background. In addition, it would have negative impacts on the preachers' work. *Al-Monitor*, 16 July 2016, <https://www.al-monitor.com/pulse/originals/2016/07/egypt-unified-text-friday-sermon-criticism-mosques.html#ixzz4FDAnKXaP> (last accessed 13 August 2020).
3. *Faaliyet Raporu 2006*: 44.
4. The figure 4,455 was reached by multiplying the number of *hutbes* – fifty-three Friday and two religious festival (*Ramazan Bayramı* and *Kurban Bayramı*) *hutbes* – making up fifty-five *hutbes* for a year, by eighty-one, the number of provinces.
5. *Din Hizmetleri Raporu 2011*: 19.
6. *Din Hizmetleri Raporu 2013*: 31.
7. *Din Hizmetleri Raporu 2011*: 28.
8. *Din Hizmetleri Raporu 2011*: 28–9.
9. *Din Hizmetleri Raporu 2012*: 33–4.
10. *Din Hizmetleri Raporu 2013*: 40–1.
11. *Din Hizmetleri Raporu 2014*: 33.
12. *Din Hizmetleri Raporu 2015*: 36.
13. *Din Hizmetleri Raporu 2016*: 32.
14. *Din Hizmetleri Raporu 2017*: 22.
15. *Din Hizmetleri Raporu 2018*: 25.
16. Two minor changes may be noticed: instead of 'woman' (2013) it says 'woman, child and adolescent' (2018) and instead of 'belief/doctrine (*itikat*)' (2013) it says 'faith' (*iman*) (*Din Hizmetleri Raporu 2018*: 27).

17. The only other – conspicuous – exception in official contexts to the dark suit was the Navy commander's white summer dress.

18. *Din Hizmetleri Raporu 2011*: 30; *Din Hizmetleri Raporu 2014*: 34.

19. *Din Hizmetleri Raporu 2013*: 41 and *Din Hizmetleri Raporu 2014*: 34.

20. *Din Hizmetleri Raporu 2012*: 35.

21. *Din Hizmetleri Raporu 2015*: 55–80.

22. This is also a reflection of amendments made in Law 633, regulating Diyanet as an institution, especially in 2010 and 2018. Available at: <https://www.mevzuat.gov.tr/MevzuatMetin/1.5.633.pdf> (last accessed 2 February 2021).

23. The style of expression in the compared mission reports is also different: one is simpler and more lucid (2009), containing fourteen articles (222 words), while the other (2018) is ponderous and repetitive, containing twenty-nine articles (645 words). See *Faaliyet Raporu 2009*: 3–4; *Faaliyet Raporu 2018*: 6–7.

24. *Faaliyet Raporu 2009*: 3–4; *Faaliyet Raporu 2018*: 6–7.

25. *Faaliyet Raporu 2009*: 3–4; *Faaliyet Raporu 2018*: 6–7.

26. *Faaliyet Raporu 2009*: 3–4; *Faaliyet Raporu 2018*: 6–7.

27. *Kendi Dilinden FETÖ – Örgütlü Bir Din İstismarı* (2017): 7–11.

28. *Dini İstismar ve Tedhiş Hareketi DEAŞ* (2016): 1–4.

29. The official state news agency Anadolu Ajansı, 26 July 2017. Available at <https://www.aa.com.tr/tr/turkiye/diyanetten-feto-raporu/869839> (last accessed 27 February 2021).

30. Fehim Taştekin: Understanding Turkey's vision of medical schools for small Syrian town, *Al-Monitor*, 12 February 2021, <https://www.al-monitor.com/pulse/originals/2021/02/turkey-syria-new-turkish-school-sign-of-further-entrenchment.html> (last accessed 18 February 2021).

31. *Suriye Fırat Kalkanı ve Zeytin Dalı Faaliyet Raporu*: 28.

32. *Suriye Fırat Kalkanı ve Zeytin Dalı Faaliyet Raporu*: 29–30.

33. *Suriye Fırat Kalkanı ve Zeytin Dalı Faaliyet Raporu*: 38–9, 42.

34. *Suriye Fırat Kalkanı ve Zeytin Dalı Faaliyet Raporu*: 43.

35. By 2021 more than 450 mosques (Fehim Taştekin, ibid.).

36. *Suriye Fırat Kalkanı ve Zeytin Dalı Faaliyet Raporu*: 45–63.

37. *Din Hizmetleri Raporu 2017*: 140.

# CONCLUSIONS: THE SECULAR
# ORDER UNHINGED?

Secularism has from the very beginning of the Republic been an integral part of Turkey's modernisation project. Just like the building of dams, power plants, railways, industrial complexes and educational institutions, 'secularism' was a deliberate governmental venture meant to help the country reaching the level of development of other European countries. The institution created to implement that part of the reform programme was Diyanet, the organisation through which religion, on the one hand, was deprived of its official status and, on the other, turned into an ordinary governmental agency, and in that form was drawn closer into the orbit of the steadily growing, complex state apparatus. An important aspect of the increasingly more rigid incorporation of religious affairs into the governmental network was that the traditional ulema were stripped of many of their previous functions.

With the *medrese*s closed and the judicial system taken over by secular courts, the religious professionals were eventually reduced to employees on Diyanet's payroll, in other words to ordinary state officials (*memur*). In this process the old Ottoman ulema suffered degradation in at least three respects: stripped of their educational and judicial functions, their area of action shrank; as state employees, nothing really separated them from other officials in the bureaucratic hierarchies; and, deprived of support from various private foundations, *vakıf*s, they lost much of their previous comparative independence. Clerics on various levels were thus pushed into the background, less visible to the public eye than had previously been the case. However, from this partly degraded and hidden backstage, religion still came to play an important role in the formation of the modern Turkish nation. As a matter of fact, under secularism Islam actively came to promote the development of modern Turkish nationalism. The affinity between Islam and nationalism in the Turkish case is widely recognised, in scholarly circles and beyond, and is therefore not a novel idea (Karpat 2001; Lewis 1968; Özdalga 2009; White 2013; Zürcher 2010). Still, what the present study aims to contribute is the as yet less examined role of official oratory in that process. When summing up the findings, I will start by linking up with the theoretical classification delineated in the Introduction: *the nation as a political community*, where emphasis is on the relation between state and individual and the notion of modern citizenship; and *the nation as a cultural community*, where various aspects of cultural standardisation and streamlining are the focus.

## The Nation as a Political Community

The political discourse permeating the official Friday sermons as they were prototyped in the early decades of the Republic was based on the notion that the fundamental building blocks of the contemporary political community was the state and the individual citizen. This Enlightenment-inspired, liberal doctrine had left important marks also on the Tanzimat reform programmes of nineteenth-century Ottoman society, but with the establishment of the Republic in 1923, the citizens, that is the people of the Turkish nation, became the ultimate source of sovereignty. The symbol and executive manifestation of this supreme power was the state. No other intermediate estate or community could challenge that order, and rights and obligations vis-à-vis that uppermost authority were articulated only in the name of individual citizens. However, what applied in theory did not fit with social realities, especially not in those parts of the country where tribal or semi-tribal networks still flourished, as was the case in many Kurdish and Alevi-dominated areas. Therefore, positioning the individual citizen at the centre of the oratorical discourse meant that it fell out of tune with large parts of the population.

Tribalism went hand in hand with Sufism, or Islamic mysticism, a branch of Islam with deep roots throughout Anatolia. The prohibition of all kinds of Sufi brotherhoods in 1925 and the closure of their lodges was therefore a heavy blow to the religious organisation and ideological superstructure of tribal society. The assault on tribalism was in line with the logic of modern nationalism (Gellner 1983), but here, half a century before the 1970s and 1980s, when identity politics got high into the agenda, Alevi as well as Kurdish communities found themselves dissociated from the mainstream discourse of official oratory.

Concerning mainstream Sunni Islam, the situation was different. Instead of alienation, there was even a kind of discursive affinity between orthodox Islam's emphasis on the individual believer's direct and unmediated relation to God, and that of the state–citizenship-oriented, liberal political discourse. Sunni Islam, therefore, found a suitable ally in the modern republican order, in spite of its secularism.[1] However, stripped of its previous coexistence and dialogue with various Sufi communities and their every so often unorthodox interpretations of Islam, Sunnism drifted into a straighter, less imaginative path. The official version took on a tighter jacket, with narrowing effects also on which identities could be accepted within the boundaries of Turkish nationhood.

The reflections on the general social consciousness of an individual- and citizenship-oriented discourse, coupled as it was to mainstream Sunni interpretations of Islam, should not be exaggerated. The impact of such a notion did not exceed that of a dull bass chord, hardly audible to the mosque audiences around the country, that is, it was a hidden (latent), rather than an overt (manifest) process. Even if hard to substantiate, a fusion or adaptation of Sunni Islam and republicanism took place over the following decades and it was in that amalgamated form it encountered the new political and identity-related challenges gaining impetus at the end of the 1960s. Because, as modernisation and urbanisation took hold of Turkish society during the post-war decades, tribal and semi-tribal structures eventually grew weaker with noticeable consequences, especially regarding the position of Kurdish ethnic and Alevi ethno-religious minorities. In the wake of vanishing tribal hibernation, Kurds and Alevi, in their different ways, required a fair say in the republican project. However, as seen in Chapter 4, whenever demands related to ethnic, religious or any other social injustice issue triggered political confrontation, the standard response of official oratory was an appeal to 'unity and togetherness' (*birlik ve beraberlik*). The question was around what cultural values that pact was going to build. That it would be in the spirit of increasing cultural homogeneity is in the nature of modern nationalism, but what did that mean in the oratorical context of contemporary Turkey?

## The Nation as a Cultural Community

On the road towards 'congruence of culture and polity' (Gellner 1983: 111), signified by cultural homogenisation, nationhood found an obliging companion in official preaching. A fundamental starting point was the religious abode: the mosque. The ban in 1925 against all places for religious veneration other than the mosques, such as Sufi lodges and shrines, meant a decisive step on the road towards standardisation of the physical environment of worship. The architectural shaping of mosques constituted an important aspect of that context. During the single-party period, when Kemalism was at its height, very few new mosques were built, both for ideological reasons and due to lack of funding.[2] It was only after the first free elections in 1950, when the restrictions against the building of new mosques was lifted and the economy recovered, that new mosques were built; and it was only during the 1960s that their numbers really increased. Traditionally, mosques were built on the initiative of wealthy or powerful individuals and well-to-do foundations. However, linked to the mass migration from rural areas to the cities, the building of mosques was left to ordinary people's own initiative. Local associations, often collecting money from the Friday congregations, turned into the real mosque-builders, opening a lucrative market for firms specialising in mosque construction. To be sure, once built, Diyanet took over responsibility for staff and administration.

The fact that mosques have been built through local initiative has not stood in the way of architectural standardisation. Quite the contrary, a conventional, cliché type of classical Ottoman design has come to dominate in new, middle and lower class urban districts.[3] Maybe trivial, but still with significant symbolic meaning, is the increased use of mass-produced, synthetic carpets, often with prayer-rug patterns woven into the fabric, creating a dull, monotonous atmosphere. This should be compared to the traditional floor covering made up of bestowed woolen carpets or *kilim*s (flatwoven rugs): on the one hand, randomly arranged carpets in different sizes and colours; on the other, huge, one-piece synthetic floor-coverings with the same repetitive pattern, promoting associations to Orwell's famous *1984* dystopia. Gellner's (1983) description of the difference between culture in agrarian and industrial society could hardly have found a more telling symbolic representation.

The language used during preaching likewise became subject to standardisation. Not only was the Kurdish language, spoken by around 20 per cent of the population, forbidden;[4] local dialects were also substituted by standard modern Turkish, which, during the language reforms of the 1930s, was actively cleansed of un-Turkish or 'old-fashioned' (Ottomanish) words originating in the Arabic and Persian languages. In line with these policies, the Turkish Linguistic Association introduced Turkish neologisms, representing allegedly purer forms of the language, with roots in medieval, Central Asian Turkish dialects. Thereby the language spoken from the pulpits eventually took on the form of the standard 'school' Turkish, spoken among professionals and other educated elites in the big cities. It should also be added that sermons linked to special memorial days, especially those reminding of key events of the War of Independence (1919–22), were a product of the early modern Republic. Early on, these took on a standardised form; a mould that has been slavishly reproduced over the decades, even to the extent that the same texts have been replicated verbatim year after year.

Also, the education of religious personnel has been homogenised. Turkish public education on primary and secondary levels is well known for its extremely centralised organisation. Week by week, the same topics based on the same textbooks are taught all over the country. The fact that Imam-Hatip education – re-established in 1951 several years after shutting down – falls under the Ministry of Education (Akşit 1991: 146) has therefore bolstered streamlining also in religious education, especially when compared to the local variations characterising pre-republican Ottoman *medrese* education. True, *hutbe*s distributed through Diyanet have generally been of a higher quality than what has generally been brought about by local sermonisers. In that respect, official *hutbe*s have represented an overall and in scholarly terms more advanced level of preaching, but nonetheless the standardisation and routinisation of preaching has taken away much of the local naturalness and spontaneity, which the achieved improvement in learning and erudition hardly could compensate for. Another effect of centralisation was that the Hanefi law school of Sunni Islam – prevalent among Ottoman Turks – came to prevail over the Shafii law school, common in the eastern, Kurdish parts of the country.

Last, but not least, concerning official preaching itself, the oratorical messages delivered from the pulpits around the country have over the decades become increasingly standardised. The fact that *hutbe*s are categorically kept at a distance from what is happening in the political arena, both locally and nationally, has deprived them of the vibrant dynamics and tensions of real daily life. Instead, a stereotyped notion of a harmless, small-scale society made up of idealised and allegedly tightly knit families, artisans, small traders and shop-owners has flourished as the background against which the religious admonitions are given. As publication and distribution technologies have improved, the same, centrally produced, *hutbe*s have been put to practice more and more often.

It is difficult to tell how much these symbolic expressions have in fact affected the sense of national unity. Quite the contrary, some of them have instead spurred further antagonisms. This is especially true for those sizable minorities, who fall outside of the official definition of Turkish nationhood. For example, emphasis on mosques as the only acceptable abode of worship has alienated many Alevi, who for decades have fought an uphill battle for official recognition of their *cemevi*s as sacred abodes of praying; while the open hostility against manifestations of Kurdish ethnicity, especially language, has since the beginning of the 1980s degenerated into outright military confrontation between the PKK and the Turkish Armed Forces. Much hope has over the years been placed on Islam as a unifying factor between Turkish and Kurdish ethnicities, an idea especially common in religious circles, but without tangible results. Instead, with the Islamists in power the antagonisms have increased, with still unknown consequences for the Turkish nation, as its borders are known today.

## National Unity, Religion and the State

'Unity and togetherness' has been used as a mantra in official Turkish oratory throughout the Republic. In guarding its status as a tightly unified nation, the official discourse has especially concentrated on shared values, sameness and uniformity, which should not be mistaken for a representation of how things are, but what the composing mind behind the oratory wish they were or think they ought to be. Because Turkey is not only facing exigent challenges in relation to its Kurdish and Alevi minorities; also, hidden behind an ethnically, linguistically and religiously relatively homogenous majority stands an essentially heterogeneous society saturated with potential small-scale and large-scale conflicts.

There are two opposing ways to handle disarray and social unruliness: either by authoritarian means, that is, suppression; or by opening the public sphere to freer exchange of ideas and expressions of political and cultural identities. While the first speaks of narrow-mindedness and chauvinism, the other is based on trust and tolerance – reminders that the impact of the form of government is decisive in the formation of nationalism. In that regard, modern Turkey has experienced a spectrum of different regimes: one-party system during the mid-war period; liberal, parliamentary democracy after 1950, interrupted by several more or less repressive military regimes; and lastly, an authoritarian Islamist-oriented regime defying the rule of law with disastrous effect on official institutions, including Diyanet.

However, the fact that Turkey has been a kind of testing ground for different forms of government also allows for comparisons. In that perspective, religion, both as oratorical discourse and organisation, has fared best during periods of relative democratic openness. The period best corresponding to such conditions started during the second half of the 1980s and continued, with shorter interruptions, until the AKP took a firmer, clearly authoritarian grasp on power after its third straight election victory in 2011. Just like other cultural articulations – science, art and literature – religion needs free space to develop. In that respect, religion is not fundamentally different from other cultural expressions. True, there is a core of orthodoxy in any belief system, but the cultural attributes surrounding that dogmatic idiom is certainly subject to change concurrently with the course of history. That is also the justification of an institution like Diyanet, whose mission it is to organise and oversee the multitude of religious articulations.

I do not agree with those who in Diyanet see a brake-block to social, economic and political progress, in other words as a reactionary force promoting Islamist leanings (Lord 2018: 79ff.; Şen 2010). That this institution has been especially called on by networks and political parties with an Islamist agenda (MSP, RP, FP[5] and AKP), does not mean that those factions have been the only actors with interest in or claims on this institution. As deliberated upon in Chapter 4, the former director of Diyanet, Tayyar Altıkulaç (1978–86) made arduous efforts in favour of strengthening Diyanet as an autonomous institution, both vis-à-vis the hard core of the state – the military – and emerging Islamist networks, thereby laying the ground for comparative independence – a tendency safeguarded well into the 2000s. It is not the existence of the institution itself that is a problem. The critical point is how its jurisdiction and authority are defined and managed within the larger governmental system. That this arrangement is closely linked to how secularism, that is, the relation between state and religion, is understood goes without saying.

The former director of Diyanet, Mehmet Nuri Yılmaz, appointed by Süleyman Demirel in 1992 and removed from office by Recep Tayyip Erdoğan in 2003,[6] has been an outspoken figure in the public debate over secularism and democracy.[7] After his years at Diyanet, Yılmaz was writing weekly (Fridays) articles in the best-selling, liberal-conservative Istanbul daily *Hürriyet*. Worth noting are topics such as: 'Democracy' (20 July 2007); 'There is no contradiction between religion and science' (24 August 2007); 'Religion and the state' (29 June 2007); 'On secularism' (22 June 2007); 'Islam is not a theocratic system' (1 June 2007); and 'No development without reading' (17 August 2007). Upon a reader's question, claiming that democracy is but an idol (*put*), Yılmaz answers: 'Dear Reader, Islam is a religion. Democracy, however, is a form of government . . . Democracy, in fact, is the form of government that suits the essence of Islam the best' ('Democracy', 20 July 2007). The articles also contain criticisms against corruption and other forms of abuse of power as in 'Political degeneration' (13 July 2007).[8] Several years later, in connection to the 7 June 2015 general elections, he criticised Prime Minister Recep Tayyip Erdoğan for postponing the *ezan* because of a rally led by the leader himself.[9]

During these years of relative openness, criticism was also directed inwards, towards Diyanet itself. For example, to address the complex congregations of Turkish believers with the same sermon had proved counter productive. That oratorical standardisation had its limits had been widely recognised by preachers, audiences and leading cadres alike. As mentioned above, efforts had been made from within Diyanet to break this vicious circle, but these attempts lagged and were eventually shelved, when the whole governmental apparatus, including Diyanet, fell prey to the ruling party's exceeding power ambitions. Under no other regime has religion, as oratorical discourse and administrative institution, suffered more than under the AKP. Not only was the political opposition silenced and the rule of law torn to pieces, Diyanet also got its share. Increased financial resources and more personnel are of little consequence as long as they are used to promote an increasingly authoritarian and narrow-minded nationalist agenda and, linked to that, an expansionist foreign policy.

Does this mean the end of secularism? With an Islamist-oriented and increasingly authoritarian political party in power it may seem so. Leading AKP cadres would hardly stand up for 'secularism', but neither have they made efforts of any note in the direction of having the principle of laicism eliminated from the constitution. It therefore seems that secularism has been left hanging in the air. What really seems to have suffered, however, is the trust in religion itself. Meddling with revered institutions comes at a price. Politicisation, or what amounts to the same thing, instrumentalisation of religion is a venture with unpredictable outcomes. Religious sentiments are not written in stone. Sooner than anticipated they may turn into new forms of disappointment and disbelief.

## At Last: A Vision Still Waiting to Come Through

When Mustafa Kemal Atatürk mounted the pulpit in Zağnos Paşa mosque in Balıkesir on 7 February 1923, addressing the congregation gathered to meet the hero of the War of Independence, he set out a vision. After praising Islam, he expounded on the tasks awaiting the country's congregations. Mosques were not built for religious worship only but were places where citizens should come together in order to exchange ideas on matters vital to society at large.[10] To carve out the aims of the nation was a duty to be shouldered by all members of society, not just a narrow elite. The vision put forward was that of an open, participatory society.

What happened to that vision?

Turkish citizens have continued to congregate during the Friday *hutbe*s, thereby corroborating a sense of symbolic unity nourished by religious beliefs and rituals. However, the advised dialogue between preacher, congregations, authorities and the wider society on common national issues has not been forthcoming. True, there have been periods marked by serious efforts to infuse fresh life into *hutbe* oratory, but in general the formation of an open-minded elevating discourse has failed to appear. The fact that Atatürk's '*Balıkesir hutbesi*' is cited so often reveals the existence of a still alive, but unfulfilled dream of captivating preaching. That the *hutbe*s leave a great deal to be desired is a common contention among preachers, administrators and audiences alike. Throughout the chapters of this book, the self-experienced deficiencies and predicaments have been analysed from different angles – an effort which clearly represents but part of a much longer story. Because it must be kept in mind that what happens within the field of *hutbe* oratory is closely linked to the problem of consolidating democracy and an open society – two faces of the same vision, still waiting to come through.

### Notes

1. See Shankland (2003) for an analysis of the affinity between Sunni Islam and republican ideology in a comparative Sunni–Alevi perspective.
2. A note of irony: while mosques that had fallen into disrepair were sometimes used for storage and other non-religious purposes, deserted churches (heavy decimation of the Armenian and Greek Orthodox populations during the First World War and the War of Independence) could be turned in mosques to meet the need for religious abodes. 'Camilerimiz değerlerini nasıl kaybetti?' (How our mosques lost their values) NTV, 2 August 2012. Available at <https://www.ntv.com.tr/turkiye/camilerimiz-degerlerini-nasil-kaybetti,pl9sPawcyEqQAey0wSvi8g> (last accessed 1 February 2021).
3. For economic reasons, it is not uncommon that such mosques are built in combination with supermarkets, kebab houses, barber shops, or other firms (Shankland 2003).
4. Publications in Kurdish were forbidden in 1924. In 1983, following the September 1980 military intervention, the language was banned all together (Başaran 2017: 17, 29).
5. The Virtue Party (Fazilet Partisi, FP) was established in 1997 and closed in 2001. For a well-informed – and rare – analysis of its short history, see Jonasson (2004).
6. Holding office for eleven years (1992–2003), he was second only to Mehmet Rıfat Börekçi (1924–41) in keeping that position for the longest period.
7. Another public figure was the professor of theology, Mehmet Aydın, who, as the AKP's minister of state (2002–2011), travelled widely at home and abroad exhibiting a distinctly liberal discourse.

8. All articles available at <https://www.hurriyet.com.tr/yazarlar/mehmet-nuri-yilmaz/> (last accessed 21 September 2020).

9. Available at <https://odatv4.com/meydanlarda-kuran-sallanmaz-2405151200.html> (last accessed 21 September 2020).

10. The fact that Atatürk held his address from the pulpit gave it the character of a *hutbe*, even if this particular speech was not held on a Friday. Another thing that particularly hints at a Friday *hutbe* was that it was held by Mustafa Kemal [Atatürk] in his capacity as a victorious commander and national hero. It should also be borne in mind that a *hutbe* (Arabic: *khuṭba*) by tradition also carries the meaning of speech in general.

# APPENDIX I: EXCERPTS IN THE ORIGINAL TURKISH FROM AHMET HAMDİ AKSEKİ'S 1927–8 *HUTBE* COLLECTION (CHAPTER 2)

Note: the numbers in square parenthesis refer to the number given to the translated quotation in Chapter 2. The number given after each citation refers to the number given to the *hutbe* (in all fifty-one *hutbe*s) in Akseki's collection (Akseki 2005 [1928]).

[1] Dünyada ve ahirette mutlu olmak için efendimizi kendimize örnek almak, onun ahlakıyla ahlaklanmak, her hususta ona uymak lazımdır. İyi biliniz ki, Rasuli Ekrem'in ahlakı Kur'an'dan ibarettir. Şimdi dinleyiniz de Efendimizi size biraz anlatayım:

Önce Peygamberimizin her hareketi akilane ve doğru idi. Ömründe hiçbir defa yalan söylemediler. Hiç kimse ile alay etmezdi, kimsenin gıybetini yapmaz, kimseyi kıskanmazdı. İftira ve hafiyelik gibi halleri hiç sevmez, bu gibi kötü huyları şiddetle yasaklardı. Dünyaya ve ahirete faydası olmayan sözlerle vakit geçirmezdi. Kimseye küsmez, küs duranları sevmezdi (hutbe 11).

[2] Kullarına lütuf, merhamet, kerem ve inayet sahibi olan Allahü Teala geceyi istirahatimize uygun şekilde yaratmış, gündüzleri ise her türlü çalışmamıza mutabık bir halde halk etmiştir.

Öyleyse, her sabah, bizi ışığıyla mutluluğa davet eden, güneşin altında tembel tembel oturmak, boş boş gezinmek Müslümanlığa yakışmayan bir şeydir. İslamda çalışmanın büyük bir önemi vardır. Kar ve kazançla uğraşmak nafile ibadetten evla ve efdaldir.

Rasulullah, bir sabah eshabu kiramıyla sohbet ederken güçlü kuvvetli bir gencin geçtiğini gördüler. Sahabeyi kiramdan bazıları 'Yazık! Şu genç, gençliğinin, gücünü ve kuvvetini Allah yolunda sarf etseydi ne olurdu?' demeleri üzerine, Peygamberimiz şöyle buyurdu:

'Böyle söylemeyin, eğer o genç, kendi nefsini veya küçük çocuklarını yahut ihtiyar annebabasını geçindirmek için öyle sabahleyin hayata atılmış ise, onun hareketi Allah yolundadır. Eğer gösteriş veya aleme çalım satmak için yapıyorsa Allah yolunda değildir.'

Hz. Ömer (r.a.) buyuruyor ki: 'Rızık için çalışmayı terk edip de Allah bana rızık ver demeyin. Bilirsiniz ki gökten ne altın ne gümüş yağar. Rızkı çalışarak arayınız' (hutbe 16).

[3] Efendimiz cömert idi. Herkese ikram eder, bizlere de böyle yapmayı emrederdi. Hem mütevazi hem ciddi hem de ağırbaşlı idi. Bir kimsenin evine, odasına girmek istediği zaman, önce kapısını çalarak izin ister, ondan sonra içeri girerdi. Selam vermeden oturmazdı. Gördüklerine selam verir ve ellerini sıkardı. Bir meclise girdiği zaman nerede boş yer bulunursa hemen oraya otururdu. Bulundukları meclislerde herhaliyle örnek olurdu. İnsanları sıkmak istemezdi. Meclis adabını çok iyi bilirdi veya onlara sıkıntı verecek halleri bulunmazdı.

Efendimiz herkese karşı tatlı dilli, güler yüzlü idi. Kimseye kötü söz söylemez, kötü muamele yapmazdı. Kimsenin sözünü kesmezdi. Hiç kimsenin gizli hallerini, ayıplarını araştırmaz, bunun son derece kötü bir şey olduğunu söylerdi. Hizmetçilerini son derece hoş tutar, onları incitmezdi. Kendisi ne yerse, hizmetçilerine de onu yedirirdi. Kendisi ne giyerse hizmetçilerine de onu giydirirdi (hutbe 11).

[4] Efendimiz son derece temiz ve pak idi. Temizliği çok tavsiye ederlerdi. Kendini temiz tutmayan kimsenin imanının noksan olduğunu söylerlerdi. Dişlerin misvak ile sık sık yıkanmasına çok önem verirlerdi. Ümmetine de bu yolda çok sıkı emirler vermiştir. Gusül icap etmese bile haftada bir kere gerektiğini söylerlerdi. Saçını sakalını daima yıkar, tarar, güzel kokular sürerlerdi. Kötü kokulardan, kirden, pastan hoşlanmazdı (hutbe 11).

[5] Ey cemaati Müslimin!

Peygamberinizi iyice bilmeye bakın. O iki cihan güneşine karşı muhabbetinizi artırmaya gayret edin. Dinleyiniz de ben size Peygamberimizi anlatayım.

Peygamber Efendimiz kendisini gayet temiz tutar, her hususta temizliğe son derece dikkat ederlerdi. Asla perişan gezmezlerdi. Üst dudaklarının kırmızısı görünecek kadar bıyıklarını güzelce kesip saçlarını bazen tıraş ederlerdi. Bazen de kulaklarının yumuşağını geçecek kadar uzatırlardı. Lakin sakallarını bir tutamdan fazla uzatmazlardı.

Sadece bayağı zamanlarda değil, hatta savaşa gittikleri zamanlarda bile tarak, makas, misvak, ibrik gibi temizliğe ait şeyleri yanlarından ayırmazlardı. Saçlarını sakallarını daima temiz tutar, aynaya bakıp taranırlardı. Hiç güzel koku sürünmeseler bile mübarek terleri de misk gibi kokarlardı. Öyleyken yine daima güzel güzel kokular sürünürlerdi. Dünyada iken en çok sevdiklerinden biri de güzel koku olduğunu söylerlerdi.

Peygamber Efendimiz dünyada eşi bulunmaz bir insan güzeli idi.

Allah onu öğmüş de öyle yaratmıştı, boy bos, endam hep yerinde idi. Hiçbir noksanı yoktu. Peygamberimizin pembe beyaz olup pek sevimli ve güzel olan yüzünden nurlar akardı. Mübarek dişleri de konuşurken, gülümserken inci gibi parlardı. Bu bir Allah vergisidir ki, vücudu ne kadar güzelse ahlakı da o derecede güzeldir. Güler yüzlü, tatlı sözlü olup ağzından fena laf çıkmazdı. Kimsenin gönlünü kırmaz, asla hırçınlık etmezdi. Kendine hizmet edenleri de pek hoş tutardı. Kibirlenmez ve kurum satmazdı. Daima ciddiyetini muhafaza ederdi. Peygamberimizi ilk defa gören kimsenin içine bir korku düşerdi. Lakin görüşüp konuştukça kendisine gönül vermemek elden gelmezdi (hutbe 45).

[6] Ey cemaati Müslimin!

Hakk Teala şimdi okuduğum ayeti kerimede buyuruyor ki 'Ey Müminler! Allah'tan korkunuz. Her şahıs yarın için hazırladığını göz önüne getirsin ve Allah'dan sakınsın, çünkü Allah yaptığınız her şeyi bilir.'

Evet Allahü Teala her şeyi bilir. İnsanlar daima kalplerinden Allah korkusunu çıkarmamalıdır. Çünkü, hikmetin başı Allah korkusudur. Allah'tan korkmayan kimse, her kötülüğe yeltenir. Böylesinden insan hayır görmez. Onların kalbinde nurdan ve faziletten eser bulunmaz.

Allahü Teala bizlere emrediyor, hem de dünyada iken ahiret için hazırlamış olduğumuz şeyleri göz önüne getirmemizi ferman buyuruyor.

Binaenaleyh, hayatımızı nasıl geçiriyoruz? Kıymetli vakitlerimizi nasıl kaybediyoruz? Uhrevi saadetimizi temin edebilecek güzel amellerde bulunuyor muyuz? Şimdiye kadar ne yaptık? Gelecek için ne hazırladık? İşte bütün bunları düşünmemiz gerekiyor. Son pişmanlık fayda vermez (hutbe 35).

[7] Ey cemaati Müslimin!

Bütün alemleri, görülen görülmeyen, bilinen bilinmeyen, her çeşit yaratığı yaratan yalnız Cenab-ı Allah'tır. Allahü Teala Hazretleri bizleri topraktan, bir damla sudan insan haline getirmiş; akıl vermiş, fikir vermiş, kudret ve irade vermiş; göz kulak, el ayak gibi sayısız nimetler ihsan etmiştir. Bunları iyilere de vermiş iman etmeyenlere de! Bu nimetleri verirken hiçbirini ayırt etmemiştir (hutbe 1).

[8] İşte insanların bu hale gelmemesi için, herkese Allah'ını unutturmamak, herkesin göğsüne adeta bir bekçi koymak lazımdır. Bu da olsa olsa ancak namazla gerçekleşebilir. Çünkü namaz insanın kötülük yapmasına engel olur. Namaz insana Mevlasını unutturmaz. Namaz insanı çeker çevirir. Biraz düşündürüp kendine getirir. Namaz insanı Hakk'ın divanına sokar. Daha doğrusu her zaman Allah'ın huzurunda bulunduğunu insanın zihnine koyar. Yirmi dört saatte hiç olmazsa beş kere dünya işlerini bırakıp Allah'ın divanına durmak az şey değildir.

Böylece sürekli Mevlasını unutmayan kimse asla kötülük yapamaz. Böyle bir kimseye dünyanın hazineleri bile bırakılsa hıyanet etmesi, ona el sürmesi mümkün değildir. Çünkü o daima huzurda bulunur. O daima kendini Allah ile görür. Artık böyle olan bir kimse, bir kere böyle dereceyi bulan kimse, alemin malına, canına, ırzına, namusuna hiç göz diker mi? Hiç öyle fena şeylere tenezzül eder mi? Hiç öyle adilikleri kendine yakıştırır mı?

Gördünüz mü ey cemaat, namazın büyüklüğünü? Bu ilim dininin tevekkülünü insanlara bildiriyor. Bu şey boşuna mı ki Cenab-ı Hakk bize, 'Namaz kılın,' buyuruyor? Namazın ne olduğunu bilmeyenler, işin zevkine iyice varmayanlar, namazı sadece yatıp kalkmaktan ibaret sanıyorlar. Bilmiyorlar ki namaz insanı melekleştirir. Namaz insanı Mevlası ile birlikte bulundurur. Dünyada bundan daha büyük bir ibadet bulunamaz. Dünyada bundan daha büyük gönül sefası bulunamaz. İşte siz de namazı böyle bilin. Siz de namazın zevkine böyle varın. Müezzin 'Allahü Ekber' dediği zaman, hemen kendinize gelin. Elinizi eteğinizi dünyadan çekin. O sırada iş, uyku, soğuksıcak demeyin, hemen namaza kalkın. Hiçbir şekilde namazınızı geçirmemeye gayret edin. Elinizden gelen itinayı gösterin. Öyle baştan savma namaz kılmayın. Kalıbınızı secdede bırakıp aklınızı ve fikrinizi orada burada gezdirmeyin. Sadece vücudunuza değil, gönlünüze de namaz kıldırın. Gönülsüz kılınan namazdan fayda çıkmaz. Öyle kılınan bir namaz, insanı Allah'ın huzuruna çıkaramaz.

Bir insan kırk yıl böyle namaz kılsa ne gönlü yumuşar ne ahlakı düzelir ne de ruhu zevk alır. Bunun için ne yaptığınızı bilerek, kimin divanına varmak istediğinizi düşünerek namaza durun. Eğer böyle yaparsanız, namazı böyle kılarsanız, hiç şüphe etmeyin ki gökleri aşar, melekleri geçersiniz. Hiç olmazsa bir anlık Allah ile bir olup kendinizi unutursunuz. İşte bu da sizin Miraçınızdır. Ne mutlu namazı böyle bilip, böyle kılanlara. Yazıklar olsun Rahman'a secde etmeyip Mevlasını unutanlara (hutbe 9).

[9] Uygulamasız bir iman açıkta yanan bir kandile benzer. Hafif bir rüzgar bile onu söndürür. O kandil güzel bir fenerin içine konulursa artık hiçbir tehlike kalmaz. İşte imanı böylece ibadetlerle, iyi işlerle daima muhafaza ederseniz kimse sizin imanınızı çekip çalamaz. Siz kendi imanınıza sahip olmazsanız, iyi amellerde bulunmadığınız gibi gece gündüz fenalık içinde yüzerseniz, gitgide gönlünüz kararır, imanınız zayıflar. Günün birinde o devlet kuşu başınızın üstünden uçar gider de haberiniz olmaz. O vakit sizin önceden getirdiğiniz şehadetler neye yarar. O kuru Müslümanlık davasının ne faydası olur? (hutbe 7).

[10] Ey cemaati Müslimin!

Dikkat ediyor musunuz Cenab-ı Peygamber ne buyuruyor? Tam bir Müslüman olmak için ne dünyadan ne de ahiretten vazgeçmemek lazımdır. Dünyayı bırakıp da yalnız ahiret için çalışanlar hayırlı bir Müslüman değildir. Ahireti bırakıp da yalnız dünya için çalışanlar da böyledir. İnsanın hayırlısı dünyası için ahiretini, ahireti için dünyasını terk etmeyip her ikisi için çalışan ve halkın başına yük olmayandır. İnsan hiç ölmeyecekmiş gibi dünyaya sarılmalı, yarın ölecekmiş gibi ahiret için hazırlanmalıdır (hutbe 33).

[11] Ticaretle ve ziraatle, elindeki hüneri ile para kazanıp nafakasını çıkarmak, her Müslümanın üzerine farzdır. Aynı zamanda büyük bir ibadettir. Dünya ve ahiretimizi mamur etmeye çalışmak şahsi vazifemizdir (hutbe 33).

[12] Ey cemaati Müslimin!

Ey Allah'ın kulları! Düşmana karşı kuvvet hazırlamak üzerimize farzdır. Bu kuvvetlerin en mühim kısımlarından biri de şüphe yok ki askerdir . . . Asker, düşmanlara karşı dinimizi, yurtlarımızı, ırz ve namuslarımızı bilfiil koruyan silahlı bir kuvvettir. Bunun için askerlik çok büyük, çok mukaddes bir vazifedir. Allah'ını, Peygamberini, yurdunu, yuvasını seven; ırz ve namusunun kıymetini bilen her insan, askerlik görevini seve seve yapmalıdır.

Bizim dinimizde askerliğin mertebesi çok yüksektir. Ölürse şehit, kalırsa gazidir. Peygamberlik rütbesinden sonra en yüksek rütbe şehitlik mertebesidir. Bir insan için bu iki unvan ne büyük ve şerefli bir ünvandır. Onun için askere çağrılınca koşa koşa ve sevine sevine gitmek lazımdır.

Peygamberimiz 'Silah altına davet olunduğun zaman hemen icabet et!' buyurmuştur (hutbe 51).

[13] . . . bilmiş olunuz ki, akıl, irade, ihtiyaç sahibi olarak yarattığı insanlara sonraki nimetleri bir değildir. Onlara vereceği nimetleri gayret ve çalışma kanununa bağlamıştır. Dünyada çalışan kazanır ve çalıştığının karşılığını alır. Çalışmayanlar da tembelliğinin cezasını muhakkak görür. Bunun içindir ki Allahü Teala hazretleri ahirette vereceği nimetleri de herkesin gayretleri ve çalışmasına göre verecektir. Kullarına iradelerinin sarf ettikleri kamil iman ve güzel amele göre ahirette mükafat olarak bağışlayacak ve ihsanda bulunacaktır. Dünyada hayır işleyen, iyi ve güzel işlerle uğraşlarda bulunanlar ahirette Allah'ın nimetlerine kavuşacaklar, mükafatını da göreceklerdir. Salih işleri olmayanlara ahirette nimet de yoktur (hutbe 1).

[14] Her Müslüman, hem dünyasını hem de ahiretini mamur etmek için çalışacaktır. Kendi nafakasını, çoluk çocuğunun nafakasını çıkarmak, dinine, milletine, vatanına faydalı olmak için çalışıp para kazanmak her Müslümanın üzerine farzdır. Bu niyetle çalışmak büyük bir ibadettir. Bu niyetle helalinden mal kazanmak, Allah yolunda mücadele etmek kadar

hayırlıdır. İnsan bu niyetle ne kadar çalışır ne kadar zengin olursa, Allah'ın ve peygamberin yanında kıymeti o derece artar. İyi ve namuslu insanlar için para ve mal çok iyi bir şeydir. Namuslu bir zengin, her türlü hayrı yapar hem kendisine hem ailesine hem de memleketine hayırlı işler görür. Milletinin yükselmesi için çok faydalı olur. Fakir olan insan ne yapabilir? Bir fakir başkalarına yük olmaktan başka ne iş görebilir? İnsan bu zamanda parasız hiçbir iş göremez. Para olmadığı sürece ne dinini muhafaza edebilir ne namusunu ne de dünyasını! Bunların hepsi para ve inançla güzeldir. Peygamber efendimizin buyurduğu gibi, Hiç ölmeyecek gibi çalışmak, yarın ölecek gibi ibadet etmek lazım (hutbe 15).

[15] Müslümanlar!

Böyle olunca, meşru bir şekilde ve gayret göstermekten geri durmayın. Bir sanatla veya ticaretle yahut ziraatla iştigal edin. Oğullarınızı ve torunlarınızı da böyle faideli mesleklere yönlendirin. Milletimizin refahı, memleketimizin ilerlemesi ancak bu sayede gerçekleşebilir. Cenab-ı Hakk da bu şekilde çalışan Mümin kullarından razı olur.

Çalışmayan insan millete ve devlete yük olur. Cemiyette de yeri yoktur. Hergün biraz daha söner ve sevilmeyen bir yaratık olur.

Dedelerimiz de dinimiz de devamlı olarak tembelliğin insanlığa bile yakışmadığını bildirmektedir (hutbe 17).

[16] Ey cemaati Müslimin!

Bilmiş olun ki, Allah'a ibadetten sonra boynumuzun büyük borçlarından biri de anaya babaya itaattir. Onlara karşı hürmet ve riayettir. Bu o kadar önemli bir şeydir ki, Allahü Teala Kur'an-ı Kerim'inde tekrar tekrar bundan bahsediyor. Hatta bazı ayeti kerimelerde kendisine ortak koşulmamasını emredip, hemen arkasından anaya babaya iyi muamele edilmesini emir buyuruyor. Sonra da onlara karşı kötü muamele etmemizi değil, 'Of, aman' bile dememizi yasaklıyor. Peygamberimiz de anayı babayı hoş tutmamız için pek çok emirler veriyor. İhtiyar anası babası olup da onlara iyi muamele edemeyenlere, bu sebepten cennete giremeyenlere yazıklar olsun buyuruyor (hutbe 12).

[17] Evet, annenin babanın hakkına riayet çok büyük bir ibadettir (hutbe 13).

[18] Ey cemaati Müslimin!

Annenize babanıza hayatlarında itaat ettiğiniz gibi ölümlerinden sonra da dua ve istiğfarda bulununuz. Onların yerine getiriniz, akrabalarına ve dostlarına ikram ediniz ki, onlar hakkındaki görevlerinizi yerine getirmiş olasınız. Bir zat Aleyhisselatü Vesselam Efendimizin huzuruna gelerek, 'Ya Rasulallah! Annem ve babam öldükten sonra onları memnun edebilmek için yapacak bir şeyim kalır mı?' diye sormuş. Peygamber efendimiz de 'Evet, annenin babanın vefatlarından sonra onlara dua ve istiğfar etmek, vasiyetlerini yerine getirmek, dostlarına ikram etmek, akraba ve taallukatına ihsan ve iyilik etmek kalır. Sen bunlar ile sorumlusun,' buyurmuştur. Peygamberimiz bu hadisi şerifinde ümmetine İslam kardeşliğinin, milli muhabbetin korunmasını emir buyurmuş oluyor. Zira bir kimse ölmüş olan babasının mesleğini muhafaza, dostlarının haklarını korursa, içtimai ve dini görevlerini yerine getirmiş, Müslümanlar arasında görülmesi arzu edilen birlik ve beraberliği kuvvetlendirmiş olur (hutbe 13).

[19] Ey cemaati Müslimin!

Dünyada düşmansız insan olmaz. İnsanın dostu bir ise düşmanı bindir derler. Bunlar, boşuna söylenmiş sözler değildir. Düşmanın açığı var, gizlisi var, bilineni var, bilinmeyeni var, küçüğü var, büyüğü var. Fakat düşman değil mi, hepsi fırsat kollar, hepsi bir zamanını bekler. Onun için insan daima uyanık olmalı, düşmanı korkutacak, düşmanın tecavüzüne meydan vermeyecek kadar kuvvetli, o kadar uyanık bulunmalı. Düşmana küçük büyük dememeli, düşman karınca olsa bile yine önem vermeli ve çalışmalı. Bütün gücünü sarfedip, daima kuvvetli ve hazır bir vaziyette bulunmalı. Başka şekilde dünyada rahat yaşanmaz ve yaşatmazlar (hutbe 51).

[20] Ey cemaati Müslimin!

Cenab-ı Hakk, Kur'an-ı Kerim'inde ve şimdiki ayeti kerimede şöyle buyuruyor: Düşmanlarınıza karşı gücünüzün yettiği kadar kuvvet hazırlayınız!

Bu ayeti kerime biz Müslümanlara daima hazırlıklı bulunmanın lüzumunu hatırlatıyor. Memleketin, istiklalin, şeref ve namusun nasıl muhafaza edileceğini gösteriyor. Mülkü muhafaza etmek için hem düşmana karşı hem de düşmanlığı açık olanları değil, açıktan dost görünüp de içinden düşman olanları da hesaba katın, bunların hepsini korkutacak, hepsini sindirecek, hepsinin gözlerini yıldıracak 'kuvvet' hazırlayın diyor. Öyle ise bu uğurda var gücümüzü var kuvvetimizi sarf etmek, üzerimize farzdır. Bu hususta ne kadar çalışır ne kadar emek verirsek o nisbette faydasını görürüz. Emeklerimiz kesinlikle boşa gitmez (hutbe 2).

[21] Allah bize, Dünya ve ahiretimizi mamur etmek için çalışın, birbirinizin malına, ırzına, canına göz dikmeyin, düşmanı korkutacak, memleketi muhafaza edecek kuvvet hazırlayın; Bunun için gücünüzün yettiği kadar çalışın, buyuruyor. Adaleti elden bırakmayın, emanete riayet edin, birbirinize yardımda bulunun, hakkı tanıyın, fitneden ve ayrılıktan sakının, buyuruyor (hutbe 25).

[22] Ey cemaati Müslimin!

Cenab-ı Hakk, Kur'an-ı Kerim'inde buyuruyor ki: 'Hem Allah'a hem de onun Peygamberine itaat ediniz; birbirinizle uğraşmayınız, sonra güveniniz kaybolur, kuvvetten düşersiniz, heybetiniz de elinizden gider. Bir de hiçbir düşman, hiçbir tehlike karşısında dayanma gücünü elden bırakmayınız. Şüphe yoktur ki, Allah sabredenlerle beraberdir.'

Ey Müminler, ey Allah'ın sevgili kulları!

Dünyada sefil, ahirette rezil olmayalım dersek bu ayeti kerimenin gösterdiği yolu takip etmeliyiz. Evet Allah'a itaat eden, Peygamber'in yolundan giden, fertleri arasında birlik beraberlik olan bir İslam milleti, ululuktan ve azametten mahrum kalmaz. Lakin Allah'a itaat etmeyen, Peygamberin emirlerini dinlemeyen, fertleri birbirlerini çekemeyen, birbiriyle boğuşan bir millet zayıf düşer, kudretten, kuvvetten kesilir. Harici düşmanlara karşı varlığını muhafaza edebilecek ne maddi kuvvetler hazırlamaya vakit ne de iman bulabilir. Sonra kendisine korkaklık gelir, mali gücü kırılır, böylece uçuruma yuvarlanır. İşte bunun içidir ki, Cenab-ı Hakk bizi kendisine ve Peygamberine itaate davet ve birbirimizle çekişmekten men ettikten sonra birbirinize sabırlı olun diye emrediyor (hutbe 34).

[23] Ey Allah'ın kulları kardeş olunuz! Müslüman Müslümanın kardeşidir. Dolayısıyla ona zulmetmez, yardıma muhtaç olduğu bir zamanda onu kendi haline bırakmaz, ona yalan söyleyip aldatmaz. O'na hakaret gözüyle bakmayın. Takva kalptedir. Bir kimse Müslüman kardeşine hakaretle baktı mı, işte, şer olarak bu kadarı ona yeter de artar. Müslümana Müslümanın her şeyi; canı, malı, ırzı haramdır (hutbe 31).

[24] Namaz kılmak, oruç tutmak, zekat vermek de bize farzdır. İslam milletinin saadetine çalışmak, milletimizin varlığını devam ettirmesi için lazım gelen maddi ve manevi kuvvetleri temine gayret etmek de bizim vazifemizdir (hutbe 35).

[25] Fertleri birbirine küsmüş olan bir aile, bir ev halkı düşününüz. Böyle bir ailede, böyle bir evde dirlik, düzenlik ve rahat olur mu? Böyle bir aile arasında emniyet, birbirine güven kalır mı? Böyle bir evde didik, düzenlik olur mu? Bu aile dışa karşı kuvvetli olabilir mi? Dışardan meydana gelebilecek bir saldırıya karşı kendini koruyabilir mi? Asla. İşte bir millet de böyledir. Fertleri arasında samimiyet olmayan bir millet ne içeride ne de dışarıya karşı kuvvetli olabilir. Bir milletin fertleri birbirinin kardeşi demektir. Öyleyse, kardeşlik bağını gevşetecek olan her şey Müslümanlıkta yasaklanmıştır (hutbe 31).

# APPENDIX II: *HUTBE* TOPICS IN TURKISH AND ENGLISH FROM AHMET HAMDİ AKSEKİ'S 1936–7 *HUTBE* COLLECTION (AKSEKİ 1936 AND AKSEKİ 1937) (CHAPTER 2)

**Table II.1** *Hutbe* topics in Turkish and English, Volume I (1936)

| Topics of *hutbe*s (in Turkish) | Topics of *hutbe*s (in English) |
| --- | --- |
| 1. *Yaradanı tanı. Verdiği nimetlere şükret* | 1. Recognise the Creator and give thanks to His blessings |
| 2. *Mevlid. Peygamberimiz Muhammed (aleyhisselam)'in büyüklüğü ve doğduğu gecenin şerefi* | 2. *Mevlid.* On the greatness of the Prophet Muhammad (p.b.u.h.) and the honour of the night he was born |
| 3. *Tayyarenin ehemmiyeti* | 3. On the importance of the Aeroplane |
| 4. *İslam'ın temeli* | 4. The foundation of Islam |
| 5. *Kur'an yolu, hak yolu* | 5. The Koran shows the right way |
| 6. *Allah korkusu, iki cihan saadetinin anahtarıdır* | 6. God-fearing is the key to happiness in this world and the next |
| 7. *İbadet* | 7. Worship |
| 8. *Hayatın kıymeti, vücud sağlığı* | 8. Health, an important life value |
| 9. *Temizlik* | 9. Cleanliness |
| 10. *Müslümanlık ve ahlak güzelliği* | 10. Islam and the beauty of ethics |
| 11. *Emanet ve emanete hıyanetin cezası* | 11. Entrustment and the punishment of betraying entrustment |
| 12. *İftira* | 12. Slander |
| 13. *Müslümanlık hastalıktan korunmayı emreder* | 13. Islam commands taking care of your health |
| 14. *Cihad ve düşmanla savaşmak* | 14. Jihad and making war against the enemy |
| 15. *Yalancılık en kötü bir huydur* | 15. Telling lies is the worst of habits |
| 16. *Gençliğin kıymeti* | 16. The value/preciousness of youth |
| 17. *Kişi dünyada ne ekerse ahirette onu biçer* | 17. Whatever one sows in this world, one will harvest in the next |

*(Continued)*

| Topics of *hutbe*s (in Turkish) | Topics of *hutbe*s (in English) |
|---|---|
| 18. *Kamil ve olgun mümin* | 18. Mature and experienced believer |
| 19. *Allah'tan korkmak ve nas ile hoş geçinmek* | 19. God-fearing, getting along well with people |
| 20. *Cenab-ı Hakk'ın sayısız nimetleri* | 20. The innumerable blessings of Allah the Almighty |
| 21. *Allah'ı sevmek, Peygambere uymakla olur* | 21. Love for Allah comes through abiding by the Prophet |
| 22. *İslam dininde çalışmanın kıymeti* | 22. The value of work in Islam |
| 23. *Allah'ın ve Peygamber'in hayat verici emirleri* | 23. The life-giving commands of Allah and the Prophet |
| 24. *Müslümanlık hayati bir dindir* | 24. Islam is a religion that is vital to life |
| 25. *Kalbin salahı ve fesadı hakkında* | 25. Peace and disorder of the heart |
| 26. *Beşeri vazifelerimiz* | 26. Our duties as human beings |
| 27. *İbadetlerimizde ihlas* | 27. Sincerity in worship |
| 28. *Hakk'ın rızası ve halkın muhabbeti nasıl kazanılır* | 28. How to obtain Allah's consent and people's affection |
| 29. *Mekarim-i ahlak* | 29. Good/exemplary morals (characteristic for the Prophet Muhammad) |
| 30. *Buhul ve israfın mazzaratı, iktisad ve tasarrufun ehemmiyeti* | 30. On the harm of greediness and waste, the importance of thrift and saving |
| 31. *Buhul ve israfın mazzaratı, iktisad ve tasarrufun ehemmiyeti* | 31. On the harm of greediness and waste, the importance of thrift and saving |
| 32. *Buhul ile israf arasında itidal ve tasarruf* | 32. Sobriety and saving between greediness and waste |
| 33. *Dünya iş yeri, ahiret ceza ve mükafat mahalli* | 33. The world is a place for work, the other world is one of punishment and reward |
| 34. *Allah'ın emirlerinde bir takım hikmetler var* | 34. Allah's commands contain a set of divine wisdoms |
| 35. *Namaz* | 35. *Namaz* (ritual prayer) |
| 36. *Namazın farz olmasındaki hikmetler* | 36. The wisdom of *namaz* as obligatory worship |
| 37. *Namazda duyulan yüksek duygular* | 37. The exalted feelings experienced during *namaz* |
| 38. *İmanı muhafaza eden ibadetlerimizdir* | 38. Worship protects our faith |
| 39. *Ramazanı karşılamak* | 39. Greeting Ramadan |
| 40. *Ramazan hesab görme ve mağfiret dileme ayıdır* | 40. Ramadan is the month of settling accounts and asking forgiveness of God |
| 41. *Orucun ruhlarımız üzerindeki arıtıcı tesirleri* | 41. The purifying effects of fasting on our souls |
| 42. *Sıyamın ve Ramazanın kıymeti* | 42. The value/preciousness of fasting and Ramadan |

*(Continued)*

| Topics of *hutbe*s (in Turkish) | Topics of *hutbe*s (in English) |
| --- | --- |
| 43. *Orucun ahkamı* | 43. Regulations related to fasting |
| 44. *Zekat ve ahkamı* | 44. Regulations related to alms-giving |
| 45. *Kadir gecesi* | 45. The Night of *Kadir* (the first verses of the Koran revealed) |
| 46. *Makbul ibadet devam üzere yapılandır* | 46. The desirable worship is the one, which is carried out regularly |
| 47. *Ramazan bayramı* | 47. The religious holiday of Ramadan |
| 48. *Kurban bayramı* | 48. The feast of the sacrifice |
| 49. *Hicri yılbaşı, muharrem hutbesi* | 49. The hijri new year, the Muharram *hutbe* (first month in the Muslim calendar). |
| 50. *Miraç gecesi* | 50. The Night of *Miraç* (heavenly ascension) |
| 51. *Berat gecesi* | 51. The Night of *Berat* (of fortune and forgiveness) |
| 52. *İslam'ın alametleri ve imanın kökleri ve dalları* | 52. The manifestations of Islam and the roots and ramifications of faith |
| 53. *Müslümanlıkta iman ve ahlak arasında münasebet* | 53. The relation between faith and morals in Islam |
| 54. *Allah'ın razı olduğu şeyler* | 54. Things that Allah complies with |
| 55. *İbadetle ahlaki vazife arasındaki münasebetler* | 55. The relation between worship and moral duties |
| 56. *İslam dininde aklın payesi ve akıllı adamların mertebesi* | 56. The state of reason in Islam and the position of knowledgeable men |
| 57. *Müslümanlıkta ilmin payesi* | 57. The position of science in Islam |
| 58. *Sanat ve hüner* | 58. Crafts and skills |
| 59. *Ticaret* | 59. Trade |
| 60. *Ziraat* | 60. Agriculture |
| 61. *Muhtelif kazanç yolları* | 61. Various ways to make earnings |
| 62. *Allah'a, Peygamber'e ve Kur'an'a karşı borçlarımız* | 62. Our debts to Allah, the Prophet and the Koran |
| 63. *Muhtaçlara yardım* | 63. Help to those in need |
| 64. *Sabrın doğru manası* | 64. The true meaning of patience |
| 65. *Koğuculuk ve cezası* | 65. Slander and its punishment |
| 66. *Suizan, casusluk, arkadan çekiştirmek* | 66. Defamation, spying and back-biting |
| 67. *Alay etmek, kötü ad takmak ahlaksızlıktır* | 67. Ridicule, nick-naming is immoral |
| 68. *Kumarın ferdi ve içtimai zararları* | 68. The individual and social malignancy of gambling |
| 69. *Cana kıymanın ağır cezası* | 69. The heavy punishment of murder |
| 70. *Dargınları barıştırmak* | 70. To make peace between offended |
| 71. *Müslümanlık şefkat dinidir* | 71. Islam is a religion of compassion |
| 72. *Herkes kazancına bağlıdır* | 72. Everyone is tied to his earnings |

*(Continued in Table II.2)*

**Table II.2** *Hutbe* topics in Turkish and English, Volume II (1937)

| Topics of *hutbe*s (in Turkish) | Topics of *hutbe*s (in English) |
|---|---|
| 73. *Fatiha'nın öğrettiği yüksek hakikatler* | 73. The eminent truth of Fatiha (opening sura in the Koran) |
| 74. *Öksüzlere yardım edelim* | 74. Let us help orphans |
| 75. *Birbirimize hürmet ve yardım edelim* | 75. Let us respect and help each other |
| 76. *Dünya ve ahiret için çalışmak, fesat çıkarmamak gerektir* | 76. Work for this world and the afterlife, do not cause trouble |
| 77. *Allah'a ve Resul'üne itaat etmek, tefrikadan sakınmak* | 77. To obey Allah and His Prophet, to stay away from discord |
| 78. *İçki her kötülüğün başıdır* | 78. Alcohol is at the beginning of all evils |
| 79. *İçki belası* | 79. The malignancy of alcohol |
| 80. *İçkinin içtimai zararları* | 80. The malignancy of alcohol for society |
| 81. *Eksik ölçenler, yanlış tartanlar* | 81. Those who use deficient measures and incorrect weights |
| 82. *Ağaç dikmenin faydaları* | 82. The benefit of planting trees |
| 83. *Peygamber Efendimizin ahlakı* | 83. The moral of our beloved Prophet |
| 84. *Doğruluk* | 84. Truth |
| 85. *Kardeşlik, dargınlık* | 85. Brotherhood and resentment |
| 86. *Kötü huylardan kaçınmak* | 86. To stay away from bad habits |
| 87. *Tevazu, kibir* | 87. Humility and arrogance |
| 88. *Hayatını korumak herkese vacibdir. İntihar etmek vazifeden kaçmaktır* | 88. Everyone is enjoined to protect his/her life. Committing suicide means escaping from that duty |
| 89. *Hased* | 89. Jealousy |
| 90. *İnsan ne bulursa dilinden bulur* | 90. A person gets into trouble for what he/she says |
| 91. *Güzel huylar* | 91. Good habits |
| 92. *Müslümanlık temizlik dinidir* | 92. Islam is a religion of cleanliness |
| 93. *Ahlaki öğütler* | 93. Moral admonitions |
| 94. *Kabir ziyareti katı kalbleri yumuşatır* | 94. Visiting a tomb softens rigid hearts |
| 95. *Olgun müminin vasıfları* | 95. Characteristics of a mature believer |
| 96. *Doğrularla iğrilerin mevkii* | 96. The rank of the rights and the wrongs |
| 97. *Kendi vücudümüze, yerlere, göklere bakmak Tanrımızın kudretini tanımak* | 97. To understand the omnipotence of God by looking at our body, the earth and the sky |
| 98. *Allah Teala Hazretlerinin sıfatları* | 98. The attributes of Allah the Almighty |
| 99. *Peygamberlere iman* | 99. Faith in the prophets |
| 100. *Adalet ve müsavat* | 100. Justice and equality |
| 101. *Yalancı şahidliği iğrenç bir hareket ve en büyük bir günahtır* | 101. False testimony is a terrible thing and the biggest sin |
| 102. *Yalan şahitliğinin, yahud şahitlikten kaçmanın cemiyet üzerinde fena tesirleri* | 102. The vicious effects on society of false testimony or refraining from testimony. |

*(Continued)*

| Topics of *hutbe*s (in Turkish) | Topics of *hutbe*s (in English) |
|---|---|
| 103. *Yalan yere şehadetin, rüşvetin içtimai zararları* | 103. False testimony, bribery and the harm they cause society |
| 104. *Zulmün sonu* | 104. The end of oppression |
| 105. *Vatan sevgisi, vatan aşkı* | 105. Affection and passion for the homeland |
| 106. *Askerlik en şerefli bir vazifedir* | 106. Military service is the most honourable duty |
| 107. *Düşmanla savaşmanın ve şehitliğin fazileti* | 107. The virtue of going to war against the enemy and suffer martyrdom |
| 108. *Şehitlik mertebesinin yüksekliği* | 108. The high rank of martyrdom |
| 109. *Secaat ve cesaret en büyük fazilettir* | 109. Bravery and courage the highest among virtues |
| 110. *Memleketi düşmanlardan koruma yolları* | 110. How to protect the country from the enemies |
| 111. *Aile hakları* | 111. Family rights |
| 112. *Aile saadeti, karı ile kocanın karşılıklı vazifeleri* | 112. Family prosperity, mutual duties of man and wife |
| 113. *Evlenmek ve evlad yetiştirmek* | 113. Marriage and raising children |
| 114. *Evlad sevgisi* | 114. Love for your children |
| 115. *Aile halkının ve bütün insanların mütekabil vazife ve mesuliyetleri* | 115. Mutual duties and responsibilities of family members and all human beings |
| 116. *Ana, baba hakkı* | 116. The right of mother and father |
| 117. *Anaya, babaya itaat* | 117. Obedience of mother and father |
| 118. *Kur'an ahlakı* | 118. Koranic ethics |
| 119. *Ahlaki faziletler ve bunların eserleri* | 119. Moral virtues and what they create |
| 120. *Kanaatın doğru manası* | 120. The true meaning of conviction |
| 121. *Borç ağır bir yüktür* | 121. Debt is a heavy burden |
| 122. *Çocuk düşürmenin içtimai ve ahlaki zararları* | 122. The social and moral harm of abortion |
| 123. *Erkanı İslamiyeden: Namaz* | 123. Fundamental rule of Islam: *Namaz* |
| 124. *İbadetlerimizdeki müşterek faziletler* | 124. Common virtues of our worship |
| 125. *En büyük günahlar* | 125. The biggest sins |
| 126. *Allah'ın haram kıldığı şeylerin hepsinde dünyevi ve uhrevi bir zarar vardır* | 126. All things forbidden by Allah are harmful for this world and the next |
| 127. *Tevekkülün doğru manası* | 127. The true meaning of submission [putting oneself in God's hands] |
| 128. *Yeni yapılan bir camiişerifin resmi küşadında okunacak hutbe* | 128. A *hutbe* to be read at the official opening of a new mosque |
| 129. *Asılsız şeylere inanmanın zararları* | 129. Harm caused by believing in groundless things |
| 130. *Güneş ve ay tutulması* | 130. Eclipse of the sun and the moon |
| 131. *Kıyamet ne zaman kopacaktır diyenlere* | 131. To those who say, when will the Doomsday come |
| 132. *Cennet de bu dünyada kazanılır, cehennem de* | 132. Paradise is earned in this life, so is hell |

*(Continued)*

| Topics of *hutbe*s (in Turkish) | Topics of *hutbe*s (in English) |
|---|---|
| 133. *Ahiret âlemi* | 133. The world of the hereafter |
| 134. *Dünya âhiretin bir remzidir* | 134. The world is a sign of the hereafter |
| 135. *Mahşer kaygusu kimler için?* | 135. Who sustains anxiety for the Last Judgement? |
| 136. *Hesab gününe iman* | 136. Faith in the day of reckoning |
| 137. *Verem hastalığı ve bundan korunma çareleri* | 137. Tuberculosis and how to avoid it |
| 138. *Mikroplardan sakınmalı* | 138. Beware of germs |
| 139. *Kızamık, kızıl, kuşpalazı* | 139. Measles, scarlet fever, diphtheria |
| 140. *Çiçek, boğmaca, tifo* | 140. Smallpox, whooping cough, typhoid |
| 141. *Sıtma, bataklık, sivri sinek, karasinek* | 141. Malaria, swamp, mosquito, housefly |
| 142. *Göz hastalığı, trahom* | 142. Eye decease, trachoma |
| 143. *Yemin'in kısımları ve hükümleri* | 143. Components and regulations of taking oaths |
| 144. *Regaib kandili* | 144. The Night of Regaib (night preceding the first Friday in the month of Recep) |
| 145. *Allah korkusu* | 145. God-fearing |
| 146. *Hırsızlık, dolandırıcılık, yataklık* | 146. Theft/robbery, fraud, harbouring (stolen goods or a criminal) |
| 147. *Faizcilik, tefecilik* | 147. Usury, loansharking |
| 148. *Rüşvet ve yalancılık* | 148. Bribery and deceitfulness |
| 149. *Kızılay cemiyeti* | 149. The Red Crescent Association |
| 150. *Ferdlerin de, cemiyetlerin de hayatı mücahede ile kazanılır* | 150. Individuals as well as societies earn their living through struggling |
| 151. *Peygamberimiz Sallallahü Aleyhi ve Sellem Efendimizin hutbeleri* | 151. The *hutbe*s of our beloved Prophet, May Allah Honour Him and Grant Him Peace |

# APPENDIX III: TURKISH ORIGINALS OF *HUTBES* SELECTED FROM *DİYANET GAZETESİ* 1971–9 (CHAPTER 4)

**ONE:** *Diyanet Gazetesi*, 15 March 1971

*Islam is a life-sustaining (vital) religion*

İSLAM HAYATÎ BİR DİNDİR

*Ey insanlar! Rabbinizden size bir öğüt, kalplerdeki hastalıklara bir şifa, inananlara bir rehber ve rahmet gelmiştir* [Kuran 10: 57].

Akıl sahibi olan insanları doğruya, güzele hak ve hakikate ulaştırmak için Allah tarafından gönderilen İslam dini başlı başına bir hayat kaynağıdır. Bu kaynağın vazı-ı olan Allahuzülcelâl Hazretleri, âlemi her canlının yaşamasına müsait bir şekilde yarattığı gibi âlemin kanunlarını da en güzel ve en doğru ölçülerle tayin etmiştir. Bir ferdin veya cemiyetin yeryüzünde bulunduğu müddetçe hayatının idâmesini ihtiyaçlarının teminini hak ve hukukunu teminat altına alarak zararsız olan bir canlının hayatına kast etmeyi, meşru yollardan mâişetini temine çalışan kimsenin rızkına mani olmayı, hak sahiplerini haklarından mahrum etmeyi kat'iyetle men etmiş ve en büyük günahlardan saymıştır. Bu ulvî prensiplerden de anlaşıldığı gibi İslâm Dini insanlık âlemini çeşitli ihtilâflardan kurtarmak, Tek Varlığın mevcudiyetine inandırmak için tamamen akla hitap etmiş, akıl ve mantığın haricinde kalan hiç bir şey'i tasvip etmemiştir.

İslâm Dini: Tefrikanın felâketle, cehaletin, zulmetin, tembelliğin, sefaletle neticeleneceğini müteaddit emir ve yasaklarıyla beyan buyurmuştur.

İslâm Dini: İstiklâl ve Hürriyetin devamı, huzur ve sükûnunun temini, Irz ve Namusun muhafazası için mensuplarını birbirine kardeş kılarak bir nokta etrafında toplamıştır. Aklın tekâmülü için İlim ve mârifeti, iktisadın tekâmülü için gaye ile çalışmayı, fert ve cemiyetin ihtiyacı için izdivacı (evliliği) meşru kılmıştır.

İslâm Dini: Hürriyeti her ferde doğuştan bir hak olarak tanımış, esaret ve köleliği, buğz ve atâleti, hırs ve temâ'ı şiddetle takbih etmiştir. Ahlâkı, fazileti, istikâmeti, cömertlik ve cesareti İslâm ve İmanın kemâline vesile kılmıştır. Şahsi menfaat ve çıkar üzerine milli menfaati tercih ederek içtimâi hayatın dengesini sağlamıştır.

İslâm Dini: Akraba ve komşuya yardımı, Din, vatan ve millet uğrunda her türlü fedakârlığı mensuplarından isteyerek, nesil ve nesebin devamına sebep olan anne ve babaya itâatı Allaha itâattan sonra zikretmiştir.

İslâm Dini: Fert ve cemiyetin sağlığına üstün bir kıymet vererek sıhhat ve âfiyetin temeli olan temizliği İmanın yarısı olarak kabul etmiş, birçok maddî ve manevî hastalıklara sebep olan işreti, kumar ve benzeri oyunları şiddetle yasaklamıştır. Cemiyet sağlığının devamı için bulaşıcı hastalık bulunan yerlere girilmemesini, hastalığa yakalanan kimsenin, bulunduğu yerden ayrılmamasını, tehlikenin ehemmiyetine binâen bulaşıcı hastalığın mevcut olduğu yerden aslandan kaçar gibi kaçılmasını emir ve tavsiye etmiştir. Nitekim biz Ümmetleri için en müşfik bir babadan daha merhametli olan Hazreti Muhammed (S.A.S.) Efendimiz, hayat, sıhhat ve servetin kıymet ve değerini veciz bir şekilde izah ederek buyuruyorlar ki (Ölümden evvel hayatın, hastalıktan evvel sıhhatin, fakirlikten evvel servetin, meşguliyet gelip çatmazdan evvel boş vaktin ve ihtiyarlıktan evvel gençliğinizin kıymetini biliniz.)

İslâm Dini: Fert ve cemiyetin zarurî olan, ziraat, san'at ve ticareti teşvik ederek âmmenin menfaati çerçevesinde faaliyet yollarını göstermiştir. Diğer taraftan bir insanın midesine koyduğu gıdanın en helâlının, elinin emeği ile kazanacağı lokma olduğunu açıklayarak (dilenciliği) katiyyetle yasak kılmış, kendi çalışmayıpta rızkını başkalarının sırtından temine uğraşan kimseleri, en ağır lisanla itham etmiştir.

Bu prensipleri havi olan İslâm, her cihetten beşeriyetin saadetini temine yeterli olup, müntesiplerine en müreffeh yaşayışlar bahşeden hayatî bir Dindir.

Fikri Duman (Müftü, Şarkışla)

**TWO: *Diyanet Gazetesi*, 15 May 1972**

*Entrustment and betraying entrustment*

EMANET VE EMANETE HİYANET ETMEK

Muhterem Müslümanlar,

Okuduğum âyeti kerime'de [Kuran 8: 27] Allahu Teâlâ şöyle buyuruyor, '*Ey iman edenler, Allah'a ve Rasûlüne hiyânet etmeyin ki bile bile emanetlerinize hiyanet etmeyesiniz.*'

Emanet korunmak üzere yanımızda bırakılan bir haktır. Bu, ister Allah'a ait olsun, ister kullara ait bir hak olsun; maddi olsun, manevi olsun, hepsine şâmildir. Manevi emanetler Allah'ın emir ve teklifleridir ki bunların başında ibadetlerimiz gelir. Vücudumuz, sağlığımız, servetimiz ve çocuklarımız da birer emanettir. Üzerimize aldığımız görevler, bize emniyet edilen ırz ve namus, şahsi veya içtimai sır ve vatanın her karış toprağı önemli emanetlerimizdendir. Bütün bunların bize tevdî edilmiş bir emanet olduğunu ve bir gün bunlardan âlemlerin Rabbi olan Allahu Teâlâ'nın huzurunda, arada vasıta ve tercüman olmadan hesap vermek mecburiyetinde olduğumuzu bilmeli ve ona göre hareket etmeliyiz. Rasûl-i Ekrem Efendimiz, bu sorumluluğumuzu bize hatırlatarak şöyle buyuruyor:

'Hepiniz çobansınız ve hepiniz çobanlığınızdan sorumlusunuz. İmam (âmir) çobandır ve çobanlığından sorumludur. Kişi, ailesinin koruyucusu ve eli altında olanlardan sorumludur. Kadın eşinin, evinin koruyucusu ve eli altında bulunanlardan sorumludur. Hizmetçi efendisinin malının koruyucusudur ve eli altında bulunanlardan sorumludur.'

Muhterem Müslümanlar,

Her ne suretle olursa olsun, bize tevdi edilen emanetleri korumak bir vazifedir. Onlara riayet etmemek hiyanettir. Meselâ; bizleri yaratan, yaşatan ve sayısız nimetlerle donatan Allah'ın ve O'nun sevgili Peygamberinin emirlerini yerine getirmeyen ve yasaklarından sakınmayan emanete hiyanet etmiştir. Adaletle hükmetmeyen, emanetleri ehline vermeyen, üzerine aldığı görevi yapmayan, memuriyetini kötüye kullanan emanete hiyanet etmiştir. İnsanlara güzel öğüt vermeyen, onları Allah'ın kitabı ve Rasûlünün sünneti ile amel etmeye irşad etmeyen bir din görevlisi emanete hiyanet etmiştir. Çocukların eğitim ve öğretimi kendisine emanet edilip de, onların eğitim ve terbiyesini iyi yapmayan, bu saf ve tertemiz gönüllere sapık akideleri, zararlı fikirleri eken öğretmen, emanete hiyanet etmiştir. İnsanları aldatan, yalan söyleyen hile ve ihtikâr yapan tüccar emanete hiyanet etmiştir. San'atını kötüye kullanan san'atkar, işini lâyikiyle yapmayan işçi emanete hiyanet etmiştir. Kendisine tevdi edilen millî bir sırrı ifşa eden, muhafaza için yanında bırakılan malı gasbeden, kendisine emniyet edilen ırz ve namusa dokunan kimse emanete hiyanet etmiştir.

Muhterem Müslümanlar,

Rasûl-i Ekrem Efendimiz, emanete hiyanet edenlerin olgun imandan mahrum olduklarını, bu gibi kimselerin münafıklardan sayılacağını haber vermişlerdir. Millî ve içtimai olan emanetlere hiyanet etmek büyük felaketlerin doğmasına ve içtimai düzenin altüst olmasına sebep olur. Nitekim bir adam Rasûl-i Ekrem Efendimize gelerek:

'Ya Rasûlallah, kıyamet ne zaman kopacaktır?' diye sormuş.
Rasûl-i Ekrem:
'Emanet zayi olduğu zaman kıyameti bekle' buyurmuş.
Adam:
'Emanetin zayi olması nasıldır?' demiş.
Rasûl-i Ekrem:
'İşler ehil olmayanlara tevdi edildiği zaman kıyameti bekle,' buyurmuş.

Bu hadîs-i şeriften öğreniyoruz ki; millî ve içtimai olan bir emanetin zayi olmasını önlemek, her işi ehline vermekle mümkündür. Emanet ehline verilmeyince, işler aksayacak, iş sahipleri tedirgin olacak, karışıklık baş gösterecektir. Bunun içindir ki Allahu Teâlâ bu hususta da bize doğru yolu göstererek şöyle buyuruyor: 'Allahu Teâlâ size emanetlerinizi ehline vermenizi ve insanlar arasında hükmettiğiniz vakit, adaletle hükmetmenizi emrediyor. Allah size ne güzel öğüt veriyor. Şüphesiz Allah, her şeyi işiten ve görendir.'

O halde aziz Müslümanlar; emaneti ehline vermeli ve emanete riayet etmeliyiz. Ancak o zaman aradığımızı bulacak ve özlediğimiz huzura kavuşmuş olacağız.

Lütfi Şentürk (Ankara müftüsü)

**THREE:** *Diyanet Gazetesi,* **15 April 1975**

*Togetherness and Separation*

BİRLİK ve AYRILIK

*Ey iman edenler! Allah'dan nasıl korkmak gerekirse öylece sakınıp hakkıyle müttaki olun ve ancak, müslüman olarak can verin. Toptan Allah'ın ipine sımsıkı sarılın, dağılıp ayrılmayın. Allah'ın size olan nimetini hatırlayın. Hani siz birbirinize düşmanken kalplerinizin arasını bulup sizi birbirinizle uzlaştırdı da O'nun nimeti sayesinde kardeş oldunuz. Sizler ateşten bir uçurumun kenarında bulundurdunuz da Allah sizi oradan kurtardı. Artık doğru yolu bulup hak üzere durasınız diye Allah size ayetini iste böylece açıklar* [Kuran 3: 102–3].

Bu ayeti kerimeler, birlik ve beraberliğin, milletlerin hayatında ne kadar büyük bir kıymet olduğunu, ayrılık ve gayrılık gütmenin, şenlik benlik dâvasının ise milletleri nasıl perişan edip felâket uçurumlarına sürüklediğini çok açık ve veciz bir surette beyan etmekte, bu hususa dikkati çekmektedir.

Âyette evvelâ takva ile emrolunmaktadır. Takva Allah'dan gereği gibi sakınmak, O'nun buyurduklarına karşı gelmekten korunmaktır. Takvanın en derli toplu tarifi şöyledir: İşlenmesi gereken şeyi terk etmemek, yapılması gereken şeyi de işlememek yani Allah'ın buyruklarını kaçıracağım diye endişe edip bu hususta gayet titiz davranmaktır. Bir çokları tarafından rivayet olunduğu üzere Abdullah ibni Mesut hazretleri bu ayetin tefsirinde diyor ki:

> Takva Allah'a daima itaat üzere olup, isyan etmemek, Allahı her vakit anıp hiç unutmamak, herhalde şükredip hiç küfrana, nankörlüğe düşmemektir. Takva dinimizde en şerefli mertebedir. Muttaki kul olmak en büyük mutluluktur. Buna erebilmek için ayeti kerimede beyan buyurulan bilhassa şu iki noktaya önem vermek gerekir:
> 1. Allaha yapılan ahde sarılmak, Allah'a olan bağlılığı korumak.
> 2. Tefrikadan, ayrılık, gayrılık gütmekten, bozgunculuktan, milleti parçalamaktan sakınmak. Dünya ve ahiret saadetinin yolu budur.

Dinimizin buyruğu böyle. İslâm dini, vahdet dinidir. Bir Allah'a iman edenlerin birlik ve beraberlik içinde yaşamaları gerekir. İslâmiyet kalplerin ve safların bir olmasını ister. Toplum için birliğin önemi ne kadar büyüktür. İçtimai ihtiyaçları en güzel şekilde cevaplandıran İslam dini, birliğe her hususta gerektiği önemi vermiştir. Vahdet, birlik İslâm dininin yüce esasları arasında yer alır. Bu sağlam esas hiçbir surette zedelenemez. İmanda, ibâdette birliğe verilen değer, herkesin bildiği ve takdir ettiği bir husustur. Herkes başına buyruk olsun, aklına eseni yapsın. Müslümanlıkta bu olamaz. Sürüden ayrılanı kurt kapar. Cemaattan ayrılan bizden değildir yollu hükmüyle cemaate verilen önem, birliğin değerini göstermeğe yeter. Ümmetin mecmuundan hatâ kaldırılmıştır. İcmâ-i ümmet, şer'î deliller arasında yer almıştır. Allahın rahmeti, yardımı cemaat üzerindedir. Bu hususta birçok Hadisi şerifler vârit olmuştur. Hayır toplumdadır. Milleti bölenlerin sonu hüsrandır.

Kur'an-ı Kerim, imanlı toplumu birliğe ve beraberliğe davet ettikten, ayrılık gayrılık, şenlik benlik dâvasına düşmekten nehyettikten sonra Allahın mü'minlere olan nimetini hatırlatıyor. Geçmişten ibret almağa davet ediyor. Birbirlerine düşman olan fertler, din ve iman birliği sayesinde kardeş oluveriyor. Din ve iman insanları birleştirici ve barıştırıcı bir kuvvettir. Din kardeşliği insanları en şerefli ve kutsal bağlarla birbirlerine bağlar. Bir Allah'a inanan, Ona ibadet için yan yana durup Allah evi dediğimiz camilerde ve mescidlerde saf saf olan insanların, birbirlerine düşman olmaları nasıl tasavvur edilir? Gönlüne gerçek iman yerleşmiş bir insan, din kardeşine nasıl kötü muamele edebilir? Kur'an-ı Kerim; kin ve ihtiraslarına aldanıp parça parça olmuş, tefrikaya düşmüş milletlerin ateşten bir uçurum kenarında bulunduklarını, ancak bunların iman kardeşliği sayesinde kurtulduklarını hatırlatıyor ki, bu, üzerinde önemle durmağa değer bir noktadır. Bir uçurum ki, hem de ateşten, Allah esirgesin, ona düşen milletin hali nice olur? Bunu düşünmek bile kalbinde zerre kadar millet sevgisi olan insanı ürpertir. Oğul babaya küskün, baba oğluna kızgın, kardeş kardeşe dargın olan bir milletin vay haline! Bu duruma düşmüş bir millet kuvvetli bir topluluk meydana getirip hayat kavgasıyla dolu bu dünyada varlık gösteremez.

İşte Kur'an-ı Kerim, tefrikanın zararlarını gayet veciz bir uslûpla anlatarak bizi uyarıyor. Ayrılık gayrılık güden cemaatler, ateşten bir uçurumun kenarına sürüklenmişler, itilmişler demektir. Oraya düşmelerinden pek korkulur. Bundan kurtulmak için, milletin silkinip kendine gelmesi, aklını başına alıp birlik ve beraberliğe sarılması gerekir. İbn-i İshak'ın rivayet ettiği üzere Evs ve Hazreç kabileleri arasında 120 sene gibi uzun bir müddet savaşlar sürüp gitmiş, nihayet onlar Müslüman olmakla bu ayrılık gayrılık davasından kurtularak kardeş olmuşlar, bir bayrak altında toplanmışadır. Böylece de o ateşten uçuruma yuvarlanmaktan kurtulmuşlardı. Tarih buna benzer örneklerle doludur. Kur'an-ı Kerim bu gerçeği en canlı bir surette gözümüzün önüne sermekte, şenlik benlik dâvalarıyle parçalanan milletlerin kötü akibetini haber vermektedir. Bunlara kulak asmıyarak bölücü ve bozguncu hareketlere kalkışanlar, milletin başına felaket getirmeğe çalışıyorlar, demektir. Vebali boyunlarına olsun.

Ayeti Kerimede birlik Allah'ın bir nimeti olarak zikrediliyor. Bunun kadrini bilelim. Bölünmeler, tefrika ise ateşten bir uçuruma benzetiliyor, bundan ibret alalım. Millet olarak ayakta durmak istiyorsak Kur'an-ı Kerim'in uyarısına uyalım. Hakkın sesine kulak asalım. Birlikten ayrılmayalım, dirliğimizi bozmayalım. Birlik olmanın yararlarını dile getiren milli şair M. Akif Ersoy bakınız ne diyor!

'Girmeden tefrika bir millete düşman giremez.
Toplu vurdukça yürekler, onu top sindiremez.'

Osman Keskioğlu

**FOUR:** *Diyanet Gazetesi*, **15 May 1977**

*Fraternity in Islam*

İSLAMDA KARDEŞLİK

*Müminler ancak kardeştirler. O halde iki kardeşinizin arasını bulup barıştırın. Allahdan korkun. Ta ki esirgenesiniz* [Kuran 49: 10].

Muhterem Cemaat!

Allah'ü Tealaya ve Resûline inanan ve İslam'ın tevhid bayrağı altında toplanan bütün mü'minler, bir anne ve babadan doğmuş kardeş gibidirler, İslamdaki bu kardeşlik, geçici bir kardeşlik olmayıp ebedi bir kardeşliktir. (1) Müslümanın müslüman üzerindeki haklarından birisi de; aralarında meydana gelen kavga ve münakaşalarda, iki kardeş arasını bulup barıştırmaktır. Nitekim bu hususda bir âyet-i kerimede şöyle buyurulur:

'Müminler ancak kardeştirler. O halde iki kardeşinizin arasını bulup barıştırın. Allahdan korkun. Tâki esirgenesiniz.' (2) Sevgili peygamberimiz de bir hadisi şeriflerinde: 'Mü'min mü'minin (din) kardeşidir,' buyurur. (3)

Muhterem Müslümanlar!

Yüce dinimiz müslümanlar kardeşliği ve kardeşçe yaşamayı, birlik ve beraberlik içinde bulunmayı emreder. Çünkü mü'minler birbirlerine karşı bir vücudun parçaları gibidirler. Bir başka hadisi şerifte peygamberimiz (S.A.) şöyle buyurur: 'Müminler birbirlerini sevmekte, birbirlerine acımakta ve yekdiğerini korumakta bir vücut gibidirler. Vücudun herhangi bir parçası rahatsız olursa diğer kısımları da bu yüzden uykusuzluğa ve humma (hastalığına) tutulurlar.' (4) Dünyanın neresinde olursa olsun, bir müslümanın başına gelen bir felâketten, bütün müslümanlar üzüntü duyarlar. Müslümanlar birbirlerine karşı çok merhametlidirler. Çünkü merhamet; sevginin öz kardeşidir. Dinimiz, müslümanın müslümana canı, malı, ırzı ve namusunun haram olduğunu haber verir. Bize her hususda örnek olan peygamberimiz, Mekke'den Medine'ye hicret eden müslümanları göstererek, 'Ey Ensar! Bu muhacirler sizin kardeşlerinizdir,' buyurunca, Sahabe'yi-kiramdan Saad Bin Rebîa (r.a.) Mühacir kardeşini evine götürür ve ona malını göstererek: 'Bak kardeşim bu malımın yarısı senindir,' der. Bu güzel lütuf karşısında, son derece duygulanan Abdurrahman İbni Avf (r.a.) Hazretleri: 'Kardeşim, Cenab-ı Hak bütün malına bereket versin. Sen yalnız bana çarşıya giden yolu göster, gerisini bana bırak,' demiş ve çarşıdan almış olduğu bir miktar süt ve peyniri satıp akşam evine dönmüştü. (5)

Hal böyle iken bu gün bizler, dünyanın geçici menfaatleri uğruna birbirimizin boğazına sarılmakta ve canına kıymakta bir sakınca görmemekteyiz. Bu ise bizi düşmanlarımıza karsı kuvvetsiz düşürür. Birkaç kişinin yapmış olduğu bir anarşik olay, bütün milleti huzursuz eder.

Muhterem Müslümanlar!

Netice olarak, müslümanlar arasındaki kardeşlik bağlarını bozucu her türlü hareketlerden sakınalım. İnsanların en hayırlısının insanlara iyiliği dokunan kimseler olduğunu bilelim. Dilimiz, kitabımız ve kıblemizin bir olduğunu unutmayalım. (6) Kötülüğe rızanın kötülük olduğunu bilip, her türlü huzur bozucu hareketlerden uzak kalalım.

Fitne çıkarmak isteyenlere yardımcı dahi olmayalım. Birbirlerimizin kardeşleri olduğunu aklımızdan çıkarmayalım.

Kamil Şahin

**FIVE:** *Diyanet Gazetesi,* **15 January 1979**

*Come, let's forget resentments*

GELİN KIRGINLIKLARI UNUTALIM

*Yüce Allah Kuranı Keriminde, 'Şüphesiz Müminler birbirleriyle kardeştirler, öyleyse dargın olan kardeşlerinizin arasını düzeltin; Allah'tan sakının ki size acısın' buyuruyor* [Kuran 49: 10].

Muhterem kardeşlerim,

Bu Ayet-i Kerime mü'minlerin kardeş olduklarını ve kardeşliğin gereği olan birlik içinde bulunmalarını; her türlü çekişme ve bölünmelerden sakınmalarını öğütlemektedir. Millet olarak ayakta durmamızı sağlayan en büyük kuvvetin, birlik ve kardeşlik olduğunda şüphe yoktur. Bunun içindir ki Yüce Allah Kur'an-ı Keriminde, 'Toptan Allah'ın ipine sımsıkı sarılın, ayrılmayın,' buyurmuş, dayanışma içinde olmamızı emretmiştir. Millet ve memleket yararına yöneleceğimiz her alanda bizi başarıya ulaştıracak olan bu birliktir. Çünkü yüce yaratıcının yardım ve rahmeti birlik içinde bulunan topluluklaradır. Birliği bozulan topluluğun dirliği de bozulur. Fertleri birbiriyle çekişen topluluklar güçlerini kaybederler. Nitekim bu husus Enfal suresinin 46. ayetinde hatırlatılmakta ve şöyle duyurulmaktadır: 'Allah'a ve peygamberine itaat edin, çekişmeyin yoksa başarısızlığa düşersiniz ve kuvvetiniz gider. Sabredin, doğrusu Allah sabredenlerle beraberdir.' Sevgili peygamberimizde bu konuda bizleri uyarıyor ve şöyle buyuruyor: 'Birbirinize düşmanlık etmeyiniz, yekdiğerinizi kıskanmayınız, birbirinize arka çevirip ilginizi kesmeyiniz, Ey Allah'ın kulları hepiniz kardeş olunuz.'

Aziz Kardeşlerim,

Müslüman müslümanı kardeş bilir ve ona sevgiyle yaklaşır. Ona haksızlık etmez. Onu üzecek söz ve hareketlerden sakınır. Kendisine göre farklı olan düşüncelerini hoşgörüyle karşılar. İyilikte ona yardımcı olur, kötülüklere karşı onu uyarır ve sakındırır. Kendisi için sevdiği şeyi onun için de arzular.

Kardeşler arasında bölücülük yapmak, söz gezdirerek aralarını açmak büyük günahtır. Hatta Kur'an-ı Kerim, bunun insan öldürmekten daha kötü olduğunu bildirmiştir. Sevgili Peygamberimiz, toplumun huzurunu ve birliğini bozan söz ve davranışlardan sakınılmasını öğütler; küsleri barıştırmaya ve ayrılıkları önlemeye büyük önem verirlerdi. Müslümanlar arasındaki birliğin bozulmamasına bütün gücü ile çalışırdı. Hatta bir defasında arkadaşları arasında geçimsizlik çıkmıştı. Bunu duyar duymaz hemen olay yerine gitmiş ve aralarını buluncaya kadar çalışmıştı, öyle ki ikindi ezanı okunduğu halde cemaate gidememiş, namazı Hz. Ebu Bekir kıldırmıştı.

O halde Muhterem kardeşlerim, geliniz kardeşliği, üstün ahlâkı, birbirini içten sevmesiyle ün yapmış olan asil milletimiz arasında son günlerde beliren kırgınlıkları önleyelim. Birbirimize karşı kırıcı davranışlardan son derece sakınalım. İlk müslümanları ve atalarımızı örnek alarak onlar gibi birbirimizi sevelim. Büyüklerimize saygı, küçüklerimize sevgi gösterelim. Böyle yapacak olursak yüce Allah'ın hoşnutluğunu kazanmış oluruz.

Lütfi Şentürk, Başkan Yardımcısı

## SIX: *Diyanet Gazetesi*, 22 July 1974

*War*

SAVAŞ

*Ey inananlar. Sizi can yakıcı bir azabtan kurtaracak kazançlı bir yolu size göstereyim mi? Allah'a ve Peygamberine inanırsınız: Allah yolunda canlarınızla cihad edersiniz bilesiniz. Bu sizin için en iyi yoldur* [Kuran 61: 10–11].

Muhterem müslümanlar,

Yakın tarihimiz en önemli günlerini yaşıyoruz. Tarih boyunca kahramanlık destanları yazmış olan şanlı ordumuz, vatanımızın bir parçası olan Kıbrıs'daki din ve soydaşlarımıza karsı yapılan zalimane hareketlere son vermek üzere harekete geçmiş bulunmaktadır. Bu harekatta silahlı kuvvetlerimizin başarıya ulaşmasını yüce Allah'tan dileriz.

Savaş, insanlıkta doğmuştur. İnsanlar yasadıkça da devam edecektir. Sevgili Peygamberimiz bu gerçeği: 'Savaş, kıyâmete kadar sürüp gidecektir' sözleri ile ifade buyurmuşlardır. Çünkü savaş hak ile bâtılın, iyi ile kötünün, haklı ile haksızın mücadelesidir. Bunun içindir ki İslamiyet yüce Allah'a imandan sonra en üstün amelin savaş olduğunu haber vermiştir. Savaş deyince ilk akla gelen, vatan savunmasıdır. Her insan, her vatandaşın en birinci ve en esaslı görevi budur. Bunu içindir ki İslâmiyet, vatanı savunma görevi olan askerliği en şerefli görevlerden saymış. Allah rızası için askerin bir gece nöbet beklemesinin, gecesi namaz ile gündüzü oruçla geçen bin geceden daha hayırlı olduğunu haber vermiştir.

Şanlı ordumuz bu indirme ve çıkartması ile yavru vatan Kıbrıs harekâtı başlamıştır. Kıbrıs, Hz. Osman zamanından beri başta sevgili Peygamberimizin güzide arkadaşları olmak üzere müslüman ve Türk kanı ile sulana gelmiş olan, içinde binlerce şehidimizin mezarı bulunan, hatta şehit sahabi yatan bir yerdir. Orada yaşayanlar müslüman Türk kardeşlerimizdir. Yunanlılar, müslüman kardeşlerimizi öldürmek, ezan sesleri yükselen cami ve şehitlerimizin mezarlarını çiğnemek suretiyle adayı Yunanistan'a ilhak etmek üzere saldırıya geçmişlerdir. Bu durum karşısında hükümetimiz duruma müdahale kararı almış ve silahlı kuvvetlerimiz adaya çıkmışlardır.

Aziz müslümanlar,

Bu harekât, yakın tarihimizde ilk def'a bizlere cihad fırsatı vermiştir. Dikkat buyurun, 'Cihad fırsatı' diyorum, çünkü bu sayede adada süregelen haksızlıklara ve insanlık dışı davranışlara son verilecek, müslüman Türk kardeşlerimizin hakları korunmuş olacaktır. Bu uğrada ölenlerimiz şehit, kalanlarımız gazi olacaklardır. Her iki rütbe de rütbelerin en büyüğüdür. Bir adam Sevgili Peygamberimize:

– İnsanların hangisi efdal? diye sordu.

Peygamberimiz:

– Allah yolunda malı ile canı ile cihad eden inanmış kimsedir, buyurmuştur.

Bir gün sevgili Peygamberimiz Ebû Revaha oğlu Abdullah kumandasında bir bölük askeri düşmanla savaşa göndermişti. Komutan Abdullah, tan yeri ağarmadan birliğini toplayıp savaş alanına göndermiş, kendisi de sabah namazını Peygamberimiz'le beraber kılmak için mescide gelmişti. Namazı kıldılar. Peygamberimiz selâm verip yüzünü cemaate dönünce Abdullah'ı orada görmüştü. Ona: 'Savaşla görevlendirildiğiniz halde, vazifenizi niçin terk ettiniz?' diye sordu. Abdullah: 'Ey Allah'ın Resûlü, sizinle birlikte sabah namazını kılmak için onlara yetişmek üzere geri kaldım' demesi üzerine, Peygamberimiz: 'Nefsimi kudret elinde bulunduran Allah'a yemin ederim ki, gece gündüz bu mescidde başını secdeden kaldırmasan, yine de o gazi askerlerin faziletine erişemezsin. Haydi durma arkadaşlarına yetiş' buyurdu. Bu olay, cihadın faziletini ne güzel ifade etmektedir.

Müslüman kardeşlerim,

Yüce Allah Kur'an-ı Kerim'de: 'Ey inananlar, sizi can yakıcı bir azâbtan kurtaracak kazançlı bir yolu size göstereyim mi? Allah'a ve Peygamber'ine inanırsınız; Allah yolunda canlarınızla mallarınızla cihad edersiniz. Bilesiniz, bu sizin için en iyi yoldur' buyurmuştur. Yüce Rabbimizin bu emrine uyarak, önümüze çıkan bu cihad fırsatını değerlendirmeliyiz. Maddi-manevi güçlerimizle yardıma koşmalıyız. Ancak böyle fırsatlar için kazandığımız malımızla cihad etmeliyiz. Cephede savaşanlara malımızla canımızla destek olmalıyız. Sevgili Peygamberimiz savaşa giden orduyu donatan kimsenin, bizzat savaş etmiş gibi sevap alacağını müjdelemiştir. Dikkat edilirse hem âyet ve hem de hadislerde canlarımızla olduğu gibi mallarımızla da Allah yolunda savaşmamız emredilmektedir. Malla savaşmak, inançtaki sadakatin, doğruluğun sonucudur. İnanan kimse inandığını gösterir.

Sevgili Peygamberimiz Hendek harbinde Ashâb-ı Kirâm'ı savaş hazırlığı için yardıma çağırmıştır. Herkes malından bir miktarını ortaya koydu: kimi malının üçte birini, kimi yarısını, kimi daha az, kimi daha çok verdi. Bunlar arasında bir Ebû Bekir vardı ki, her şeyini ortaya koymuştu. Peygamberimiz kendisine:

– Ey Ebû Bekir, kendine, çoluk çocuğuna ne ayırdın? deyince, Hz. Ebû
  Bekir:
– Onlara Allah ile Resûlünü bıraktım, diye cevap vermişti. Çünkü
  inanıyordu. Allah için verdiği her şeyin karşılığı fazlasıyla kendisine
  Allah tarafından verilecekti.

Öyle ise, biz de Ashâb-ı Kiramı ve atalarımızı örnek alarak, bugün Kıbrıs'ta savaşan kahraman silahlı kuvvetlerimize ve orada çok zor günler yaşayan din kardeşlerimize yek vücud halinde destek olmalıyız. Hava ve Deniz Kuvvetlerimizi Güçlendirme Vakıflarına yardıma koşmalı bu maksatla açılacak kampanyalara seve seve katılmalıyız.

Böyle yaptığımız takdirde haklı olduğumuz bu davada yüce Allah bizi başarıya ulaştıracaktır.

Gazanız mübârek olsun, Allah'ın yardım ve nusreti bizimle beraber olsun.

Lütfü Şentürk (Ankara müftüsü)

## SEVEN: *Diyanet Gazetesi*, 1 August 1975

*Oneness and togetherness in Islam*

## İSLAMDA BİRLİK VE BERABERLİK

*Ey iman edenler! Topluca barışa girin, şeytanın saptırıcı adımlarına uymayın. Şeytan sizin apaçık bir düşmanınızdır* [Kuran 2: 208].

Bilindiği gibi İslam Dini, intişarından itibaren insanlar arası ilişkilerin düzeltilmesini mensuplarından istemiş ve onları bu harekete teşvik etmiştir. Allah'a imana davet ederken bile güzel sözlerle, muhatabın kalbini incitmeden çağırmayı öğütlemiştir.

Resûlü Ekrem dini yayarken, kardeşlik ve birlik fikrinin tohumlarını atmış, insanlara Tek Allah inancını aşılayıp, ibadet esaslarını öğretirken, kardeş olduklarını ve birbirlerine sevgi duymalarının gereğini de ehemmiyetle tavsiye etmiştir.

Gerçekten İslâmiyet, barış ve kardeşlik dinidir. Çünkü inanan her mü'min, kendisi için hoş görmediği, kendisine yöneltilmesini istemediği hareketleri, başkalarına da yapamaz. İnsanları huzursuz ve rahatsız edemez. Gaye olan kâmil imana erişmek için, bütün müslümanlar, ilâhi emirlere uymağa ve Resûl-ü Ekrem'in nasihatlerini tutmağa büyük gayret gösterirler.

Cenâb-ı Hak, sulh ve kardeşlik içinde olun, düşmanlarınız antlaşmaları bozup size saldırmadıkça siz onlara saldırmayın, derken, Hazreti Peygamber (S.A.S.) 'bir müslümanı inciten, beni incitir, bir zimmîye eza edenin hasmı benim, birbirinizi seviniz, kimsenin ırzına, malına, kanına dokunmayınız, gönlünüzde bütün mahlûkata şefkat ve merhamet bulunsun' diye nasihat ederken, elbette bir mü'mine bunların aksini yapmak yaraşmaz.

Müslüman kavgacı, öfke ve kin sahibi, iftiracı ve fesat çıkaran olamaz. Din kardeşlerinin canına kıyamaz. Zira imanla fitne fesat bir araya gelemez. Çirkin hareketlerin kundakçıları, değil kâmil imana kavuşmak, gerçek mü'min bile sayılamazlar.

Milleti bölenler veya bölünmesine çalışanlar, Hazreti Peygamber'in (S.A.S.) şu hadislerini iyi düşünmelidirler: 'Bölücülük yapanlar bizden değildir' (1) ve 'Bize silah çekenler, içimizde kargaşalık çıkarıp bizi karıştıranlar, bizden değildir.' (2)

Şu halde inançlı bir toplumda isyandan, kavgadan, serkeşlikten, insanların birbirlerine eza etmesinden, eğrilik ve hileden, haklara saldırmadan bahsedilemez. İslâm cemiyetinde bu tutumların asla yeri yoktur.

İslâm cemiyetinde iman ve ibâdetlerle, güven ve karşılıklı sevgiyle vücut bulmuş huzurlu bir asayiş vardır. Bu güzel nizam içerisinde her mü'min emniyet ve neş'eyle çalışarak mensubu bulunduğu toplumu ayakta tutma ve ileriye götürme gayreti içerisindedir. Çünkü kâmil imana erişmeye çalışan her müslüman, canından çok sevdiği Peygamber'inin: 'Birlikte rahmet, bölünmelerde azap vardır.' (3) 'Müslüman, müslümanın kardeşidir, ona hiyanet etmez, onu yalanlamaz, onu mahcup edip küçük düşürmez.' (4) 'Mazlumu zulümden kurtarmada, zalimi, yaptığı kötü hareketten vazgeçirmede, din kardeşlerine yardımcı ol,' (5) diyen öğütlerini hiçbir suretle unutamaz.

Sevgi, saygı, kardeşlik, sulh, iyilik ve güzelliğe büyük ölçüde ehemmiyet veren dinimiz, bunları imân-ı Kâmile (Olgun imâna) erişmenin de esaslarından olarak kabul etmiştir. Hiçbir menfaat ve hiçbir düşünce gerçek mü'minin kalbinden bu duyguları söküp atamaz. Onu bu sıfatlarını terke mecbur edemez. Çünkü bu sayılan vasıfları unutup, zıtları olan çirkin ve menfi hareketlerde bulunmak, şeytana uymaktır. Oysaki, Cenâb-ı Hak: 'Ey iman edenler! Topluca barışa girin, şeytanın saptırıcı adımlarına uymayın. Şeytan sizin apaçık bir düşmanınızdır,' (6) buyuruyor. Düşmanının taktiğine uyup kendini helâk etmek, herhalde akıl ve mantık sahibi bir kimsenin yapacağı bir iş değildir. Gerçek şu ki, selim akıl taşıyan hiç bir fert, böyle sakim bir yol tutamaz.

Müslüman, içinde yaşadığı cemiyetin bir ferdi olduğunu unutmaz. Bir bütünü meydana getiren parçalardan, herhangi birinin menfi davranışı, bütünü zedeler, bütün yaralanınca onun parçaları da işe yaramaz hale gelir. O halde akıllı müslüman cemiyete zarar verecek her hareketin, kendi nefsine de zararlı olacağı şuuru içindedir. Cemiyetin bekası, sıhhatlı olması, normal bir düzenle çalışması, onu teşkil eden fertlerin karşılıklı sevgi, gayret ve beraberliği ile mümkündür. Yoksa Allah korusun, toplum yok olunca, artık fert kalır mı?

Sevgili Peygamberimiz (S.A.S.) diyor ki: 'Birbirinize öfke ve kin beslemeyiniz, birbirinizle kardeşlik alakanızı kesmeyiniz, birbirinize sırt çevirmeyiniz. Ey Allah'ın kulları! Allah'ın size emrettiği gibi kardeş olunuz. Bir Müslüman için din kardeşine, üç günden fazla dargın durmak helal olmaz.' (7)

Hakiki Müslümanlar, toplumu dargınlık ve kırgınlıklardan, düşmanlık ve nefretten, kibirlilik ve zalimlikten, hasılı her türlü fesat ve kötülüklerle, ne biçimde olursa olsun bütün çirkin hareketlerden uzak, tek kelimeyle melekleşmiş insanlardan teşekkül etmiş bir cemiyettir. Tarihi boydan boya okumaya lûzum yok, şüphe edenler Hazret-i Peygamber ve Ashabına baksınlar. Kuşkusu olanlar, yakın tarihimizde İstiklal Harbinin öncesi, Anadolu'muza baksınlar. Fikir vermeye, ibret almaya bu iki manzara yeter. Bugün Kuvay-ı Milliye ruhunu bir abide gibi ortaya çıkarmış olan dedelerimizin, babalarımızın kardeşlik şuuruna çok ihtiyacımız var. Birbirimizi Allah'ın (C.C.) ve Resûlü'nün (S.A.S.) dedikleri gibi sevelim, kardeş olalım, Cenâb-ı Hakkın ve Resûl-ü Ekremin rızasını kazanalım.

Talat Karaçizmeli, Planlama Müşaviri

**EIGHT: *Diyanet Gazetesi*, 1 February 1977**

*Let's protect our national and moral values*

## MİLLİ VE MANEVİ DEĞERLERİMİZİ KORUYALIM

*Peygamberin getirdiklerini alınız. Yasak ettiği şeylerden sakınız* [Kuran 59: 7].

Bir cemiyeti ayakta tutan, onun varlığını devam ettiren iki unsur vardır. Bunlardan birincisi maddiyat, ikincisi de maneviyattır.

Bir binanın taş ve tuğlasını bir cemiyetin maddiyatına benzetirsek, bu parçaları birbirine bağlayan harç da cemiyetin maneviyatına benzer. Binaenaleyh harç kullanılmadan kuru kuruya örülen bir duvar ve bu duvarın meydana getirdiği bina nasıl ki harçla örülen duvarların meydana getirdiği bina kadar sağlam olamazsa, sırf maddiyata dayanan maneviyatsız bir cemiyet de tıpkı harçsız örülmüş duvarlar gibi çürüktür, yıkılmaya mahkûmdur.

Bizim manevi değerlerimizin kaynağı olan dinimiz iki ana temele dayanır. Bunlarda biri Allah'ın kitabı Kur'an-ı Kerim, diğeri de âlemlere rahmet olarak gönderilen Peygamberimizin (s.a.) sünnetidir. Sonra bunlara uyan selef-i sâlihinin içtihatları, güzel ahlâk ve amelleri ile ecdadımızın kitap ve sünnete uygun düşen örf ve âdetleridir.

Yüce Allah, Kur'an-ı Kerim'de müminleri kitap ve sünnete uymaya çağırır ve mealen buyurur ki:

'Peygamberin getirdiklerini alınız, yasak ettiği şeylerden sakınınız.' (1)

Yine Yüce Allah, Kur'an-ı Kerim'in Ahzâb suresinde Resûlüllah'a uymanın önemine ve gereğine işaret eder ve mealen buyurur ki:

'Andolsun ki Resûlüllah da Allahı ve ahiret gününü umar olanlar ve Allahı çok zikredenler için güzel bir örnek vardır.' (2)

Erkek ve kadın her müslüman, itikad, ibadet, ahlâk ve bütün muamelâtında Kur'an-ı Kerime ve Peygamber Efendimizin (s.a.) sünnetine ve onun kıymetli ashabının güzel ahlâk, adet ve geleneklerine uymaya çalışmalı, ecdadının güzel adetlerini de yaşatmalıdır. Dine uymayan kötü örf ve adetler ecdaddan da kalsa derhal terkedilmelidir. Hele bu kötü adetler gayr-i müslimlerden gelmişse mutlaka en kısa zamanda bırakılmalıdır. Maalesef zamanımızda hıristiyan Avrupa'nın kötü örf ve adetleri gün geçtikçe milletimizin fertleri arasında geniş çapta yayılmaktadır.

Hıristiyan Avrupa'yı öylesine taklid ediyoruz ki iyi kötü, faydalı faydasız ayırd etmeden ne görürsek alıyoruz. Bu da bizi küçültüyor. Bir millet olarak gerçek kişiliğimizi kaybettiriyor. Avrupa'nın faydalı olan tekniğini ve müspet ilmini almalıyız. Bunu almakta dinen bir sakınca yoktur. Zira sevgili Peygamberimiz (s.a.):

'İlim ve hikmet müminin kaybedilmiş malı gibidir, onu nerede bulursa alır,' buyurmuştur. Fakat gayr-i müslimlerin bize hiç faydası dokunmayan, hatta zararlı olan örf ve adetlerini, dini inançlarını almamalıyız. Bizi bir millet olarak bir arada tutan, bizi birbirimize sevdiren ve bağlayan kendi örf ve adetlerimizdir. Bir milleti yıkmak, içinden çökertmek isteyen düşmanlar, o milletin önce dinini, dilini, tarihini, kültürünü, örf ve adetlerini millet fertlerinin ruhundan söküp artmaya sonra da bunların yerine kendi dinlerini, gelenek ve göreneklerini, kendi kültürlerini yerleştirmeye çalışırlar.

Ebu Said Hudri (r.a.) nin rivayet ettiği bir hadisde, Resulü Ekrem (s.a.): 'Muhakkak siz, kendinizden önce gelen milletlerin karış karış, arşın arşın yolunda gideceksiniz. Öyle ki şayet onlar bir kelerin deliğine girseler siz de onlara tabi olacaksınız' buyuruyor. Eshab da ya Resûlüllah! Bu ümmetler yahudilerle hıristiyanlar mı? diye sorar. Resulü Ekrem: 'Onlardan başka ya kim olacak?' buyurur.

Bu hadis-i şerifde hıristiyanlarla yahudilerin gayri ahlâki hal ve hareketlerini takip ve taklid etmekten İslâm ümmeti sakındırılmıştır. Taklidin kötülenmesi yalnız bunlara münhasır kalmayıp tarihte gelip geçmiş bütün başka milletlerin kötü adet ve törelerini taklide de şamildir.

Şüphesiz ki, her dinin ve her içtimai kuruluşun kendisine has bir medeniyeti ve diğerlerinden ayıran bir özelliği vardır ki, milletler arasındaki varlığını ancak bu özel nitelikleriyle korur.

Bir Müslüman-Türk mensup olduğu milletin ve bağlı olduğu ümmetin örf ve adetlerini bırakır da gayr-i müslümlere benzemeye çalışırsa Hz. Muhammed (s.a.) in şu hadisi gereğince, o, benzemeye çalıştığı zümreden sayılır. Resûlüllah (s.a.) buyuruyor ki:

'Her kim bir kavme benzerse artık o kimse onlardandır.' (3)

İbn Mes'ud'un rivayet ettiği başka bir hadis-i şerifde de şöyle buyuruluyor:

'Her kim bir kavmin yaptıklarına razı olursa onlardan olur.' (4)

Şüphesiz bir kimse bir kavmin, bir zümrenin, hayatını, örf ve adetlerini taklid ederse, o kimse onlara hayran ve kalben bağlı demektir. Allah biz müslümanları gafletten kurtarsın.

Ârif Erkan

# APPENDIX IV: ECONOMIC INDICATORS AND DİYANET STATISTICS IN TABLES (CHAPTER 7)

**Table IV.1** Population, Gross Domestic Product and GDP/cap (in current US dollars), and rates of change 1998–2020

| Year | Population (million) | GDP (billion US dollar) | GDP/cap (US dollar) | GNP/cap change rate (per cent) |
|------|------|------|------|------|
| 1998 | 61.3 | 276.0 | 4,500 | – |
| 1999 | 62.3 | 256.4 | 4,116 | -8.5 |
| 2000 | 63.2 | 274.3 | 4,337 | 5.3 |
| 2001 | 64.2 | 201.8 | 3,143 | -27.1 |
| 2002 | 65.1 | 240.2 | 3,688 | 17.3 |
| 2003 | 66.1 | 314.6 | 4,760 | 29.1 |
| 2004 | 67.0 | 408.9 | 6,101 | 22.0 |
| 2005 | 67.9 | 506.3 | 7,456 | 22.2 |
| 2006 | 68.8 | 557.1 | 8,102 | 8.7 |
| 2007 | 69.6 | 681.3 | 9,792 | 20.9 |
| 2008 | 70.4 | 770.4 | 10,941 | 11.7 |
| 2009 | 71.3 | 649.3 | 9,104 | -16.8 |

*(Continued)*

| Year | Population (million) | GDP (billion US dollar) | GDP/cap (US dollar) | GNP/cap change rate (per cent) |
|------|------|------|------|------|
| 2010 | 73.3 | 777.0 | 10,742 | 18.0 |
| 2011 | 73.4 | 838.8 | 11,421 | 6.3 |
| 2012 | 74.7 | 880.6 | 11,795 | 3.3 |
| 2013 | 75.9 | 957.8 | 12,614 | 6.9 |
| 2014 | 77.2 | 938.9 | 12,157 | -3.6 |
| 2015 | 78.5 | 864.3 | 11,006 | -9.5 |
| 2016 | 79.8 | 869.7 | 10,895 | -1.0 |
| 2017 | 81.1 | 859.0 | 10,591 | -2.8 |
| 2018 | 82.3 | 778.4 | 9,456 | -10.7 |
| 2019 | 83.4 | 761.4 | 9,127 | -3.5 |
| 2020 | 83.6 | 717.0 | 8,599 | -5.8 |

*Source: World Bank*

**Table IV.2** Number of Diyanet personnel in absolute numbers and per 100,000 inhabitants from 1970 to 2020

| Year | Number of personnel | Personnel per 100,000 inhabitants |
|------|------|------|
| 1970 | 25,236 | 72 |
| 1973 | 30,970 | 83 |
| 1981 | 43,197 | 96 |
| 1982 | 44,369 | 96 |
| 1983 | 46,665 | 99 |
| 1984 | 49,784 | 104 |
| 1985 | n.a. | |
| 1986 | 61,929 | 124 |
| 1987 | 65,361 | 128 |
| 1988 | 70,099 | 135 |
| 1989 | 74,930 | 141 |
| 1991 | 74,789 | 136 |

*(Continued)*

| Year | Number of personnel | Personnel per 100,000 inhabitants |
|------|---------------------|-----------------------------------|
| 1992 | 76,232 | 137 |
| 1993 | 75,090 | 133 |
| 1994 | 74,772 | 130 |
| 1995 | 75,043 | 128 |
| 1996 | 76,087 | 128 |
| 1997 | 81,492 | 135 |
| 1998 | 79,685 | 130 |
| 1999 | 77,795 | 125 |
| 2000 | 75,433 | 119 |
| 2001 | 76,037 | 119 |
| 2002 | 74,368 | 114 |
| 2003 | 74,108 | 121 |
| 2004 | 74,114 | 111 |
| 2005 | n.a. | |
| 2006 | 79,779 | 116 |
| 2007 | 84,157 | 121 |
| 2008 | 83,116 | 118 |
| 2009 | 81,816 | 115 |
| 2010 | 84,115 | 115 |
| 2011 | 98,516 | 134 |
| 2012 | 105,431 | 141 |
| 2013 | 121,809 | 160 |
| 2014 | 119,692 | 155 |
| 2015 | 117,323 | 149 |
| 2016 | 119,692 | 150 |
| 2017 | 109,289 | 135 |
| 2018 | 107,139 | 130 |
| 2019 | 104,752 | 126 |
| 2020 | 127,892 | 153 |

Sources: Diyanet Activity Reports 2006–20 (DİB Faaliyet Raporları); Çakır and Bozan (2005)

**Table IV.3** The Diyanet budget 2006–20 (TL and US dollars) and rates of change

| Year | Yearly budget (million TL) | Yearly budget (million US dollar) | Rate of change (per cent) TL (US dollar) |
|------|------|------|------|
| 2006 | 1,453 | 1,074 | – |
| 2007 | 1,770 | 1,222 | 21.8 (13.8) |
| 2008 | 2,100 | 1,795 | 18.6 (46.9) |
| 2009 | 2,553 | 1,659 | 21.6 (-7.6) |
| 2010 | 2,733 | 1,834 | 7.1 (11.2) |
| 2011 | 3,393 | 2,179 | 24.1 (18.8) |
| 2012 | 4,254 | 2,252 | 25.4 (3.3) |
| 2013 | 4,971 | 2,793 | 16.9 (24.0) |
| 2014 | 5,705 | 2,622 | 14.8 (-6.1) |
| 2015 | 6,038 | 2,569 | 5.8 (-2.0) |
| 2016 | 6,517 | 2,236 | 7.9 (-13.0) |
| 2017 | 7,247 | 2,017 | 11.2 (-9.8) |
| 2018 | 8,356 | 2,206 | 15.3 (9.4) |
| 2019 | 10,213 | 1,916 | 22.2 (-13.1) |
| 2020 | 10,930 | 1,836 | 7.0 (- 4.2) |

*Sources: Diyanet Activity Reports 2006–20 (DİB Faaliyet Raporları); Turkish Central Bank Statistics*

# BIBLIOGRAPHY

**Primary Sources**

Akseki, Ahmet Hamdi ([1928] 2005) *Türkçe Hutbe* (Sermon in Turkish), translated from Ottoman into modern Turkish and edited by Emine Şeyma Usta as *Atatürk'ün Hazırlattığı Cuma Hutbeleri* (Friday sermons initiated by Atatürk), Istanbul: İleri Yayınları.

Akseki, Ahmet Hamdi ([1933] 2014) *İslam dini. İtikat, İbadet, Ahlak* (Islamic religion. Belief, worship and ethics), Istanbul: Nur Yayınları.

Akseki, Ahmet Hamdi (1936) *Yeni hutbelerim* (My new sermons), Vol. 1, Ankara: Diyanet İşleri Reisliği.

Akseki, Ahmet Hamdi (1937) *Yeni hutbelerim* (My new sermons), Vol. 2, Ankara: Diyanet İşleri Reisliği.

Altıkulaç, Tayyar (2011) *Zorlukları Aşarken* (Overcoming the difficulties), 3 vols, Istanbul: Ufuk Yayınları.

Atatürk, Mustafa Kemal (2008) *The Great Speech*, Ankara: Atatürk Research Center.

al-Bukhari, Muhammad (1979) *Ṣaḥīḥ al-Bukhārī*, translated into English by Muhammad Muhsin Khan, 9 vols, Lahore: Kazi Publications.

al-Bulaqi Azizi, Ali b. Ahmad (d. 1659) (1887) *al-Sirāj al-munīr bi-sharḥ al-Jāmiʿ al-ṣaghīr*, 3 vols, Cairo: al-Matbaʿat al-Khayriyya.

Diyanet İşleri Başkanlığı, DİB (2012) *Din Hizmetleri Raporu 2011*, https://dinhizmetleri.diyanet.gov.tr/sayfa/384 (last accessed 12 November 2021).

Diyanet İşleri Başkanlığı, DİB (2013) *Din Hizmetleri Raporu 2012*, ibid.

Diyanet İşleri Başkanlığı, DİB (2014) *Din Hizmetleri Raporu 2013*, ibid.

Diyanet İşleri Başkanlığı, DİB (2015) *Din Hizmetleri Raporu 2014*, ibid.

Diyanet İşleri Başkanlığı, DİB (2016) *Din Hizmetleri Raporu 2015*, ibid.

Diyanet İşleri Başkanlığı, DİB (2017) *Din Hizmetleri Raporu 2016*, ibid.

Diyanet İşleri Başkanlığı, DİB (2018) *Din Hizmetleri Raporu 2017*, ibid.

Diyanet İşleri Başkanlığı, DİB (2019) *Din Hizmetleri Raporu 2018*, ibid.

Diyanet İşleri Başkanlığı, DİB (2016) *Dini İstismar ve Tedhiş Hareketi DEAŞ* (Exploitation of religion and terrorist organisation DAESH), https://diyanetamerica.org/wp-content/uploads/2016/10/ISIS_Report.pdf (last accessed 25 November 2021).

Diyanet İşleri Başkanlığı, DİB (2017) *Exploitation of Religion and Terrorist Organisation DAESH*, https://yayin.diyanet.gov.tr/File/Download?path=520_1.pdf&id=520 (last accessed 12 November 2021).

Diyanet İşleri Başkanlığı, DİB (2007) *Faaliyet Raporu 2006*, https://stratejigelistirme.diyanet.gov.tr/sayfa/22/Faaliyet-Raporlari (last accessed 12 November 2021).

Diyanet İşleri Başkanlığı, DİB (2008) *Faaliyet Raporu 2007*, ibid.

Diyanet İşleri Başkanlığı, DİB (2009) *Faaliyet Raporu 2008*, ibid.

Diyanet İşleri Başkanlığı, DİB (2010) *Faaliyet Raporu 2009*, ibid.

Diyanet İşleri Başkanlığı, DİB (2011) *Faaliyet Raporu 2010*, ibid.

Diyanet İşleri Başkanlığı, DİB (2012) *Faaliyet Raporu 2011*, ibid.

Diyanet İşleri Başkanlığı, DİB (2013) *Faaliyet Raporu 2012*, ibid.

Diyanet İşleri Başkanlığı, DİB (2014) *Faaliyet Raporu 2013*, ibid.

Diyanet İşleri Başkanlığı, DİB (2015) *Faaliyet Raporu 2014*, ibid.

Diyanet İşleri Başkanlığı, DİB (2016) *Faaliyet Raporu 2015*, ibid.

Diyanet İşleri Başkanlığı, DİB (2017) *Faaliyet Raporu 2016*, ibid.

Diyanet İşleri Başkanlığı, DİB (2018) *Faaliyet Raporu 2017*, ibid.

Diyanet İşleri Başkanlığı, DİB (2019) *Faaliyet Raporu 2018*, ibid.

Diyanet İşleri Başkanlığı, DİB (2020) *Faaliyet Raporu 2019*, ibid.

Diyanet İşleri Başkanlığı, DİB (2021) *Faaliyet Raporu 2020*, ibid.

Diyanet İşleri Başkanlığı, DİB (2017) *Kendi Dilinden FETÖ – Örgütlü Bir Din İstismarı* (FETÖ in his own words – organised religious exploitation), https://www.aa.com.tr/uploads/TempUserFiles/haber/2017/07/KENDI-DILINDEN-FETO-20170725son.pdf' (last accessed 12 November 2021).

Diyanet İşleri Başkanlığı, DİB (2018) *Suriye Fırat Kalkanı ve Zeytin Dalı Faaliyet Raporu* (Report on the Operation Euphrates Shield and Operation Olive Branch), https://dinhizmetleri.diyanet.gov.tr/ResimKitapligi/FKB-ZDB%20Faaliyet%20Raporu.pdf (last accessed 12 November 2021).

Ebüssuud Efendi (d. 1574) (1928) *Tefsiru Ebüssuud: İrşadü'l-akli's-selim ila mezaya'l-Kur'ani'l-Kerim*, 5 vols, Cairo: Matba'at Muhammed Ali Sabih wa avladih.

Ibn Hacer el-Askalani, Ahmed (d. 852) (1967) *Bülüğü'l-Merâm Tercümesi ve Şerhi: Selâmet Yolları* (Bulugh al-Meram translation and commentary: the roads to salvation), edited and translated into Turkish by Ahmed Davudoğlu, Vol. 4, Istanbul: Sönmez Neşriyat.

Ibn Hisham, Abd al-Malik (d. 833) [from Ibn Ishaq (d. 768)] (1955) *al-Sīra al-nabawiyya* [edited by Mustafa al-Saqqa, Ibrahim al-Abyari, and 'Abd al-Hafiz Shalabi, Cairo: Maktabat wa-Matba'at Mustafa al-Babi al-Halabi], translated by A. Guillaume as *The Life of Muhammad: A Translation of Isḥāq's Sīrat Rasūl Allāh*, Oxford: Oxford University Press.

Ibn Malak Izz al-Din Abd al-Latif b. Abd al-Aziz (d. after 1418) (1886) *Mabāriq al-āzhār fī sharḥ Mashāriq al-ānwār*, 2 vols, Istanbul: Hacı Muharrem Efendi Matbaası.

Kara, Ismail (2015) *Kutuz Hoca'nın Hatıraları* (Kutuz Hoca's memories), Istanbul: Dergah, 2015.

Makal, Mahmut ([1954] 1965) *A Village in Anatolia*, London: Valentine, Mitchell.

Muslim ibn al-Hajjaj (d. 875) (1975) *Ṣaḥīḥ Muslim*, 4 vols, translated into English by Abdul Hamid Siddiqi, Lahore: SH Muhammad Ashraf.

al-Nabhani, Yusuf b. Isma'il (d. 1932) (1932) *al-Fatḥ al-kabīr fī zamm al-zīyāde ilā al-Jāmī' al-ṣaghīr*, 3 vols, Cairo: Manshurat Mustafa el-Babi al-Halabi.

Nedvi, Muinüddin Ahmed and Said Sahib Ansari (1963) *Asrı Saadet: Peygamberimiz'in ashabı* (Age of happiness: the companions of the Prophet), edited by Eşref Edip, translated into Turkish by Ali Genceli, 4 vols, Istanbul: Sebilürresad Nesriyatı.

al-Raghib al-Isfahani (d. 1108) (1961) *al-Mufradāt fī Gharīb al-Qur'ān*, ed. Muhammed Sayyid Kilani, Cairo: Manshurat Mustafa al-Babi al-Halabi.

Turkey State Institute of Statistics (1977) *1977 Statistical Yearbook of Turkey*, Ankara: Turkey State Institute of Statistics.

Yazıcıoğlu, M. Said (2013) *Ne Yan Yana Ne Karşı Karşıya. Anılar* (Neither side by side, nor up against. Memories), Istanbul: Alfa Yayınları.

## Secondary Sources

Abrams, Philip (1988) 'Notes on the Difficulty of Studying the State', *Journal of Historical Sociology*, 1: 1, pp. 58–89.

Afet İnan, Ayşe ([1931] 1969) *Medeni Bilgiler ve M. Kemal Atatürk'ün El Yazıları* (Civics and M. Kemal Atatürk's writings), Ankara: Türk Tarih Kurumu.

Akşit, Bahattin (1991) 'Islamic Education in Turkey: Medrese Reform in Late Ottoman Times and Imam-Hatip Schools in the Republic', in Richard Tapper (ed.), *Islam in Modern Turkey: Religion, Politics and Literature in a Secular State*, London: I. B. Tauris, pp. 145–70.

Anderson, Benedict (1983) *Imagined Communities: Reflections on the Origin and Spread of Nationalism*, London: Verso.

Antoun, Richard (1989) *Muslim Preacher in the Modern World*, Princeton: Princeton University Press.

Armağan, Mustafa (2015) *Türkçe Ezan ve Menderes: Bir Devrin Yazılamayan Gerçekleri* (Turkish *ezan* and Menderes: an epoch's realities that could not be written), Istanbul: Timas.

Arslan, Elif (2015) 'Mütevazi Bir Aile Mektebi: Diyanet Aile Dergisi', *Diyanet Aylık Dergi*, Nr 300, pp. 38–41.

Aytürk, İlker (2004) 'Turkish Linguists against the West: The Origins of Linguistic Nationalism in Atatürk's Turkey', *Middle Eastern Studies*, 40: 6, pp. 1–25.

Aytürk, İlker (2008) 'The First Episode of Language Reform in Republican Turkey: The Language Council from 1926–1931', *Journal of Royal Asiatic Society*, 18: 3, pp. 275–93.

Azak, Umut (2010) *Islam and Secularism in Turkey: Kemalism, Religion and the Nation State*, London: I. B. Tauris.

Başaran, Ezgi (2017) *Frontline Turkey: The Conflict at the Heart of the Middle East*, London: I. B. Tauris.

Becker, Carl (2006) 'On the History of Muslim Worship', in Gerald Hawting (ed.), *The Development of Islamic Ritual*, Aldershot: Ashgate, pp. 49–74.

Berkes, Niyazi ([1964] 1998) *The Development of Secularism in Turkey*, New York: Routledge.

Berkey, Jonathan (1992) *Transmission of Knowledge in Medieval Cairo*, Princeton: Princeton University Press.

Bernières, Louis de (2005) *Birds Without Wings*, London: Vintage Books.

Birand, Mehmet Ali, Rıdvan Akar and Hikmet Bila (1999) *12 Eylül Türkiye'nin Miladı* (12 September, milestone for Turkey), Istanbul: Doğan Kitap.

Bloch, Maurice (ed.) (1975) *Political Language and Oratory in Traditional Society*, London: Academic Press.

Bora, Tanıl (2003) 'Nationalist Discourses in Turkey', *The South Atlantic Quarterly*, 102 :2–3, pp. 433–51.

Breuilly, John (1993) *Nationalism and the State*, Manchester: Manchester University Press.

Bulut, Mehmet (2006) 'Diyanet İşleri Başkanlığının Yayımladığı İlk Hutbe Mecmuası Türkçe Hutbe', *Diyanet Aylık Dergi*, Nr 184, pp. 48–50.

Bulut, Mehmet (2015) 'Kuruluş Yıllarında Diyanet İşleri Başkanlığının Yayın Hizmetleri', *Diyanet Aylık Dergi*, Nr 300, pp. 12–17.

Bulut, Mehmet (2019a) 'Hatiplerin Ellerinden Kütüphane Raflarına Hutbe Mecmuaları', *Diyanet Aylık Dergi*, Nr 345 pp. 34–7.

Bulut, Mehmet (2019b) 'Başkanlığın Hutbe Kitapları. "Yeni Hutbelerim" ve Diğerleri', *Diyanet Aylık Dergi*, Nr 346, pp. 30–3.

Büyüker, Kamil (2015) 'Mecmua'dan Dergi'ye. Sırat-ı Müstakim'den Diyanet'e Süreli İslami Yayıncılığa Dair Notlar', *Diyanet Aylık Dergi*, Nr 300, pp. 18–23.

Çakır, Ruşen and İrfan Bozan (2005) *Sivil, Şeffaf ve Demokratik Bir Diyanet İşleri Başkanlığı Mümkün Mü?* (Is a civil, transparent and democratic Diyanet possible?), Istanbul: TESEV Yayınları.

Clark, Bruce (2006) *Twice a Stranger: How Mass Expulsion Forged Modern Greece and Turkey*, London: Granata Books.

Cook, Michael (2006) *Commanding Right and Forbidding Wrong in Islamic Thought*, Cambridge: Cambridge University Press.

Cündioğlu, Dücane (1998) *Türkçe Kur'an ve Cumhuriyet İdeolojisi*, Istanbul: Kitabevi.

Doğan, Recai (1998) 'Cumhuriyet Öncesi Dönemde Yaygın Din Eğitimi Açısından Hutbeler', *Ankara Üniversitesi İlahiyat Fakültesi Dergisi*, 39, pp. 491–533.

Doumanis, Nicholas (2013) *Before the Nation: Muslim–Christian Coexistence and its Destruction in Late-Ottoman Anatolia*, Oxford: Oxford University Press.

Dressler, Markus (2015) 'Rereading Ziya Gökalp: Secularism and Reform of the Islamic State in the Late Young Turk Period', *IJMES*, 47, pp. 511–31.

Eisenstadt, S. N. and W. Schluchter (1998) 'Introduction: Paths to Early Modernities – A Comparative View', *Daedalus*, 127: 3, pp. 1–18.

Eliade, Mircea (1974 [1954]) *The Myth of the Eternal Return, or, Cosmos and History*, Princeton: Princeton University Press.

Gaffney, Patrick (1994) *The Prophet's Pulpit: Islamic Preaching in Contemporary Egypt*, Berkeley: University of California Press.

Gellner, Ernest (1983) *Nations and Nationalism*, Ithaca: Cornell University Press.

van Gennep, Arnold ([1960] 2004) *The Rites of Passage*, London: Routledge and Kegan Paul.

Gerber, Haim (2002) 'The Public Sphere and Civil Society in the Ottoman Empire', in Miriam Hoexter, Shmuel N. Eisenstadt and Nehemia Levtzion (eds), *The Public Sphere in Muslim Societies*, New York: SUNY, pp. 65–82.

Gibran, Kahlil ([1926] 1992) *The Prophet*, London: Penguin Books.

Gökalp, Ziya ([1923] 2014) *Türkçülüğün Esasları* (The basic principles of Turkism), Istanbul: Ötüken Neşriyat.

Görgülü, Faruk (2015) 'Dini Dergicilik ve Süreli Yayınlarımız', *Diyanet Aylık Dergi*, Nr 300, pp. 24–7.

Hall, Stuart and Bram Gieben (eds) (1992) *Formations of Modernity*, Cambridge: Polity Press.

Halldén, Philip (2005) 'What is Arab Islamic Rhetoric? Rethinking the History of Muslim Oratory Art and Homiletics', *IJMES*, 37: 1, pp. 19–38.

Hanioğlu, Şükrü (1995) *The Young Turks in Opposition*, Oxford: Oxford University Press.

Hanioğlu, Şükrü (2001) *Preparation for a Revolution: The Young Turks 1902–1908*, Oxford: Oxford University Press.

Hanioğlu, Şükrü (2008) *A Brief History of the Late Ottoman Empire*, Princeton: Princeton University Press.

Haywood, J. A. (1997) 'al-Suyūṭī', *The Encyclopaedia of Islam*, 2nd edn, Vol. IX, Leiden: Brill, pp. 913–16.

Hefner, Robert W. (2000) *Civil Islam: Muslims and Democratization in Indonesia*, Princeton: Princeton University Press.

Heyd, Uriel (1950) *The Foundations of Turkish Nationalism: The Life and Teachings of Ziya Gökalp*, London: The Harvill Press.

Heywood, Andrew (2007) *Politics*, New York: Palgrave.

Hjärpe, Jan (2005) *Sharīʿa: Gudomlig Lag i en Värld i Förändring* (Sharia: divine law in a changing world), Stockholm: Norstedt.

Hobsbawm, Eric (1990) *Nations and Nationalism Since 1780: Programme, Myth, Reality*, Cambridge: University Press.

Hoesterey, James Bourk (2016) *Rebranding Islam: Piety, Prosperity, and a Self-Help Guru*, Stanford: Stanford University Press.

Hoexter, Miriam, Shmuel Eisenstadt and Nehemia Levtzion (eds) (2002) *The Public Sphere in Muslim Societies*, Albany: SUNY Press.

Hodgson, Marshall (1974) *The Venture of Islam: Conscience and History in World Civilizations*, 3 vols, Chicago: University of Chicago Press.

Inalcık, Halil (1973) *The Ottoman Empire: The Classical Age, 1300–1600*, London: Weidenfeld and Nicolson.

*İslam Ansiklopedisi* (Islam Encyclopedia] (2013), Istanbul: Türkiye Diyanet Vakfı.

Itzkowitz, Norman (1972) *Ottoman Empire and Islamic Tradition*, Chicago: University of Chicago Press.

Iz, Fahri (1976) 'Ottoman and Turkish', in Donald P. Little (ed.), *Essays on Islamic Civilization Presented to Niyazi Berkes*, Leiden: Brill, pp. 118–39.

Jäschke, Gotthard (1972) *Yeni Türkiye'de İslamlık* (Islam in the new Turkey), Ankara: Bilgi Yayınevi.

Jonasson, Ann-Kristin (2004) *At the Command of God? On the Political Linkage of Islamist Parties*, Gothenburg: Gothenburg University, Department of Political Science.

Jones, Linda (2006) 'Ibn Abbad of Ronda's Sermon on the Prophet's Birthday Celebration: Preaching the Sufi and Sunni Paths of Islam', *Medieval Sermon Studies*, 50, pp. 31–49.

Jones, Linda (2012) *The Power of Oratory in the Medieval Muslim World*, Cambridge: Cambridge University Press.

Jones, Linda (2020) 'Discourses on Marriage, Religious Identity and Gender in Medieval and Contemporary Islamic Preaching: Continuities and Adaptations', in Simon Sternholm and Elisabeth Özdalga (eds), *Muslim Preaching in the Middle East and Beyond: Historical and Contemporary Case Studies*, Edinburgh: Edinburgh University Press, pp. 173–200.

Jusdanis, Gregory (2001) *The Necessary Nation*, Princeton: Princeton University Press.

Juynboll, Th. W. (1986) 'Adhān', *The Encyclopaedia of Islam*, 2nd edn, Vol. I, Leiden: Brill, pp. 187–8.

Kaplan, Abdurrahman (2014) *Kurtuluş Savaşı'nın Manevi Reisi M. Rifat Börekçi* (M. Rifat Börekçi, the moral leader of the Independence War), Ankara: Hitabevi.

Karaosmanoğlu, Yakup Kadri ([1932] 2008) *Yaban* (Stranger), Istanbul: İletişim.

Karpat, Kemal H. (2001) *The Politicization of Islam: Reconstructing Identity, State, Faith, and Community in the Late Ottoman State*, Oxford: Oxford University Press.

Kedourie, Elie (1993) *Nationalism*, Oxford: Blackwell.

Kieser, Hans-Lukas (2011) 'Dersim Massacre, 1937–1938', *Online Encyclopedia of Mass Violence*, 27 July 2011, <http://bo-k2s.sciences-po.fr/mass-violence-war-massacre-resistance/en/document/dersim-massacre-1937-1938>, ISSN 1961-9898 (last accessed 2 October 2020).

Kieser, Hans-Lukas (2018) *Talaat Pasha: Father of Modern Turkey, Architect of Genocide*, Princeton: Princeton University Press.

Kinross, Patrick ([1964] 2001) *Atatürk: The Rebirth of a Nation*, London: Phoenix.

Kushner, David (1977) *The Rise of Turkish Nationalism, 1876–1908*, London: Frank Cass.

Lagerlöf, Selma ([1891] 2009) *The Saga of Gösta Berling*, London: Penguin Books.

Lane, Edward William ([1860] 2003) *An Account of the Manners and Customs of the Modern Egyptians*, Cairo and New York: The American University in Cairo Press.

Lewis, Bernard (1968) *The Emergence of Modern Turkey*, Oxford: Oxford University Press.

Lord, Ceren (2018) *Religious Politics in Turkey: From the Birth of the Republic to the AKP*, Cambridge: Cambridge University Press.

Mardin, Şerif (1962) *The Genesis of Young Ottoman Thought: A Study in the Modernization of Turkish Political Ideas*, Princeton: Princeton University Press.

Mardin, Şerif (1989) *Religion and Social Change in Modern Turkey: The Case of Bediüzzaman Said Nursi*, New York: SUNY Press.

Marshall, T. H. (1950) *Citizenship and Social Class and Other Essays*, Cambridge: Cambridge University Press.

Moore, Barrington (1978) *Injustice: The Social Bases of Obedience and Revolt*, London: Macmillan.

Olsson, Tord, Elisabeth Özdalga and Catharina Raudvere (eds) (1998) *Alevi Identity: Cultural, Religious and Social Perspectives*, Richmond: Curzon Press.

Owen, Roger and Şevket Pamuk (1998) *A History of Middle East Economies in the Twentieth Century*, London: I. B. Tauris.

Özbudun, Ergun and Ömer Faruk Gençkaya (2009) *Democratization and the Politics of Constitution-Making in Turkey*, Budapest and New York: Central European University Press.

Özdalga, Elisabeth (1978) *I Atatürks spår. Det Republikanska Folkpartiet och Utvecklingsmobilisering i Turkiet, från Étatism till Populism* (In the footsteps of Atatürk. The Republican People's Party and development strategies in Turkey, from étatism to populism), Lund: Dialogus.

Özdalga, Elisabeth (1998) *The Veiling Issue, Official Secularism, and Popular Islam in Modern Turkey*, London: Curzon Press.

Özdalga, Elisabeth (2009) 'Islamism and Nationalism as Sister Ideologies: Reflections on the Politicization of Islam in a Longue Durée Perspective', *Middle Eastern Studies*, 45: 3, pp. 407–23.

Özdalga, Elisabeth (2020) 'Friday Sermons in a Secular State: Religious Institution-building in Modern Turkey', in Simon Stjernholm and Elisabeth Özdalga (eds), *Muslim Preaching in the Middle East and Beyond: Historical and Contemporary Case Studies*, Edinburgh: Edinburgh University Press, pp. 83–106.

Poulton, Hugh (1997) *Top Hat, Grey Wolf and Crescent: Turkish Nationalism and the Turkish Republic*, London: Hurst & Co.

Qutbuddin, Tahera (2019) *Arabic Oration Art and Function*, Leiden: Brill.

Retsö, Jan (2020) 'The Framework of Islamic Rhetoric: The Ritual of the *Khuṭba* and its Origin', in Simon Stjernholm and Elisabeth Özdalga (eds), *Muslim Preaching in the Middle East and Beyond: Historical and Contemporary Case Studies*, Edinburgh: Edinburgh University Press, pp. 19–29.

Robson, J. (1986) 'Abū Hurayra', *The Encyclopaedia of Islam*, 2nd edn, Vol. I, Leiden: Brill, p. 9.

Rowson, E. K. (1995) 'al-Rāghib al-Iṣfahānī', *The Encyclopaedia of Islam*, 2nd edn, Vol. VIII, Leiden: Brill, pp. 389–90.

Sayarı, Sabri (2010) 'Political Violence and Terrorism in Turkey, 1976–80: A Retrospective Analysis', *Terrorism and Political Violence*, 22: 2, pp. 198–215.

Schacht, J. (1986) 'Muḥammad Abū'l-Suʿūd', *The Encyclopaedia of Islam*, 2nd edn, Vol. I, Leiden: Brill, p. 152.

Şen, Mustafa (2010) 'Transformation of Turkish Islamism and the Rise of the Justice and Development Party', *Turkish Studies*, 11: 1, pp. 59–84.

Shankland, David (2003) *The Alevis in Turkey: The Emergence of a Secular Islamic Tradition*, London: RoutledgeCurzon.

Shissler, A. Holly (2003) *Between Two Empires: Ahmet Ağaoğlu and the New Turkey*, London: I. B. Tauris.

Skovgaard-Petersen, Jakob (1997) *Defining Islam for the Egyptian State: Muftis and Fatwas of the Dār al-Iftā*, Leiden: Brill.

Smith, Anthony (1971) *Theories of Nationalism*, London: Duckworth.

Stirling, Paul (1965) *Turkish Village*, New York: John Wiley & Sons.

Turner, Victor ([1969] 2008) *The Ritual Process: Structure and Anti-Structure*, New Brunswick, NJ and London: Aldine Transaction.

Watt, William Montgomery ([1962] 1987) *Islamic Philosophy and Theology*, Edinburgh: Edinburgh University Press.

Wensinck, A. J. (1986) 'Khuṭba', *The Encyclopaedia of Islam*, 2nd edn, Vol. V, Leiden: Brill, pp. 74–5.

White, Jenny (2013) *Muslim Nationalism and the New Turks*, Princeton: Princeton University Press.

Yazıcı, Nesimi (1996) 'Osmanli Son Döneminden Cumhuriyete Hutbelerimiz Üzerine Bazı Düşünceler (Reflections on our *hutbe*s from late Ottoman times until the Republic), paper presented at a symposium organised by the Faculty of Theology, Marmara University, Istanbul, 24–7 October.

Zilfi, Madeline C. (1988) *The Politics of Piety: The Ottoman Ulema in the Postclassical Age (1600–1800)*, Minneapolis: Biblioteca Islamica.

Zürcher, Erik J. (1994) *Turkey: A Modern History*, London: I. B. Tauris.

Zürcher, Erik J. (2010) 'The Importance of Being Secular: Islam in the Service of the National and Pre-National State', in Celia Kerslake, Kerem Öktem and Philip Robins (eds), *Turkey's Engagement with Modernity: Conflict and Change in the Twentieth Century*, Basingstoke: Palgrave Macmillan, pp. 55–68.

Zürcher, Erik J. (2019) 'The Young Turk Revolution: Comparisons and Connections, *Middle Eastern Studies*, 55: 4, pp. 481–98.

## Online Databases

Diyanet İşleri Başkanlığı, DİB, *Faaliyet Raporları* (Activity Reports) https://stratejigelistirme.diyanet.gov.tr/sayfa/22/Faaliyet-Raporlari (last accessed 12 November 2021).

Diyanet İşleri Başkanlığı, DİB, *Din Hizmetleri Raporları* (Religious Services Reports) https://dinhizmetleri.diyanet.gov.tr/sayfa/384 (last accessed 12 November 2021).

*İslam Ansiklopedisi*: <https://islamansiklopedisi.org.tr/ Türkiye Diyanet Vakfı> (last accessed 18 June 2021).

*The Qur'ān: English Meanings*: <https://alrashidmosque.ca/wp-content/uploads/2019/05/The-Quran-Saheeh-International.pdf> (last accessed 18 June 2021).

*The Hadith of the Prophet Muhammad*: <https://sunnah.com> (last accessed 18 June 2021).

# INDEX